DATE DUE

The Impact of
War on Children

Graça Machel

The Impact of War on Children

A review of progress since the 1996 United Nations
Report on the Impact of Armed Conflict on Children

Photographs by Sebastião Salgado

Contributing editors: Jennifer F. Klot and Theo Sowa

palgrave

palgrave

THE IMPACT OF WAR ON CHILDREN

Text © UNICEF, 2001
All photographs are copyright © Sebastião Salgado/Amazonas Images, with
the exception of the photograph of Mrs. Machel.

First published in the United States by PALGRAVE, 175 Fifth Avenue,
New York, NY 10010.
Companies and representatives throughout the world. PALGRAVE is the new
global imprint of St. Martin's Press LLC Scholarly and Reference Division
and Palgrave Publishers Ltd. (formerly Macmillan Press Ltd.).

Printed in Malaysia

ISBN 0-312-29422-0

Cataloging-in-Publication Data available from the Library of Congress

The statements in this publication are the personal views of the author and do
not necessarily reflect the views of the United Nations Children's Fund or any
other United Nations organisation.

This book is dedicated to the indomitable spirit of the children who inspired its preparation. Their hopes and aspirations live throughout this text.

Contents

Preface

"Adults go to war, but they don't realise what damage they are doing to children."

— A Nicaraguan child[1]

My journey began in Rwanda. It was September 1994, one month after the United Nations Secretary-General had asked me to carry out a global human rights assessment of children in armed conflict. Rwanda was the first of many field visits that I would take to war-ravaged countries.

Throughout this odyssey I met remarkable children who had survived catastrophic atrocities. I witnessed pain, fear and desperation. I saw courage and resilience.

I remember vividly when a Palestinian child asked me in earnest, "How long will it take before things get better? A month, a year?" His question crystallised for me the desperate circumstances of war. It pitted hope against hopelessness. Potential against lost opportunities.

When I began my journey, I had no idea how deeply I would be moved, how compelled I would feel to act or how impatient for change I would become.

The Report on the Impact of Armed Conflict on Children that I submitted in 1996 was a *cri de cœur.*

It was an urgent call to end the cynical exploitation of children as soldiers. To end impunity for war crimes against children. To end the scourge of landmines. To protect children from sanctions. To help children recover from their physical and psychological wounds. To provide education, health care, nutrition and safety for all war-affected children. To shatter the political inertia that has allowed armed conflict to destroy millions of children's lives.

It was the young Palestinian boy who moved me to call for a five-year review of progress made in support of the agenda we had crafted. I recommended that this review take place in the year 2000, ten years after the World Summit for Children and the entry into force of the Convention on the Rights of the Child.

So when the Government of Canada decided to convene an International Conference on War-affected Children in September 2000, it gave me great pleasure to accept their invitation to prepare a formal review of progress made and obstacles encountered since my 1996 Report. The information gathered for that review, together with my original Report, form the basis of this book.

The stories and images in this book are both challenging and tragic. They tell how eight landmines in my own country, Mozambique, prevented more than 20,000 people from returning to their villages in the Mahniça valley for seven years. They tell of girls being forced to exchange sex for safe passage or food and of their exploitation as soldiers and sexual slaves.

This book exposes new threats to children's security. It charts the rise of HIV/AIDS as the single most powerful new factor compounding the dangers for children in armed conflict. It attests to the way in which the proliferation of small arms and light weapons ignites and sustains the wars that victimise children.

But the book also showcases programmes that have been put in place since 1996 that have made a real difference in the lives of children caught in desperate circumstances. It shows how new information technologies are being used to reunite families separated by conflict. And it shows the powerful role that women play in building peace and reconstructing their families and communities. This book explores how education has brought stability into the lives of uprooted children, and it argues for education to be at the centre of what must become a renaissance – a transformation of schools into safe havens for communal care, learning and support.

I salute the many individuals and organisations that have shown leadership on behalf of war-affected children. The United

Nations Children's Fund, the Office of the United Nations High Commissioner for Refugees, the Office of the High Commissioner for Human Rights and the Special Representative of the Secretary-General for Children and Armed Conflict have strengthened significantly the humanitarian response for children. Coalitions have formed across sectors to improve children's protection in conflict. Civil society groups in particular have shown outstanding perseverance and concern. They continue to be at the cutting edge of innovative policy development, research and field practice. A small but growing number of governments have carried out their commitments to children by improving the standards for their protection, mobilising resources for their care and establishing programmes to meet their needs.

So, collectively, we can be encouraged by the progress made over the past five years. But we still have very far to go before we can say that our promises to children are fulfilled.

This book is a second *cri de cœur*. It is an appeal to spare children from the pernicious effects of war and to consider them zones of peace. It is a desperate plea to respect childhood as inviolate. It is an urgent call for the compassion, the commitment and the tenacity needed to protect children from the atrocities of war.

I still maintain that children present us with a uniquely compelling motivation for mobilisation. Our collective failure to protect children must be transformed into an opportunity to confront the problems that cause their suffering. The impact of armed conflict on children is everyone's responsibility. And it must be everyone's concern.

Graça Machel

Acknowledgements

Since 1994, I have been privileged to collaborate with Stephen Lewis. I value deeply his friendship, wisdom and courage, and want to acknowledge, with affection, his contributions to the analysis of the issues tackled in this book. And I am deeply grateful to my other special advisers, Marta Santos Pais and Kimberly Gamble-Payne, for their unflagging commitment, innovative ideas and insightful analysis.

I am honoured that my dear brother Sebastião Salgado has contributed his photographs to this volume. His internationally acclaimed photographs are both dignified and painfully evocative. They testify to the horrific plight of children caught up in conflicts while showing us the haunting beauty of children's resilience, their strength and their courage.

This book draws from the findings of my 1996 Report on the Impact of Armed Conflict on Children. I wish to acknowledge the support given to its preparation by the following group of eminent persons: Belisario Betancur, Francis Deng, Marian Wright Edelman, Devaki Jain, Julius K. Nyerere, Lisbet Palme, Wole Soyinka and Archbishop Desmond Tutu.

The technical advisers who shaped the report and guided its preparation included Thomas Hammarberg (Chair of the Advisory Group), Philip Alston, Rachel Brett, Victoria Brittain, Maricela Daniel, Ibrahima Fall, Helena Gezelius, Jim Himes, Duong Quynh Hoa, Elizabeth Jareg, Helga Klein, Salim Lone, Jacques Moreillon, Vitit Muntarbhorn, Olara A. Otunnu, Sadig Rasheed, Everett Ressler, Jane Schaller, Anne Skatvedt and Jody Williams.

The secretariat for the 1996 Report was managed by Jennifer F. Klot. It was supported by many people, including Nigel Fisher, Scholastica Kimaryo, Theo Sowa, Beth Verhey, Nalinee Nippita, Alethea John, Florette Brown and Peter Stalker. Financial contributions for the 1996 Report were received from Redd Barna (Save the

Children Fund-Norway) and the Committees for UNICEF of Germany, Greece, Hong Kong, Japan, the Netherlands, Portugal, Spain, Sweden, Switzerland, the United Kingdom and the United States.

The present book would not have been possible without the committed secretariat that supported its preparation, led by my co-authors, Jennifer F. Klot and Theo Sowa. Saudamini Siegrist's thoughtful research, boundless dedication and gifted editing skills were essential to this process. Invaluable and dedicated research was also provided by Ivy Lam, Richard Leonard and Lieke van de Wiel. Support in the early compilation of materials was provided by Jelagat Ronoh and Bertra McGann. The inspired work of three editors, David Pitt, Janet Solberg and Peter Stalker, sharpened the text and made it more vivid and accessible. Rijuta Tooker and Liliana Potenza provided a calming influence and superb administrative support.

A great debt is owed to the following experts who gave so generously of their time and insight in reviewing the many iterations of each chapter: Hodan Addou, Noeman Al-Sayyad, Philip Alston, David Angell, Anatole Ayissi, Yumi Bae, Sam Barnes, Jo Becker, Elizabeth Bernstein, David Biggs, Lyndsay Bird, Sherazade Boualia, Rachel Brett, Peter Buckland, Francesc Claret, Roberta Cohen, Christopher Coleman, Mark Connolly, Patrick Couteau and UNHCR colleagues, Joanne Csete, Catarina de Alberqueque, Maria de la Soudiere, Enrique Delamonica, Laketch Dirasse, Carol Djeddah and WHO colleagues, Paula Donovan, Glenda Fick, Rana Flowers, Virginia Gamba, Richard Garfield, Gulbadan Habibi, Eva Jespersen, Gareth Jones, A.J. Jongman, Kate Joseph, Eylah Kadjar-Hamouda, Randolph Kent, James Kunder, Robert Lawson, Jean-Claude Legrand, Iain Levine, Ludmila Lhotska, Ernest Ligteringen, Jane Lowicki, João Madureira, Mark Malan, Monty G. Marshall, Una McCauley, Roeland Monasch, Erin Mooney, Maha Muna, Rory Mungoven, Bo Viktor Nylund, Valerie Oosterveld, Agostino Paganini, Allison Pillsbury, Francisco Quesney, Robert Scharf, Jens Schlyter, Yasmine Sherif, Wendy Smith, Carmen Sorger, Crispin Stephen, Bert Theuermann, Patrick Tigere and UNHCR colleagues, Marjatta Tolvanen, Jan Vandemoortele, Beth Verhey, Margaret Vogt, Mary Wareham,

Marc Weil, Markus Werne, Beth Woroniuk and Jane Zucker.

Although responsibility for the views expressed rests with the author, the breadth of knowledge, analysis and innovation benefited hugely from the contributions of these reviewers.

This book would never have been published without the warm and continuous support of Patricia Lone, who handled the publication process remarkably in the face of changing deadlines. Her team provided exceptional support: Vicky Haeri, Jaclyn Tierney, Hashi Roberts, Hirut Gebre-Egziabher, Yvonne Lester, Arati Rao, Sonia Yeo and Petra Morrison. Thanks are due to Ellen Tolmie and Amazonas Images for selecting and facilitating the use of Sebastião Salgado's photos.

Financial and administrative support from the United Nations Development Fund for Women and the United Nations Children's Fund made this publication possible. Financial support for the preparation of a previously published summary of this book was provided by the Governments of Canada and Norway.

Contributing editors

Jennifer F. Klot served as a policy adviser on peace and security at the United Nations Children's Fund and has worked on issues of human rights, gender and development with various international non-governmental organisations and private foundations. She is currently the Senior Governance Adviser at the United Nations Development Fund for Women.

Theo Sowa is an independent consultant working in the areas of African development, youth policy development, conflict resolution and communications. Born in Ghana, she has worked with various national, international, intergovernmental and non-governmental organisations. Ms. Sowa is a board member of Conciliation Resources and the Comic Relief Africa Grants Committee.

Editorial note

The United Nations General Assembly, at its forty-eighth session in 1993, adopted resolution 48/157 on the "Protection of children affected by armed conflicts," in which it requested the UN Secretary-General to appoint an independent expert to undertake a comprehensive study on the impact of armed conflict on children.

Mrs. Graça Machel, former Minister of Education of Mozambique, was appointed in September 1994 and carried out a two-year process of research, consultation and mobilisation, with the support of the United Nations Children's Fund (UNICEF), the then United Nations Centre for Human Rights (now the Office of the High Commissioner for Human Rights) and the Office of the United Nations High Commissioner for Refugees.

In November 1996, the Secretary-General of the United Nations presented to the General Assembly the Report prepared by Mrs. Machel on the Impact of Armed Conflict on Children (A/51/306 and Add.1).

This book draws upon the findings and analysis of the 1996 report and assesses progress made and obstacles encountered in efforts over the past five years to protect children in armed conflict and to fulfil their rights. It highlights many of the significant developments within each of the themes of the original report and gives new focus to five additional areas: HIV/AIDS; small arms and light weapons; women and the peace process; media and communications; and peace and security.

A summary of the findings contained in this book was prepared at the request of the Government of Canada and published as a review document for the International Conference on War-affected Children, held in Winnipeg (Canada) in September 2000.

Chapter 1

Wars against children

"I tell you, you cannot feel the pain of
this suffering if you don't see it physically.
If you only glance at it, a sword of sorrow
will pierce your heart . . . ."

– Ugandan schoolgirl who escaped abduction by the Lord's Resistance Army[1]

Throughout history, war has exacted an horrific toll on children. But modern warfare kills, maims and exploits children more callously and more systematically than ever before. Caught up in complex conflicts that have multiple causes and little prospect of early resolution, children are being sucked into seemingly endless endemic struggles for power and resources. During the 1990s, more than 2 million children died as a result of armed conflicts, often deliberately targeted and murdered. More than three times that number were permanently disabled or seriously injured.[2] Even greater numbers have fallen victim to disease, malnutrition and sexual violence. Modern-day conflicts are particularly lethal for children because little or no practical distinction is made between combatants and civilians. In recent decades, the incidence of civilians killed and wounded has risen dramatically, from 5 per cent to over 90 per cent of all casualties.

Today's warfare is often marked by appalling levels of violence and brutality, from systematic rape and the destruction of crops to the poisoning of wells and outright genocide. Ferocious assaults are unleashed against children and their communities, resulting in some 20 million children currently uprooted from their homes, either as refugees or internally displaced.[3] And children themselves can be drawn in as fighters, caught up in a general maelstrom in which they are not just the targets of warfare but even the perpetrators of atrocities. At any given time, more than 300,000 children are being used in hostilities as soldiers.[4]

The end of the Cold War raised hopes for an end to warfare fuelled by superpower rivalry. Instead the world has seen a proliferation of armed conflicts more often than not within States rather than between them. But even these so-called internal conflicts have regional and international dimensions. Frequently dismissed as "tribal wars" or "ethnic clashes," many of these internecine conflicts are fuelled and financed by those countries, corporations and individuals with strategic interests. Vestiges of colonialism reverberate in the disintegration of public order. Ethnicity and religion are manipulated to serve personal or narrow group interests, with devastating effects.

Without limiting the discussion, the current review identifies several factors further accelerating modern-day conflicts:

• Struggles over natural resources: Diamonds finance long-running wars in Angola and Sierra Leone. In Sudan and elsewhere, civil conflict revolves around crude oil. And the profits from illicit narcotics figure prominently in fighting in Afghanistan and Colombia.

• None of these situations could exist for long without markets in affluent parts of the world. Global businesses, some legal, some illegal, have spawned international complicity that makes war not just possible but highly profitable.

• International weapons sales, especially of small arms, help ignite and sustain wars that victimise children. Indeed, small arms, light and easy to use, are now so readily available that the poorest communities can gain access to deadly weapons capable of transforming any local conflict into a bloody slaughter.

• Constrained by external debt and the demands of structural adjustment, many developing countries have been forced to restructure their economies, cut basic services and reduce the size of the public sector. In the process, they often weaken their economies and unwittingly open the gates to predatory outside interests hungry for power and profit.

Aggravating the situation further, international emergency relief for victims of armed conflict is inadequate and uneven. Between 1994 and 1999, the United Nations sought $13.5 billion for emergency relief; it received less than $9 billion. And in 1999, while donor countries provided the equivalent of 59 cents per person each day to assist 3.5 million war-affected people in Kosovo province (Federal Republic of Yugoslavia) and other parts of south-eastern Europe, in Africa, the 12 million war-affected people each received the equivalent of 13 cents per day.[5]

Beyond emergency assistance, the international community has responded to the proliferation of armed conflict by focusing increasingly on peacekeeping, peacemaking and peace-building. There have been a number of successes – in El Salvador, Namibia and Nicaragua, for example. But there have also been some tragic failures, such as in Somalia, the former Yugoslavia – and in Rwanda, where 800,000 people were slain.[6]

Brutalities routinely committed against children in war pose a profound challenge to international law, despite the fact that the international community has fashioned formidable instruments to uphold human rights and to prosecute the perpetrators of genocide. But these treaties are only as effective as the willingness of States parties and others to uphold them, and many have ignored their obligations and responsibilities with impunity.

In examining global actions to increase children's protection in armed conflict, this book examines a wide range of important issues. The following overarching themes form the basis of an urgent call to action:

1. Ending impunity for crimes against children and ending tolerance for war

Massive and gross violations of child rights continue unabated. Murder, rape, mutilation, forced recruitment, displacement, injury and malnourishment are just some of the most visible examples. These atrocities must not be tolerated as either inevitable or acceptable side effects of war. There must be an end to impunity for war crimes against children. Those who wage, legitimise and support wars must be condemned. National sovereignty must never shield those directly or indirectly responsible for such crimes. And there must be national and international action to hold all perpetrators accountable.

2. Ensuring children's central place on the peace and security agenda

In recent years, the relevance of child rights to international peace and security has been given unprecedented political legitimacy. The protection of children and women must be central to all actions to promote peace, implement peace agreements and resolve conflicts. Improved collaboration between regional and subregional groups and the United Nations is essential to this goal.

3. Monitoring and reporting on child rights violations in conflict

When the lives and fundamental rights of children are at stake, there must be no silent witnesses. Protecting human rights is a fundamental element of peacemaking, peace-building and humanitarian operations, yet it is widely neglected. That is why, in situations of armed conflict, increased resources and attention must be devoted to monitoring, verifying and reporting child rights abuses and gender-based violations. All UN bodies and international and national organisations with field presence should establish regular channels to report alleged violations of child rights.

4. Responding to the gender dimensions of conflict and peace-building

The lives of children are jeopardised when women are not protected and when women's contributions to peace-building are undermined and marginalised. The insufficient understanding of the impact of armed conflict on women and girls and of women's role in peace-building undermines political, policy and programme approaches. The glaring gaps in the protection of women and girls in conflict must be addressed through better focused humanitarian relief and development assistance.

5. Engaging adolescents in rebuilding

Adolescents are at extreme risk during armed conflict. They are fodder for recruitment into armed forces and groups; targets for sexual exploitation and abuse; and at great risk of acquiring sexually transmitted infections, including HIV/AIDS. Yet adolescents have been neglected in the delivery of health services, education, vocational training and life skills. Despite this, they remain the greatest hope and the greatest resource in rebuilding war-affected communities. Their active participation in community-based relief, recovery and reconstruction programmes can strengthen and sustain these initiatives while increasing adolescents' self-esteem, identity and sense of purpose.

6. Protecting children under siege from HIV/AIDS

Over the past five years, HIV/AIDS has become the single most powerful new factor compounding the dangers for children in armed conflict. The chaotic and brutal circumstances of war aggravate all of the factors that fuel the HIV/AIDS pandemic. HIV/AIDS devastates children by leaving millions orphaned; by killing teachers, health workers and other public servants; and by straining community resources to the breaking point. At the same time, HIV/AIDS has been recognised as a threat to international peace and security. Urgent solutions are needed to address the combined effects of HIV/AIDS and armed conflict on children. Emergency humanitarian relief should support HIV/AIDS prevention, care and treatment while contributing to the establishment of longer-term national policies.

7. Improving information, data collection and analysis of children in conflict

Effective political, policy and programme approaches for children in conflict cannot be put in place without accurate and timely information. Yet there exists no systematic approach to collecting, analysing and making available sex and age disaggregated data on war-affected children. Drawing on the strengths of all relevant bodies, a collective approach should be put in place with appropriate resources made available.

8. Training and sensitisation on child rights and gender

The need for specialised training and sensitisation on the child and gender dimensions of conflict must take place at political, policy and operational levels. Key issues include the gender and child rights aspects of protection under international humanitarian, human rights and refugee law. Current, ad hoc approaches to training have been limited in their impact. To move this agenda forward in a significant way, a plan of action must be put in place to ensure: coordination and cooperation of training initiatives among UN Member States, UN agencies, regional organisations and non-governmental organisations (NGOs); mobilisation of sufficient resources; and quality, content and standardisation of training initiatives.

9. Supporting civil society to protect children

National and international civil society groups play a fundamental role in preventing armed conflict, protecting children and rebuilding societies in the aftermath of war. This review pays tribute to their contributions, especially the courageous work of national humanitarian personnel, whose protection the international community has failed to guarantee, sometimes with fatal consequences. Special measures must be put in place to protect all those who risk their lives to protect children and women in need.

10. Mobilising resources for war-affected children

The vast inconsistency in mobilising international resources for war-affected children is one of the most brutal inequalities in the world today. Sierra Leone, for example, received less than $20 per child in 1999, compared to $216 per child in Kosovo. The shortfalls and disparities in humanitarian relief also occur in the patterns of official development assistance that is so vital for post-conflict reconstruction. Appeals for war-affected children do not fit easily within often rigid and compartmentalised funding guidelines. Donors should use criteria designed to overcome disparities and to surmount the institutional, budgetary and functional barriers between relief assistance, rehabilitation and development cooperation.

In addressing issues of children in armed conflict it is easy to become overwhelmed or inured to the depressing statistics. When we speak of hundreds, thousands and millions of war-affected children, it is essential to remember that each number and each statistic represents a child's life – someone's son, daughter, sister or brother.

Chapter 2

Child soldiers

"When I was killing, I felt like it wasn't me doing these things. I had to because the rebels threatened to kill me."

— 12-year-old boy abducted into rebel forces in Sierra Leone[1]

The increasingly widespread exploitation of children as soldiers is one of the most vicious characteristics of recent armed conflicts.

Over the last decade, hundreds of thousands of children under 18 have been made a part of government armies, rebel forces and paramilitary and militia groups.[2] The availability of light, inexpensive small arms like assault rifles, machine guns, pistols and hand grenades has helped accelerate the trend. The widely used AK-47 assault rifle, for example, can be easily carried and used to deadly effect by children as young as 10.

A child soldier is any child – boy or girl – under the age of 18, who is compulsorily, forcibly or voluntarily recruited or used in hostilities by armed forces, paramilitaries, civil defence units or other armed groups. Child soldiers are used for forced sexual services, as combatants, messengers, porters and cooks. Most are adolescents, though many are 10 years of age and younger. The majority are boys, but a significant proportion overall are girls.

Current estimates put the number of child soldiers at about 300,000[3] at any one time. But the cumulative total is much larger. As children are killed or wounded, or manage to grow older, their places are taken by new children. And thus the destruction of young lives is perpetuated from one generation to the next.[4]

Children at risk

As conflicts drag on, recruits tend to get younger and younger. This is partly because deteriorating economic and social conditions drive families deeper into poverty. But conflicts also shut down schools. And the longer a conflict continues, the more likely it is that armed forces, having exhausted the supplies of available adults, will turn to children to fill their ranks.

Children from wealthier and better educated families are at less risk of recruitment because their parents can buy their freedom or challenge their recruitment through legal means or political influence. Some parents resort to sending their children out of the country. Not surprisingly, it is children from the poorest families who are the most vulnerable. Children in large cities who are living and working in the streets are at particular risk, especially those living apart from their parents. So are displaced children, who are less likely to have any proof of citizenship or age.

Myanmar has one of the highest numbers of active child soldiers in the world, both in governmental forces and in armed groups. Many of these children are orphans or were living and working on the streets. According to an ILO Commission of Inquiry, children as young as 10 have been used as porters, or to sweep roads for landmines using brooms and branches.[5]

Minority and indigenous children are another especially vulnerable group. During the civil war in Guatemala, adolescent boys from Mayan communities were forcibly recruited into the Guatemalan army. Government forces and right-wing militias systematically raped girls as a way of terrorising indigenous communities.[6] In Somalia, where up to one-third of the population is estimated to be made up of minority groups, low status can place the children of these groups outside "clan law" – and thus make them vulnerable to recruitment.[7]

Recruitment

Children become soldiers in a variety of ways. Some are conscripted, others press-ganged or kidnapped, still others join armed groups because they are convinced it is a way to protect their families. In addition to being recruited for government armed forces or armed opposition groups, children have been dragooned into government-aligned paramilitary groups, militias or civil defence forces.

Angola currently has an estimated 3,000 child soldiers, a significant number of whom have been forcibly recruited from neighbouring countries.[8] In 1997, UNITA forcibly recruited an estimated 200 Rwandan refugee children who had been living along the border between Angola and the Democratic Republic of the Congo (DRC). In 1998, boys and girls as young as 13 were reportedly being abducted. Government forces also forcibly recruited refugee children from Rwanda. In 1999, groups of up to 250 youths were press-ganged from markets by the Angola Armed Forces (Forças Armadas Angolanas or FAA).[9]

Even in countries where the legal minimum age of recruitment is 18, the law is not necessarily a safeguard. In many parts of the world, birth registration is inadequate or non-existent. Worldwide, one-third of all births – about 40 million children – go unregistered every year.[10] In such circumstances, children themselves may not know how old they are. So recruiters guess, and many will record a child's age as 18 to lend the appearance of legal compliance.

In December 1999, a UN report asserted that Taliban commanders in Afghanistan were enlisting child warriors younger than 14. Taliban forces denied the report, citing an earlier decree that banned any male from fighting who had yet to grow a beard. It also set up a commission to punish commanders found to be recruiting minors.[11] The age of recruits in the Taliban forces is still in dispute, but with no birth registration system in Afghanistan, the ages of Taliban fighters cannot, in fact, be verified.

In countries where government administration is weak, it is not possible to recruit systematically from a register. Instead, armies may arbitrarily seize children from the streets, or even from schools or orphanages. In other cases, well-organised military governments may carry out forced recruitment campaigns. In Myanmar, the army has been known to surround schools and forcibly recruit groups of children from 15 to 17 years of age; those who can prove they are under age may be released, but not necessarily.[12]

Aggressive recruitment in Sri Lanka

The Liberation Tigers of Tamil Eelam (LTTE) – the "Tamil Tigers" – have recruited thousands of girls and boys as young as 10 to further their struggle against the Sri Lankan Government. So dependent are the guerrillas on child recruits that two armed units – the "Baby Brigade" and the elite "Leopard Brigade" – are made up entirely of children. The child soldiers of the Leopard Brigade come from LTTE orphanages. The LTTE recruit and train children inside schools in areas under their control. Recruitment of children soared in 1999 and 2000, amid a step-up in guerrilla attacks. Girls made up the majority of new recruits in a recent drive held in Sri Lankan schools.

Children who escape from the LTTE may face new dangers from the Sri Lankan Special Task Force and the Terrorism Investigation Division of the police, who allegedly use torture as an interrogation technique against child suspects. Despite continued high levels of violence, there are signs that people living in LTTE-controlled areas are beginning to challenge the external and internal terror engulfing the Tamil community. For example, the University Teachers for Human Rights, formed in 1988 at the University of Jaffna, has called for measures to make perpetrators of violence accountable. In another promising development, Sri Lanka signed and ratified in September 2000 the Optional Protocol to the Convention on the Rights of the Child on the involvement of children in armed conflict.[13]

In many cases, schools and military academies become prime recruiting grounds for child soldiers. For example, in 1997 and 1998, Islamic *madrasas* (schools) in Pakistan provided the Taliban with thousands of new Afghan and Pakistani child recruits.[14] In

August 1999, in response to an appeal made throughout the *madrasas* in Pakistan's Northwest Frontier Province, an estimated 5,000 students joined their forces.[15]

In some countries, including the United Kingdom and the United States, where the age of voluntary recruitment is under 18,[16] secondary schools and college campuses are often used as rallying points for recruitment drives.

"Voluntary" recruitment

While many children are forced to join armed forces or groups, others may present themselves for service. It is misleading, however, to consider this as "voluntary." Rather than exercising free choice, these children are responding more often to a variety of pressures – economic, cultural, social and political.

One of the most basic pressures is poverty. Parents who are impoverished can be tempted to offer their children for service, especially when armies pay the wages of a child soldier directly to the family. Children themselves may volunteer if they believe that this is the only way to guarantee regular meals, clothing and medical attention. However, a child's economic association with the army may be more complex, as in cases where whole families move with armed groups. In some cases, armed forces will take in unaccompanied children to protect them from violence. But this is no guarantee that the children will not end up as soldiers, particularly if they stay with a group long enough to identify it as their protector or "new family."

Some children feel obliged to become soldiers for protection. Seeing violence and chaos all around, they may feel safer if they, too, have guns in their hands. Other children have joined armed opposition groups after being harassed by government forces. Many young people have joined the Kurdish rebel groups, for example, as a reaction to scorched-earth policies and extensive human rights violations.[17]

Children fighting with civil defence forces and other militia have been described as volunteers when, in fact, they were offered up by parents who may have been pressured by authorities seeking to fill recruitment quotas. For example, children of the local chieftains of the Kamajor in Sierra Leone and of the Mayi Mayi in eastern Democratic Republic of the Congo may be given over for service as a "duty" to the community.[18]

Adolescence is a period of enormous and often stressful transition in a child's life in terms of physical and psychosocial development. That is precisely why adolescents are especially susceptible to the lure of military life and the sense of power associated with carrying deadly weapons.

Adolescents, like adults, can be attracted by specific ideologies, identifying with, and fighting for, social and political causes, for religious expression, for self-determination or for national liberation. As happened in South Africa, they may join the struggle in pursuit of political freedom.

The ideological indoctrination of child soldiers can have disastrous consequences. Children are impressionable and may even be lured into cults of martyrdom. In Sri Lanka, for example, some adults have used young people's immaturity to their own advantage, recruiting and training adolescents for suicide bombings.[19]

How child soldiers are used

Once recruited, children are treated in much the same way as adults, beginning with induction ceremonies that are often brutal. Many start out in support functions that involve great risk and hardship.

"We spent sleepless nights watching for the enemy," a former child soldier from Burundi recalled. "My first role was to carry a torch for grown-up rebels. Later I was shown how to use hand grenades. Barely within a month or so, I was carrying an AK-47 rifle."[20]

A common job for children is to serve as porters, carrying loads weighing up to 60 kilograms that can include anything from ammunition to wounded soldiers. Those unable to shoulder such burdens risk savage beatings – even execution. Indeed, arbitrary beatings and other forms of violence are common in the ranks. On the other hand, children who are considered "good" fighters may receive rewards such as extra food or promotion in rank. And boys may have girls assigned to them for forced sexual services.

Children also perform household chores and other duties, including standing guard, acting as messengers, hunting for wild fruits and vegetables and stealing food. While some of these roles may seem less perilous than combat, they can imperil all children in an area by making them all objects of suspicion. In Latin America, some government forces have killed young children in peasant communities because they were convinced they were rebel spies.

Girls perform many of the same functions as male child soldiers. In the Philippines, the Moro Islamic Liberation Front (MILF) trains girls from 10 to 16 to fire M-16 Armalite rifles and to prepare for battle. Girls also prepare food, tend to the wounded and wash clothes.[21]

Both girls and boys are often compelled to provide sexual services. In the case of girls abducted into armed groups, nearly all are forced into sexual slavery – the majority of them becoming infected with sexually transmitted infections (STIs)[22] and, increasingly, HIV/AIDS. Abducted girls as young as age 10 have been kept as sexual slaves by rebel leaders. Once the leader dies, the girl is typically put aside for ritual cleansing and then given to another rebel.[23] Describing these situations as "forced marriage" is a complete misrepresentation and distortion of a child's experience.

Although children might be assigned initially to support functions, they often find themselves in the heat of battle. Here, their inexperience and lack of training leave them particularly exposed. In actual combat conditions, the youngest children rarely appreciate the perils they face. Some commanders deliberately exploit children's seeming fearlessness, to the point of plying them with alcohol or drugs before combat.

A soldier in Myanmar recalls an attack by children who may have been drugged: "There were a lot of boys rushing into the field, screaming like banshees. It seemed like they were immortal, or impervious or something, because we shot at them but they just kept coming."[24]

Children can become desensitised to suffering as a result of their exposure to extreme violence. Often they are exposed deliberately to horrific scenes to harden them and make it easier to sever links with the rest of society. In many places, including Colombia, Rwanda and Sierra Leone, children have been forced to commit atrocities against their own families and communities, ranging from beatings to mutilations and active participation in massacres.

The after-effects of such violence are emotionally devastating. Many children, even after they are demobilised, are tormented by nightmares, hallucinations and delusions that can last for years.[25] "When I was killing, I felt like it wasn't me doing these things," said a 12-year-old boy, abducted into rebel forces in Sierra Leone. "I had to because the rebels threatened to kill me."[26]

Disarmament, demobilisation and reintegration

Without the formal recognition by all parties to a conflict that children are within their ranks, the post-war healing process is unlikely to consider the special needs of child soldiers.

There are three primary aspects to rebuilding societies ravaged by war, and steps must be taken to ensure that children figure prominently in each:
• *Disarmament*: the collection of weapons within conflict zones and the safe storage or disposal of those weapons.
• *Demobilisation*: the formal registration and release of combatants from duty, providing assistance to help them meet immediate needs and transport back to their home communities.
• *Reintegration*: the process of helping former combatants return to civilian life and readjust both socially and economically.

Peace negotiations must include a specific commitment to disarm, demobilise and reintegrate children used in hostilities. Sierra Leone's 1999 Lomé Peace Agreement, though flawed, was the first such pact to recognise the needs of child soldiers and to plan for their demobilisation and reintegration into community life.

A milestone in efforts to increase the commitment to disarm, demobilise and reintegrate child soldiers into society is the February 2000 report of the Secretary-General, 'The Role of United Nations Peacekeeping in Disarmament, Demobilization

Colombia's "little bells" and "little bees"

There are thought to be around 6,000 child soldiers fighting for rebel armies or militias in Colombia.[27] Both the main rebel groups, the Fuerzas Armadas Revolucionarias de Colombia (FARC) and the Ejercito de Liberación Nacional (ELN), have forcibly recruited children as young as 12. Some 30 per cent of all child recruits are girls.

Commanders call the children "little bells" because they serve as an early warning system or "little bees" because they sting before the enemy forces can spot them.

Paramilitaries established by the army or landowners to fight guerrillas also use child soldiers, who variously serve as spies, messengers and human shields, as well as combatants.

In June 1999, the Special Representative of the Secretary-General for Children and Armed Conflict negotiated an agreement with the Government and FARC rebel forces to end the recruitment of children younger than 15.

However, the FARC continues to recruit children under the age of 15, despite public statements to the contrary. In May 2000, FARC again announced that children younger than 15 would be demobilised and sent home, but that promise has not been fulfilled either. In fact, many reports indicate that the recruitment of children under 15 has increased.

One major obstacle to demobilising these children is that Colombia's judicial system criminalises and detains former child soldiers – a process that further alienates them and labels them as outcasts.

In 1999 the Government's Family Welfare Institute opened its first home and education centre for former child soldiers – at a location kept secret because of threats against the 19 children so far enrolled.

and Reintegration'.[28] The report sets out specific "child-conscious" measures for disarmament, demobilisation and reintegration programmes within a peacekeeping environment. It also recommends a minimum three-year commitment of resources and staff to provide for children's longer-term needs, including education, vocational training and psychosocial support.

Most of all, efforts must focus on removing children from hostilities at the earliest possible opportunity, even in the absence of a peace agreement or formal disarmament, demobilisation and reintegration (DD&R) programme. There are precedents for such expedited action. Between 1996 and 1997, the FAA and UNITA rebel forces together demobilised as many as 5,000 children. But they continued to recruit children[29] despite pledges to the contrary. International pressure and negotiations with governments and with non-state actors have resulted in commitments in Colombia, the Democratic Republic of the Congo, Sierra Leone and Sri Lanka to end the use of child soldiers. In February 2001, such negotiations led to the release of more than 2,500 child soldiers by the Sudanese People's Liberation Army.

Disarmament and demobilisation

Children must have access to the benefits of demobilisation whether or not they have weapons in their possession. In Liberia, demobilisation was organised on the basis of "one man, one gun." This worked against the best interests of children, especially girls, because rebel commanders confiscated children's weapons prior to their release, making them ineligible to participate in the demobilisation process.[30]

Demobilising children requires their immediate separation from adult soldiers. They should be transported some distance from conflict zones to reduce the risk of re-mobilisation. No more than 48 hours should elapse from the time of their release until they are transferred to civilian control. By failing to separate them from adult soldiers, children can be left vulnerable to manipulation and re-recruitment by commanders.[31] During this period, but after their transfer to a civilian interim care site, children should receive essential services such as health care, counselling and psychosocial support. Former child soldiers with disabilities should receive specialised medical care and be referred to prosthetics and, where relevant, landmine-awareness programmes.

Interviews should be strictly confidential and conducted in the child's mother tongue. Children must be kept fully informed and consulted regularly to ensure that their needs and concerns are being addressed. This is especially important in relation to family reunification and vocational and educational opportunities.

If a "demobilisation package" is offered, monetary or material support for former child soldiers should be provided, not to individual children, but to the community through reintegration programmes. In Mozambique, cash payments for former child soldiers frustrated demobilisation efforts and actually encouraged children to return to military groups.

If possible, a commitment should be obtained from government forces or armed groups to ensure that children will not be re-recruited into armed conflict. For example, in Angola, a legal provision ensured that former child soldiers would not be required to undertake military service once they reached the legal age of conscription.[32]

Special efforts must be made to ensure that girls are included in all aspects of disarmament, demobilisation and reintegration. In some countries up to 40 per cent of child soldiers are girls,[33] and yet in many cases they receive no support from DD&R programmes. For example, female child soldiers were excluded from DD&R programmes in Sierra Leone because they were registered as "dependants" or "camp followers." In Mozambique, the demobilisation package for girls included men's clothing. Many girls, who had between three and five children, were released without skills training or other support.[34] In Angola, even though girls participated in both active combat and support roles in armed groups like UNITA, their commanders did not identify or present them as former combatants for demobilisation programmes.[35]

Many demobilisation programmes falter precisely because of flawed design, a lack of resources or a failure to monitor the process. In Angola, UNITA members were used as interpreters and accompanied the children through the demobilisation process, even forcing them to falsify their testimony. In Liberia, there were not enough

resources for the DD&R process. With no escorts and no transportation available, large numbers of children simply wandered away from
demobilisation centres. Ultimately 90 per cent were unaccounted for,
and many of them were certainly lost to roving armies.[36]

In some cases young children have been demobilised in one
country only to turn up a few months later fighting another country's war, much like mercenaries. One young boy fighting in
Liberia explained: "I am not thinking about school now. After this
war, I am going to another country to fight."[37]

Reintegration

Going home is seldom easy, even though most children returning from war want to rejoin their families. In Mozambique, for
example, over 90 per cent of the children interviewed in RENAMO
bases gave this as their top priority.[38] Children who escape or are
released from armies often arrive home to find their families
uprooted and their villages abandoned. And even if families and
communities can be found, they may have been shattered by conflict. Many children never find their families, either because they
have perished or have become untraceable in the conflict.

In some cases, former child soldiers may be rejected by their
community. Cultural beliefs and attitudes can make reunification
particularly difficult for girl soldiers who have been raped or sexually abused. Left with few alternatives and little support, many girls
become victims of prostitution.

Children who have lost their families or been rejected by their
communities may need a transitional period of alternative care,
such as peer-group and foster family arrangements. When such
arrangements are strongly integrated into communities, they can
be more successful than institutional care.

Even children successfully reunited with their families usually
have little prospect of a smooth return to life as they once knew it.
Former child soldiers may have spent many years with armed
groups, growing up away from their families and deprived of the
normal opportunities for physical, emotional and intellectual
development. A formerly cheerful 12-year-old may return home as
a sullen, aggressive and alienated 16-year-old.

At best, a child's return to community life is a slow process of healing that requires a network of support from parents, teachers, religious and other community leaders. It is not uncommon for children who were soldiers to harbour deep-seated feelings of shame and worthlessness. It takes time for them to rebuild their confidence and self-image and accept the possibility of a new life. Reintegration must help children to establish new foundations for their lives, based on their individual capacities. An interesting example can be found in the care offered by a project in Liberia for children who have become pariahs because of atrocities they have committed or sexual abuse they have suffered. During an intensive eight-week programme they are reunited in social settings with their peers, receive guidance in behaviour, hygiene and self-confidence and are given basic schooling and vocational training. Local elders are invited to participate fully as a way of helping to ensure that the children are welcomed in the community.

The reintegration process should include community mediation, as well as forgiveness or cleansing rituals to help former child soldiers win acceptance from their communities and reunite with their families. In all cases, child soldiers must be shielded from retribution, arbitrary detention and other punitive measures and ensured protection in accordance with the Convention on the Rights of the Child. Any judicial proceedings should be in the context of juvenile and restorative justice in order to ensure the child's physical, psychological and social rehabilitation.

Children should help identify their health needs and vocational and educational aspirations. A participative approach throughout reintegration processes is key to helping young people acquire skills and return to community life.

Finding a place in the community

One of the best ways for children to normalise their lives and develop a non-military identity is through education and vocational training. Yet they may face many obstacles. Since former combatants are likely to have fallen behind in their schooling, they may be placed in classes with younger children – but the humiliation of struggling to keep up with much younger children often discourages ex-combatants from returning to school. And teachers and parents may object to having former child soldiers enrol at all, fearing that they will have a disruptive effect on other children. One alternative is, at the outset, to have special classes for former child soldiers who can be reintegrated progressively into regular schools.

Adolescents, who make up the vast majority of child soldiers, will need training in life skills, vocational classes and specific preparation for employment. This will not only help them survive but can facilitate their acceptance at home and provide them with a sense of meaning and identity.

The transition from child soldier back to child is unimaginably hard. Many children find it difficult to disengage from the idea that violence is a legitimate means of achieving their aims, particularly when they still suffer the frustrations of poverty and injustice. The challenge for governments and civil society is to channel the energy, ideas and experience of youth into the creation of peaceful societies.

Legal standards to stop the use of child soldiers

In May 2000, the United Nations General Assembly adopted an Optional Protocol to the Convention on the Rights of the Child on the involvement of children in armed conflict.[39] The new Protocol raises the minimum age for compulsory recruitment from 15 to 18 years of age and forbids anyone under 18 from participating in hostilities.

The Optional Protocol prohibits non-governmental forces from any recruitment below the age of 18. But its application to States parties is less clear. It requires that States establish a minimum age for voluntary recruitment, but it does not specify that the age be 18. This creates a double standard, allowing governments to recruit minors on a voluntary basis, and thereby undermining the Protocol's intent. The United Kingdom took advantage of this loophole when it signed the Optional Protocol in September 2000 and simultaneously declared its intention to deploy those younger than 18 in battle in the event of a genuine military need or when the urgency of the situation called for their participation.

A campaign is under way to encourage States to move swiftly to ratify the Optional Protocol without reservations and, consistent with article 3 of the Protocol, to submit a binding declaration setting 18 as the standard minimum age for voluntary recruitment and to make the necessary changes in their national legislation. Only a "straight 18" ban will keep children off the battlefield. Any loophole allowing children younger than 18 to participate in conflict will undermine the effectiveness of the Protocol.

In June 1999, the International Labour Organization adopted Convention 182, which calls for the elimination of forced or compulsory recruitment of children for use in armed conflict and defines children as "all persons under the age of 18." The ILO Convention also establishes child soldiering as an intolerable form of child labour, opening up new possibilities of protection and enforcement. Another landmark agreement on child soldiers is the African Charter on the Rights and Welfare of the Child, the first regional treaty to establish 18 as the minimum age for all recruitment and participation in hostilities. It came into force in November 1999.

The Rome Statute establishing the International Criminal Court, overwhelmingly approved in July 1998, makes it an international war crime for children to be conscripted or enlisted into armed forces or groups – or otherwise used in hostilities. Although it sets the minimum age for recruitment at 15, the Rome Statute, now in the ratification process, is nonetheless an important step towards the enforcement of international law forbidding children's participation in hostilities.

To set an example for police and military forces worldwide, the United Nations has taken a lead role by establishing 18 as the minimum age for UN peacekeepers and recommending that no one under 21 years of age should participate in peacekeeping missions. The Secretary-General, in a recent Report to the Security Council on the Protection of Civilians in Conflict, recommended 18 as the minimum age for all military recruitment and participation in hostilities and urged that armed groups refrain from recruiting children under 18 or face the threat of targeted sanctions.

These are all important steps on the road towards ending children's participation in hostilities. Yet recent international standards and policies defining this atrocity as a war crime confirm what everyone knows instinctively: of course it is a war crime. The exploitation of children as soldiers is as unacceptable as the impunity that prevails for this egregious abuse. It is crucial to end the impunity with which children are drawn into armed conflict. For despite these recent international standards and policies defining the use of children in armed conflict as a war crime, no State or non-state actor has been brought to account, even in the face of systematic reports from Afghanistan, Angola, Colombia, Democratic Republic of the Congo, Liberia, Sierra Leone, Sri Lanka and Uganda, among others.

Concerned parents in Uganda struggle for their children

Following a series of wholesale child abductions by the Lord's Resistance Army (LRA) in northern Uganda in 1996, local parents banded together to seek the return of their children and to mobilise grass-roots support against the brutal tactics of the LRA.[40]

Over the last 14 years, at least 12,000 children have been abducted from the Kitgum and Gulu districts. Some 6,000 remain missing, but about 4,000 have managed to escape.

Once children do escape they find it very difficult to return to their families and communities. Many have been forced to commit atrocities against their own relatives, and girls who were abused as sexual slaves have returned with babies. Sexually transmitted infections, including HIV/AIDS, are common.

Only a few years ago communities were unwilling or unable to take back children abducted by the LRA, but today, thanks to the efforts of Concerned Parents Associations (CPAs) and other local groups, the children are welcomed. These groups offer

Building consensus

The adoption of the Optional Protocol was a result of a collaborative effort by governments, UN agencies and civil society groups. In June 1998, six international non-governmental organisations – Amnesty International, Human Rights Watch, the International Save the Children Alliance, Jesuit Refugee Service, the Quaker United Nations Office in Geneva and the International Federation of Terre des Hommes – formed the Coalition to Stop the Use of Child Soldiers. They were subsequently joined by many other NGOs and additional national coalitions have been formed in nearly 40 countries. The Coalition to Stop the Use of Child Soldiers

unconditional forgiveness and reconciliation. They make no judgements and administer no punishments. Children without families are received by a large extended family. There are also centres to provide community-based, rather than institutionalised, psychosocial support.

The Governments of Sudan and Uganda have agreed in principle to work together for the release of children abducted by the LRA. While such commitments remain fragile, in signing the Nairobi Agreement in 1999, the Presidents of Sudan and Uganda renounced the use of force to resolve their differences and made commitments to locate and return abductees, especially children, to their families and offer reintegration assistance. Following the agreement, several high-level meetings between representatives of the two countries have been held, including a ministerial meeting in November 2000 convened by The Carter Center, with UNICEF participation. Yet the abducted children have not been released in significant numbers and each day that passes is another day sacrificed from their childhood for political gain.

conducts research, organises regional conferences, carries out campaigns, advocacy and media work and helps strengthen NGO networks. A major goal is the earliest possible ratification of the Optional Protocol, with a clear majority of States setting a "straight 18" ban on all recruitment as well as participation.

Since 1995, Rädda Barnen, the Swedish Save the Children, has been an active participant in the campaign. The NGO has published a major book on child soldiers, publishes regular newsletters and maintains Internet databases listing recruitment ages and numbers of child solders and giving bibliographical information on the child soldiers issue.[41]

There have been many community initiatives to stop the use of children as soldiers. In El Salvador, Guatemala and Paraguay, for example, minority ethnic groups and the mothers of child soldiers have formed organisations to pressure authorities for their release. Similar groups have been formed more recently in Uganda. In Burundi, a network of national and local partners cooperates in gathering information about child recruitment. Provincial reports are then compiled to monitor the situation of child soldiers.[42]

Regional organisations have declared their support for the campaign to end the use of child soldiers. The Economic Community of West African States (ECOWAS), in March 1999, issued a declaration by their Ministers of Foreign Affairs, strongly condemning the conscription of children into armed groups. The Organization of African Unity (OAU) Summit Declaration, July 1999, calls upon all member states to prohibit recruitment and use of child soldiers under 18 years of age. The Organization of American States (OAS) Summit Declaration, June 2000, calls upon member states to sign and ratify the Optional Protocol to the Convention on the Rights of the Child, raising the minimum age for the participation of children in hostilities.

But more effective measures should be taken to prevent the recruitment of children. These include monitoring and enforcing legal commitments to prevent recruitment below the age of 18, introducing or re-establishing reliable birth-registration systems, especially among displaced children and children of minority groups, and providing education and vocational opportunities for young people. Training military and non-state actors on issues of child rights can help also.

In spite of progress, the abduction and recruitment of child soldiers continues. In some recent conflicts, children have been recruited much more deliberately, not just because of their availability and relative cheapness, but also because they are capable of being more thoroughly indoctrinated into the use of violence and thus more willing than adults to carry out atrocities.

Chapter 3

Children forced to flee

"We left our village when the bombs began falling. Some people stayed, but we were afraid of being killed. The bombs were like earthquakes that didn't stop. You spend many years building up a home, and then, in one moment, it is destroyed."

— Aygun, age 17, Azerbaijan [1]

Wars drive millions of people from their homes. An estimated 20 million are children, deprived of the security of their communities and exposed to multiple dangers. In all, about 1 in every 150 people on earth – a total of 40 million – have fled their homes because of armed conflict or human rights violations. [2]

People who remain within their own national borders – the "internally displaced" [3] – make up some two-thirds of the total, while others who flee across borders are designated as refugees. [4] The term "displaced people" refers to both groups.

Families abandon their homes in fear of death or torture. They leave behind property, relatives, friends, familiar surroundings and established social networks. Their anguish and sense of loss can be overwhelming. Though the decision to leave is usually made by adults, even the youngest children can sense their parents' fear and uncertainty. Escape itself is fraught with peril. Families risk everything from ambush and shelling to snipers and landmines, often walking for days with limited quantities of water and food. Under such circumstances, children become acutely undernourished and prone to illness. Girls in flight are at special risk of sexual abuse.

And both boys and girls may be seized and forcibly recruited into armed groups.

Children separated from their parents

In the chaos of conflict and escape, many children fall into harm's way because they are separated from their parents. Deprived of physical care and emotional security, they become more vulnerable to hunger, disease, violence, military recruitment and sexual assault. "Unaccompanied children" are those who are separated from both parents and are not in the care of another adult who, by law or custom, has taken responsibility for them. "Separated children" or "separated minors" include those children and adolescents who are separated from both parents, but not necessarily from other relatives.[5]

Parents living in war zones can become so concerned for the safety of their children that they send them to friends or relatives outside of the conflict area or have them join evacuation programmes. But large-scale evacuation programmes may risk exposing children to the trauma of family separation while increasing the danger of trafficking or of illegal adoption. When evacuations from conflict areas are essential, UNHCR and UNICEF guidelines recommend that whole families be moved together. If this is not possible, children should be moved with their primary caregivers. Those who are organising evacuations should document the process carefully to ensure that children can maintain contact with other family members and rapidly be reunited with them.

Children separated from their immediate families should be cared for by other relatives or adults known to them, who share their customs and traditions. It is essential that brothers and sisters are kept together. This helps maintain a child's emotional security and cultural and linguistic ties. During emergencies pressures to make separated children available for adoption in country or internationally must be resisted. Adoption severs family links permanently. In Bosnia and Herzegovina, some evacuations were organised by groups intent on exploiting international adoption markets. Under the 1993 Hague Convention on Protection of Children and

Co-operation in Respect of Intercountry Adoption, the adoption of separated children should not be considered until all family-tracing efforts have been exhausted.[6] But even when agencies acting in good faith find suitable foster parents in country, there may be reluctance to return the child to his or her family. Many foster families take excellent care of children, but under the pressures of

Tracing children in the Great Lakes region

The 1994 genocide in Rwanda left an estimated 800,000 dead[7] and caused the flight of 2 million internally displaced persons and 2 million refugees.[8] In the panic during and after the slaughter, between 75,000 and 120,000 children lost contact with their families.[9]

Between 1994 and 2000, ICRC, UN agencies and NGOs in the Great Lakes region have helped reunite more than 67,000 unaccompanied children with family members. Between 1995 and 2000, the number of centres for unaccompanied children dropped from 77 to 37.[10] Yet statistics cannot convey the persistence and patience needed to bring so many children home, sometimes after years of separation. As recently as 1999, nearly 100 children a month were being reunited.[11] And because of current conflicts in the region, displacements and separations are still occurring.

A number of factors have contributed to the overall success of the Great Lakes reunification programme. From the beginning the programme was collaborative, combining the efforts of ICRC, UNHCR, UNICEF, IFRC and a number of NGOs. Altogether some 150 humanitarian organisations have participated.[12] Another key factor was the central database in Nairobi maintained by ICRC that served as a register for unaccompanied and separated children. The computer network, keeping data on all separated children, was regularly updated and accessible through ICRC offices in the region. That allowed for mass tracing, using

extreme poverty in war, some may exploit children in their care. For that reason, community-based systems are needed to monitor the well-being of children in foster families. For example, records kept by agencies and NGOs working with unaccompanied children can further family reunification efforts at a later date.

Wherever possible, institutional care should be avoided. While

lists of information organised by area of origin.

In Rwanda, during the peak of the programme, over 1,000 children and family members were identified each month.[13] Photo tracing, initiated by UNICEF, was especially helpful for children too young or distressed to provide information on their families. In the refugee camps around Goma in former Zaire, in 1995, 12,000 unaccompanied children were photographed and display boards organised in camps and areas where families and other refugees might recognise a child. This experience led to the creation of photo albums of children in centres in Rwanda. The photo albums were distributed for parents to identify their missing child. Many reunions were facilitated, even after years of separation.[14]

As the work of reunification in the Great Lakes region continues, another phase of the work is under way: addressing the plight of children whose families have never been found. Between October 1999 and April 2000, the files for nearly 700 children were turned over to the Rwandan Ministry of Social Affairs to arrange for foster families.[15] Thousands of Rwandan children remain separated from their families. Many are not in the care of centres or agencies conducting the tracing but are living in child-headed households. World Vision and UNICEF have estimated that there were 60,000 child-headed households in Rwanda.[16] For the most part, those children remain isolated, exposed to violence and extreme exploitation, struggling to survive without access to school, health care or community support.

orphanages and other institutions can meet children's basic needs, experience has shown that they do not provide sufficient emotional support. In 1994, in the Great Lakes region of Africa, a large number of centres were created specifically for separated children. The centres attracted media attention and, in the process, humanitarian aid. Some took in unnecessary numbers of separated children in order to increase financial support given to their centre. In other cases, parents thought it best to leave their children where they would be guaranteed food and health care. And there is an additional risk that temporary centres may become permanent.

Tracing programmes, to reunite unaccompanied children with their families, have improved in recent years. In the Great Lakes region of Africa in 1994, a number of agencies, including the International Committee of the Red Cross (ICRC), the International Federation of the Red Cross and Red Crescent Societies (IFRC), UNHCR, UNICEF, Save the Children Fund and other NGOs, set up a vast tracing programme that reunited almost 90 per cent of unaccompanied children who had been identified.[17]

Sophisticated tracing techniques were used in the Balkans throughout the Kosovo crisis in 1999. During the NATO aerial bombardment, communications links established by British Telecom and Eutelsat helped hundreds of thousands of Kosovar refugees contact relatives in other countries free of charge.[18] A number of other information technology companies, including Microsoft, Compaq and Hewlett-Packard, helped create a database to register 400,000 refugees in Albania. UNHCR used high-tech field kits to gather data and issue photo identification cards on the spot. Each kit included a laptop computer, a digital camera, a signature pad and an ID card printer.[19] ICRC maintains a global family tracing network with over 60 computer databases. In Kosovo, ICRC registered the names of nearly 5,000 missing persons and so far has helped reunite 1,500 people.[20]

Women and girls in camps

While camps for displaced persons should be places of safety, offering protection and assistance, they are in fact often highly militarised.

Power struggles and conflicts existing in communities prior to their displacement are likely to be reproduced in camp settings, while traditional social systems can come under strain or break down completely. Family disputes are frequent, as are high levels of violence, sexual assault, and alcohol and substance abuse. Women and adolescent girls are particularly affected. Violence prevails within families, between refugee and host communities and even from the civilian and military security forces that are meant to provide protection.

In the United Republic of Tanzania, so many Rwandan women arrived at refugee camps without their husbands that orange tents were set up to house them in specially marked "safe" areas. But the bright orange tents only called attention to the women's vulnerability, and the number of sexual attacks increased.

UNHCR has issued guidelines on preventing sexual violence against refugees. Locating the latrines in areas that are well lit, guarded and close to sleeping areas is one of the practical measures recommended. Providing water and firewood within the camps to limit the necessity of women and children venturing outside of patrolled areas is another. Appointing women guards is another essential security measure. In Tanzania, when female guards were appointed, the reporting of sexual violence increased and harassment at distribution centres decreased.[21] Despite the simplicity and effectiveness of the UNHCR guidelines, they have been inadequately enforced.

Many women in displaced communities also lack basic reproductive health care. The United Nations Population Fund (UNFPA) has responded by supplying reproductive health kits that provide women with essential medications, as well as surgical tools for home birth.

Women, youth and children should be involved actively in all aspects of camp management and especially the planning and distribution of services. Control over resources like food and plastic sheeting represents power. Men, usually in charge of distribution, often abuse this power by demanding bribes or sexual favours. Distribution points should therefore be controlled by women. In 1994, the Representative of the Secretary-General on Internally Displaced Persons visited a camp for internally displaced people in

Burundi. When he asked to meet with the camp spokespersons, among a population of several thousand women and just 25 men, only men were presented.[22] Excluding women from leadership positions, within camps or elsewhere, can undermine the effectiveness of humanitarian assistance.

Building a focus on adolescents

The special needs of displaced adolescents have been, for the most part, overlooked. The few programmes that focus on adolescent health care, education or vocational training demonstrate that the participation of young people in programme design is a key to success. For example, during the Kosovo crisis in 1999 adolescents formed Youth Councils and helped improve conditions in a number of refugee camps.

UNHCR has made children's and adolescents' issues a centrepiece of its work through its Country Operations Plans and has established four Regional Policy Officers for children and youth. UNHCR youth programmes are under way in East and West Timor to provide vocational training and formal education for some adolescents.

In 1997, UNHCR and the Save the Children Alliance developed a training programme for humanitarian workers called Action for the Rights of Children (ARC). In 1999, UNICEF and the Office of the High Commissioner for Human Rights (OHCHR) joined ARC's Steering Committee. One of the ARC resource packs is focused on strategies to address the needs of adolescents in conflict situations.[23]

In Guinea, Kenya, Liberia, Sierra Leone and Tanzania, programmes run by UNHCR and UNFPA address sexual and gender-based violence against adolescent refugee girls.[24] A leadership and skills-training initiative for youth in Rwanda, run by the International Rescue Committee (IRC), was launched in 1998 and, in Georgia, another programme allows displaced adolescents who have fallen behind in school to catch up.[25] In the West Bank and Gaza, UNICEF has supported "child-friendly communities," encouraging adolescent participation through the establishment of

Kosovo Youth Councils

During the Kosovo crisis in 1999, adolescents made important contributions to social reconstruction and peace-building. In the six refugee camps near Kukes in Albania, Kosovar Youth Councils were formed, involving about 20,000 young people ranging in age from 15 to 25.

Until then, activities in the refugee community had been structured around childcare, health services and primary education, marginalising adolescent needs. Amid the trauma of displacement and the general boredom of camp life, the outlook for young people was grim. The Youth Councils provided a safety net. The Councils elected their leaders by ballot and held regular open meetings. With support from UNICEF and the local Albania Youth Club, Council members organised sports tournaments and concerts and took an active role in running the camps and keeping them clean and safe. They helped integrate newly arrived families and organised fund-raising for the poorest members of the camp community. They assisted UN agencies and NGOs in distributing landmine awareness information and materials on organised recreation and counselling for younger children.

Perhaps the greatest benefit of the programme was demonstrated during the reconstruction phase. Although the Youth Councils had been active for less than one month, the experience gained from organising and participating in them brought out new leadership and problem-solving skills, and many of the Youth Council members returned to Kosovo to help rebuild their communities.

youth community councils.[26]

Humanitarian organisations have taken measures to protect the rights of displaced children. These include safeguards to protect youth from recruitment and prevent sexual exploitation in camps for displaced people and to educate children about the danger of land-mines. In Sierra Leone, for example, the World Food Programme (WFP) runs a school-feeding project which provides prepared meals for schoolchildren only when the attendance rate of girls is 30 per cent or more. Thus the programme achieves a dual purpose of feed-ing children and promoting non-discrimination.[27]

Minority and indigenous children

Despite the special protections set out in the Convention on the Rights of the Child and a number of international instruments, minority and indigenous children are among the most vulnerable within displaced populations. In a climate of lawlessness, attacks on these communities are especially fierce. Whether a minority is expressly targeted by more powerful groups – as in Bangladesh and Guatemala – or suffers through being relatively defenceless in a sit-uation of virtual anarchy – as was the case in Somalia – minority status increases the vulnerability of children.

When displaced from their communities, minority and indige-nous children struggle to retain their cultural identity. Finding ways to promote their language and culture can help. Minority and indigenous children are often severely disadvantaged when it comes to education and health services. In Guatemala, Mayan children have always had higher rates of malnutrition and more severe health problems than the rest of the population – inequities that were heightened by years of civil war.[28]

Internally displaced children

In practice it may be difficult to distinguish between internally dis-placed persons (IDPs) and refugees. In Liberia, for example, inter-nally displaced populations were living together with Sierra Leonean refugees. Relatives and friends often share meagre resources to provide shelter and assistance for displaced families, who are often forced to move again and again to escape conflict. This kind of displacement can increase death rates by as much as 60 per cent.[29]

When children are displaced, they may be forced to live and work on the streets. Internal displacement also limits children's access to health and education. For example, children may not be able to enrol in schools within host communities because they lack proper documentation, are not considered residents of the area or are unable to pay school fees. In Colombia, 85 per cent of displaced children have no access to primary education.[30]

When a government is unable or unwilling to assist its own dispossessed – or is itself the cause of their displacement – then the international community is called upon to take action. Although international humanitarian law guarantees the right of war victims to receive safe and timely assistance,[31] the international community has not charted a clear course of action for IDPs. Some countries do not even acknowledge displaced populations within their borders.[32] Providing assistance to internally displaced persons is further complicated by the fact that, unlike refugees, no operational agency currently has an explicit or global mandate to provide for them.

In certain instances the UN Security Council has moved to protect citizens endangered by internal conflicts, but there has been no consistent framework or consensus on which to base such interventions.

In Burundi in 1996, and again in 1999, the Government's *regroupement* policy forced over 300,000 people to leave their homes and live in camps guarded by the military, where they lack adequate food, health care, shelter and security. The *regroupement* camps have been condemned by the UN and described as "concentration camps" by former South African President Nelson Mandela, Chief Facilitator in the Burundi peace process. Following concerted international efforts, the Government began to close the camps in late 2000.[33]

With respect to children, the guidance has been more specific.[34] In Resolution 1314 on children and armed conflict, the UN

Security Council reaffirmed the need for unhindered access to children affected by armed conflict. The evidence of increased political will has yet to result in tangible action to protect and assist internally displaced children. Charting a course of action that respects national sovereignty and protects children's rights is one of the great challenges for international policy.

To this end, in 1992, the UN Secretary-General appointed Francis M. Deng as his Representative (RSG) on Internally Displaced Persons. Through field visits and advocacy, the RSG has focused world attention on displaced children. In 1998 he completed a major study, *Masses in Flight: The Global Crisis of Internal Displacement.*[35] Also in 1998, he presented to the Commission on Human Rights the *Guiding Principles on Internal Displacement.* Applicable to all phases of displacement, the 30 Principles offer a basis for protection and assistance during displacement, provide protection against arbitrary displacement and set forth guarantees for safe return, resettlement and reintegration. The Principles serve as a normative framework to guide governments, authorities and international humanitarian and development agencies in providing assistance and protection to displaced persons.

The 30 Principles direct special attention to the needs of internally displaced children. They assert that children, especially unaccompanied minors, shall be entitled to the protection and assistance required by their condition and to treatment that takes into account their special needs. They also prohibit the sale into marriage, sexual exploitation and forced labour of children and the recruitment or participation of children in hostilities. They provide for the rapid reunification of families, the education of displaced children and the equal participation of girls in education programmes.

The Commission on Human Rights has welcomed the use of the *Guiding Principles* in dialogue with governments and intergovernmental and non-governmental agencies. In the short time since their formulation, the *Guiding Principles* have been recognised as a valuable instrument for addressing the protection needs of internally displaced persons. A useful policy and practice tool, the overall impact of the Principles will depend on how effectively they are implemented.

Despite significant improvements, international response to internally displaced persons remains ad hoc and often ineffective. A lead agency may be identified to provide assistance, as for example, UNHCR in Colombia and Sri Lanka, or UNICEF in southern Sudan. But in Angola, over 1 million children have been internally displaced by a four-decades-old war between government and rebel forces, and no lead agency has been designated to care for them. A number of organisations and agencies are attempting to provide short-term emergency aid, but long-term support is lacking. The situation has been devastating for children and women – and highlights the alarming neglect of internally displaced persons over the past decade and the inadequacy of the current approach.

In some instances, as in Colombia and Chechnya (Russian Federation), UNHCR has been asked to serve a relatively small number of refugees within a much broader community of IDPs. In Colombia, UNHCR was asked to assume a leadership role after the inter-agency coordinated approach proved unsuccessful. In Tajikistan, only about 60,000 people fled to Afghanistan while 600,000 people were internally displaced. In the Federal Republic of Yugoslavia and in Timor, UNHCR took the lead role in providing for both refugees and IDPs, supported by the ICRC and other NGOs.

In order to ensure that basic assistance and protection is provided to children, a lead agency should be identified and provided with adequate resources to carry out its role in every situation where there are internally displaced persons. The agency already most involved in the country should be designated; in a majority of cases, it will be UNHCR. In those instances where UNHCR is not already directly involved, the agency most engaged should be designated. The lead agency should collaborate fully with all other agencies involved, such as UNICEF and the World Food Programme. In all cases, UNICEF should be a major partner in the protection and care of internally displaced children.

In December 1999, UN agencies outlined a series of measures to increase protection for internally displaced persons. Humanitarian agencies have been called upon to improve the monitoring of displaced children and report human rights violations.[36] At the same time, the Norwegian Refugee Council (NRC) launched a global IDP database on the Internet to provide information on internally displaced populations in more than 30 countries. The NRC is working with UNICEF and the European Commission to develop child-specific indicators for the collection and analysis of information for the database.

Refugees and asylum

Even after displaced families cross national borders, they continue to be exposed to danger. Adolescent girls and women who have been separated from their families are particularly vulnerable to exploitation and abuse from border guards and military personnel. Having crossed the border they have no guarantee of asylum. Following the end of the Cold War, governments have been more reluctant to grant asylum and some have even sought to prevent asylum seekers from reaching their borders. Asylum seekers may be detained in prisons or other institutions while governments consider their cases. Seeking asylum cannot be considered an offence or a crime, yet many women and children are being incarcerated with criminals for doing so.

Unaccompanied refugee children may find it particularly difficult to gain asylum and risk becoming stateless if they cannot establish their identity, nationality, birth place and the identity of their parents. Countries that determine refugee status on an individual basis should not refuse unaccompanied children access to asylum procedures, regardless of their age. As a minimum, governments should grant temporary asylum to all those fleeing armed conflict. Asylum procedures are lengthy, arduous and stressful, often lasting several years, with detrimental effects on child development.

Returning home and durable solutions

Whether displaced children return home, resettle elsewhere or integrate into a host community, attempts should be made to keep families together, procedures should be as efficient and expeditious as possible and the best interests of the child should be paramount. In countries disrupted by many years of conflict, there are often tensions between returnees and residents. Upon return, the legal rights of displaced populations may be at risk. Female heads of households may find that they have no rights to reclaim their property and they may lose custody of their children. Similar problems emerge for child-headed households, which are usually headed by adolescent girls and can include siblings, children of extended families or even children who are unrelated. Often lacking land, property and inheritance rights, they are in a precarious position and in need of legal and social protection. In Rwanda, NGOs worked with women's groups to promote legislation, enacted in November 1999, giving girls and women more secure access to land. In Guatemala, the 1996 Peace Accords oblige the Government to eliminate any legal discrimination against women trying to gain access to land, housing or credit.[37]

When communities are displaced for long periods of time, questions of livelihood must be addressed, especially for women and adolescents who are often unskilled and supporting younger children. For most families what begins as temporary displacement may last 6 or more years on average and frequently more than 10 years.[38] In general, short-term solutions for displaced populations have taken precedence over long-term concerns. Essential food, medicines and other emergency life-saving measures can only begin to address the long-term needs of children uprooted by war.

Long-term solutions can include programmes of voluntary return to dispossessed lands or the establishment of new homes. After the seven-year war ended in Liberia in 1997, a national Resettlement Commission was established to assist in the repatriation of refugees together with support from UNHCR. More than 1 million displaced people returned home, including large numbers of child-headed households and young girls. They were mostly left to fend for themselves, many struggling with the consequences of rape and unwanted pregnancy. With little economic support, many young girls were forced to turn to prostitution for survival. In 1998, Liberian NGOs, working with UNHCR and UNICEF, started the Liberian Children's Initiative to offer returnee and internally displaced children and adolescents catch-up schooling, vocational training and income-generating activities.[39] In

Tajikistan, UNHCR distributed shelter kits, with roofing materials, nails and plaster board, to help rebuild homes. They also sent international monitors into the area to record human rights abuses and report violations to local authorities. This twofold approach combining human rights monitoring and humanitarian assistance helped build trust among agencies, local authorities and returnees.[40] In Nicaragua, UNHCR introduced "gender clauses" into reintegration projects, stipulating that women would receive equal pay and that they would comprise half of all persons involved in the planning and implementation of assistance. But such programmes are few and far between.

In a report to the United Nations General Assembly fifty-fifth session in May 2000, the Secretary-General recommends that families be provided with long-term assistance and the means to a sustainable livelihood, including land, seeds and tools for farming. The report urges that children receive education and professional training to help ensure that they can find a future job or sustainable livelihood.[41]

Chapter 4

Children under siege from HIV/AIDS

"Fifty per cent of the new infections (HIV/AIDS) which take place today are in the age group of 15 to 25. I mean if we are the future and we're dying, there is no future."

– Mary Phiri, editor of *Trendsetters*, an HIV/AIDS news monthly produced by teenagers in Zambia[1]

Over the past five years, HIV/AIDS has changed the landscape of conflict for children more than any other single factor. The chaotic and brutal circumstances of conflict aggravate all of the factors that fuel the HIV/AIDS crisis. And HIV/AIDS reinforces the instability that prolongs conflict, spreading death, suffering and social upheaval that deprive children of their most basic rights. Together they present the most serious threat to human security that the world has ever known.

AIDS is profoundly destabilising, even in countries not at war. In January 2000, the UN Security Council identified HIV/AIDS as a significant threat to peace and security. "In already unstable societies," the UN Secretary-General Kofi Annan observed, "this cocktail of disasters is a sure recipe for more conflict. And conflict, in turn, provides fertile ground for further infections."[2]

Like armed conflict, HIV/AIDS breaks up families and communities, creating widespread social disruption. Children and women caught up in the chaos of war are more vulnerable to sexual abuse and exploitation that greatly increase the likelihood of sexually transmitted infections (STIs) and facilitate the spread of HIV. Worldwide, HIV/AIDS has already killed nearly 4 million children and orphaned 13 million more.[3] In sub-Saharan Africa, 10 times as many people are dying of AIDS as are dying in war.[4]

By killing teachers, health workers, government administrators and other public sector employees, both armed conflict and HIV/AIDS undermine the very institutions that could help mitigate the impact of the pandemic. The destruction of schools, health centres and other public buildings makes it immeasurably harder to reach young people and communities with life-saving information. And health centres, if still functioning, are usually so overburdened there is little hope of diagnosing HIV/AIDS and the diseases associated with it, much less treat them. Widespread physical violence also increases the chance that children will be exposed to HIV-contaminated blood. Even the treatment of war-related injuries can heighten the risk of infection via transfusion, since there is limited screening of blood during conflict.

Conflict, poverty and AIDS

Links between armed conflict and AIDS run in both directions – and are compounded by poverty and the gender dimensions of both. There is no question that poverty accelerates the spread of HIV/AIDS and its effects. That is why any long-term solutions in the fight against AIDS must include measures to alleviate poverty, beginning with steps to strengthen social capacity and infrastructure. Drug treatment, for example, depends on health systems for delivery – and campaigns to educate communities about HIV must rely on local and national systems of communication.

Dr. Peter Piot, Executive Director of the Joint United Nations Programme on HIV/AIDS (UNAIDS), has urged the international community to recognise the connection between debt relief and pandemic relief. African governments today spend, on average, twice as much on debt service as on their investments in basic social services. When 13 of the 17 countries with over 100,000 children orphaned by AIDS are heavily indebted poor countries

(HIPC) – and when 13 of those same 17 countries are either in conflict or on the brink – there can be no mistaking the deadly links among poverty, conflict and HIV/AIDS.[5]

National military spending consumes resources that might otherwise be used on health, education and social services in the fight against HIV/AIDS. For example, in 1998, Burundi spent 5.8 per cent of its GDP on the military, almost 10 times the 0.6 per cent allocated to health. In Ethiopia, military expenditures accounted for 3.8 per cent of the GDP, compared to 1.6 per cent for health.[6]

Drug treatments that have proven effective in industrialised countries have been prohibitively expensive in developing countries, especially those in conflict. These include the antiretrovirals (ARVs) that can slow the progress of AIDS, as well as other drugs to treat the health complications brought on by the virus, such as cryptococcal meningitis and pneumonia.

Pharmaceutical companies were slow to negotiate more affordable pricing, with some inclined to protect their market shares by locking countries into long-term purchasing commitments. In frustration, some governments and humanitarian groups moved to accept cut-rate offers by producers of generic AIDS drugs, increasing the pressure on multinational companies to reduce prices further.

Bowing to international public outrage over the inflated prices of antiretrovirals, a number of multinational pharmaceutical companies offered to lower their prices for antiretroviral drugs. But even those reduced prices remained far beyond the means of most national health services in developing countries, whether in conflict or at peace. As of April 2001, only a tiny minority of people in any developing countries had access to such treatments.

One hotly debated element in the ongoing negotiations has been international patent law, which can restrict production of generic and more affordable versions of life-extending AIDS drugs. While universal affordable access to ARVs is not enough in and of itself, if the international community waits for patents to run out on HIV/AIDS drugs, millions of people will die even more prematurely. In fact, Brazil, India and Thailand are already successfully producing generic AIDS drugs. Given the rapidly growing dimensions of the HIV/AIDS crisis, such alternative measures are not only advisable, they are imperative.

While it might be unrealistic to demand universal affordable access to the more complicated ARV therapies during armed conflict, those that can be administered more easily can and should be given priority in such emergencies. Health delivery systems in countries in conflict must be strengthened sufficiently to support and monitor the use of antiretrovirals.

The issue of drug availability goes beyond ARVs. In many conflict situations even treatment for pain relief is limited, much less treatment for opportunistic infections such as tuberculosis and pneumonia.

Underlying the call to action, on all fronts, is the recognition that greater resources are needed. "We know what to do," Dr. Piot, the UNAIDS leader, told the UN. "Prevention works. It is possible to improve treatment and care offered to people living with the virus."[7]

AIDS and the military

In conflict, sexual violence and rape involving international peacekeepers or national military and civilian security personnel highlight the additional risks to women and children of HIV/AIDS. Armed forces are estimated to have sexually transmitted infection (STI) rates two to five times greater than those of civilian populations. But during armed conflict that rate of infection can be up to 50 times higher,[8] an ominous statistic considering that STIs increase the risk of HIV transmission.

Armed forces are composed primarily of young, sexually active men who spend long periods away from their families. Aware of the potential income that soldiers bring, women and girls in the vicinity may exchange sexual services for gifts or income. When military camps are established they inevitably attract sex workers. Depending on the arrangements made, peacekeepers may live within local communities, which increases the potential for exploitative relationships as well as commercial sex. During a five-month tour of duty in Cambodia, for example, around 45 per cent of the Dutch naval personnel and marines on peacekeeping duty had sexual relations with sex workers or other local residents.[9]

Given these factors, mandatory education on HIV/AIDS prevention should be included in the training of all military forces. In July 2000, the UN Security Council called for "effective long-term strategies for HIV/AIDS education, prevention, voluntary and confidential testing and counselling, and treatment of their personnel, as an important part of their preparation in peacekeeping operations." In addition, disciplinary codes relating to sexual violence and abuse must be established and strictly enforced.

Policies that frame interactions between military, peacekeeping personnel and local communities, including those relating to family life, housing and tours of duty, should be reviewed with the purpose of ensuring the highest levels of protection for these communities. Condoms and HIV/AIDS information should be provided also to all commercial sex workers, especially those near military camps.

Under certain circumstances, some armed forces have imposed mandatory HIV testing – but experience shows that voluntary testing is far more effective when combined with confidential counselling, support and treatment. Regardless of their HIV status, all military personnel should be supplied with condoms, within the context of HIV education and prevention programmes.

Children orphaned by AIDS and war

During conflict, orphaned children are likely to find themselves in especially desperate straits. Children without adult caregivers nearly always find themselves without resources, exposed to violence and exploitation and vulnerable to HIV infection. Under such pressures, children often band together for survival, taking refuge in temporary shelters or on the streets. Older children may suddenly find themselves looking after younger siblings while still in turmoil over the loss of their parents. Without economic support or vocational alternatives, children orphaned in war-torn countries may be recruited into armed groups or enticed into the sex industry that often flourishes in societies uprooted by war. Immediate problems, such as homelessness and malnutrition, are compounded by loss of education, medical care and vocational opportunities, to say nothing of recreation.

What is needed is a unified and targeted strategy that will protect, respect and fulfil the rights of all such children, whether orphaned by conflict or by HIV/AIDS. Assistance for orphans in conflict situations should include ready access to voluntary and confidential counselling, as well as health care and educational services. Their emotional needs are best met through family and community-based care. Community-wide counselling can help to prevent and eliminate discrimination against children orphaned by AIDS. Legal frameworks to safeguard the rights of orphans during and after conflict must be put in place to protect their rights to inherit and own property and to stay together as siblings.

Young people: The power of knowledge and participation

Adolescents now have the highest rate of HIV infection:[10] at least 50 per cent of all new HIV infections occur among those between the ages of 10 and 24, with 7,000 new infections every day.[11] The special vulnerability of former child soldiers and displaced children to sexual assault and exploitation underlines the need for HIV/AIDS prevention and counselling for all war-affected young people.

A 1999 Redd Barna report describes the release by an armed group of five Ugandan girls after their commander died of AIDS. The girls arrived at a reintegration centre for former child combatants. One girl was already showing symptoms of the virus. The girls were offered confidential HIV testing and counselling, but only two agreed to be tested and then chose not to learn the results. Both tested positive.[12]

Young people need to be informed about the risks of HIV infection and how to prevent it. The sense of invulnerability that comes with adolescence affects a youg person's ability to make and carry out informed decisions even in peacetime. Trapped in the chaos of armed conflict, it is incalculably harder.

And wrenched from their schools and communities, young people may feel that sexual behaviour is one area of their lives in which they can exercise control and experience pleasure. The long-term risk of contracting HIV is seemingly diminished alongside the trauma of daily survival. Yet the risk of HIV infection under such conditions actually increases. In countries where there is little or no access to care or treatment, many young people prefer to live with the hope that they are not infected than with the knowledge that they are. Combined with taboos associated with public discussion of sex, this attitude greatly reinforces the conspiracy of silence surrounding the pandemic.

Through peer counselling, young people can support each other to cope with the daily risks presented by HIV/AIDS including its gender dimensions. The empowerment of young people has helped bring about major breakthroughs in HIV/AIDS prevention campaigns in countries such as Côte d'Ivoire, Namibia, Uganda and Zambia. Adolescents are a huge asset as communicators and counsellors for other war-affected adolescents. But their potential is only beginning to be realised.

The failure of governments and organisations to provide adequate care for people living with HIV/AIDS means that young people, especially girls, shoulder the heavy burden and are often forced to take on adult responsibilities without sufficient guidance or support.

"Vertical transmission"

Over 90 per cent of all HIV-infected children began life as babies born to HIV-positive mothers.[13] Without access to appropriate medical intervention, about a third of infected mothers will pass the infection on to their children, either during pregnancy, at birth or through breastfeeding.

Certain antiretroviral drugs can reduce greatly the risk of transmission of HIV at birth. But there is still a 15 per cent chance that an HIV-positive mother will pass HIV on to her child through breastmilk. Women must weigh this risk against the risk to their babies of not breastfeeding. In developing countries, infants who are not breastfed are six times more likely to die than those who are, when HIV is removed as a risk factor.[14]

Alternative feeding requires clean water and infant formula, both of which are scarce and expensive commodities in conflict situations. In the Democratic Republic of the Congo, only 45 per cent of the population has access to clean water; in Ethiopia, access is estimated at less than 25 per cent of the population.[15] For those living in IDP and refugee camps, the situation is far worse. Unsafe drinking water, poor sanitation and the cost and scarcity of infant formula mean that whether or not a woman knows her HIV status, breastfeeding is usually the only option and may prove to be the safest even if formula is available.

In the chaos of conflict, women still need access to HIV/AIDS testing, counselling and treatment. But that access does not yet exist for most people in developing countries, even in times of peace. Yet testing and counselling alone do not allow women to make informed choices if there are no alternatives to breastfeeding available.

During armed conflict the health of HIV-positive mothers is rarely addressed adequately. The predominant focus on protecting infants from infection has often eclipsed the health needs of HIV-positive mothers. Programme responses to HIV in conflict should provide women with access to appropriate medication, nutritional support and other care and treatment before, during and after pregnancy.

In describing the spread of HIV to babies, the medical term "vertical transmission" is popularly called "mother-to-child transmission." This term may attribute blame, directly or indirectly, to the mother. The reality is that many HIV-positive women have been unknowingly infected by their partners. Many others have been infected as a result of sexual violence and exploitation in conflict and left to face the devastating implications, both for themselves and their children.

Compounding women's risk is the fact that the rate of HIV transmission from men to women is about four times more efficient than from women to men.[16] Moreover, in most cultures, women's limited power to negotiate sexual activity is further compromised by conflict. They cannot talk about sex much less discuss condom use. And their enforced silence comes at a terrible cost.

Empowerment through education systems

When schools are functioning, they can serve as community learning centres and provide a meeting place for children and families. But during conflict they may be damaged or destroyed. In some countries, education systems are crippled because teachers and administrators have died from AIDS or armed conflict. In 1999, 51,000 Ethiopian children lost their teachers to AIDS. Education should be the centre of what must become a renaissance – a transformation of schools into safe havens for communal care, learning and support.[17]

By educating young people about prevention and treatment, schools can empower them to assist their families and the rest of the community. Education in emergencies should also include school-based feeding programmes, providing children with two meals a day and ensuring that nutrition and hygiene are integral parts of life-skills training. Providing this as a part of the regular curriculum offers the possibility of better support for children orphaned by HIV/AIDS, while helping prevent their further stig-matisation. It may also provide a conduit for attracting children who are not enrolled in school, many of whom live on the streets or in child-headed households.

In many communities, the imposition of school fees and other charges continues to block children's access to education. Many poor families – especially those affected by HIV/AIDS – simply cannot afford to send their children to school. During conflict, their resources are even more strained. As an urgent priority, governments must therefore make good on their commitment – stated in the Convention on the Rights of the Child, promoted at the 1990 World Summit for Children and reaffirmed in April 2000 at the World Education Forum in Dakar[18] – to ensure the right of every child to free and mandatory basic primary education, in peacetime or during war.

Mobilisation and information

Despite the devastating impact of HIV/AIDS, there is one positive message: HIV/AIDS is preventable. Investment in prevention by governments and international donors can save the lives of millions of children. National awareness and prevention programmes can be successful in changing the course of the pandemic.

A few governments have placed social mobilisation at the core of their national plans to confront the pandemic.[19] But overall, the response to the HIV crisis has fallen far short of the commitment needed, especially in conflict situations when effective national campaigns can play an even more important role. Where formal health and education systems have ceased to function, all efforts must be made to offer HIV-related information and health services as an integral part of emergency assistance.

Experiences in Brazil, Senegal, Thailand and Uganda have shown how essential the active support of political leaders is in promoting widespread social mobilisation in countries gripped by HIV/AIDS. In the late 1980s, despite limited financial resources, the Government of Uganda, along with national NGOs, embarked on a public campaign to fight the spread of AIDS. In 1996, highlighting its continued political commitment to this struggle, the Ugandan Cabinet adopted an "Open Declaration on AIDS." Collectively, these efforts led to a drop in the HIV-prevalence rate among antenatal clinic attendees, from a high of 31 per cent in 1990 to 14 per cent in 1998. But the same success was not evident among Ugandan military recruits, where HIV prevalence increased from 16 per cent in 1992 to 27 per cent in 1996.[20] It is not clear whether this indicates that the public campaigns have been less successful with young men in Ugandan society generally, or specifically within military populations.

In countries in conflict, information campaigns should make use of the UNAIDS/WHO/UNHCR *Guidelines for HIV Interventions in Emergency Settings.* These 1996 Guidelines should be updated to give greater focus to prevention, care and treatment issues for children. UNHCR's 1999 manual, *Reproductive Health in Refugee Situations,* provides guidance on HIV/AIDS issues in emergency settings and should be used as an integral part of information campaigns. Information campaigns should figure prominently in comprehensive national and local plans to fight HIV infection through health, education and other systems.

Emergency responses

Emergency situations thought to be temporary can drag on for years, stretching people's coping mechanisms to the breaking point. In such circumstances, reducing HIV-transmission rates hinges on the incorporation of awareness and prevention programmes into all aspects of emergency relief. In addition, humanitarian responses should include free voluntary and confidential counselling and testing, blood screening and provision of medical supplies to deal with the opportunistic infections that accompany HIV/AIDS, particularly tuberculosis.

To avoid creating an inadvertent double standard between displaced people and their neighbours, these services must be made available to both populations and should be undertaken with government collaboration and support wherever possible. Improved data collection and monitoring of HIV/AIDS prevalence, infection and transmission rates can help build a greater knowledge of appropriate policy and practice. Emergency health and life-skills programmes for youth should include HIV awareness and prevention and provide access to HIV-related health services. Condoms should be made widely available, within counselling programmes, through the health service or through other youth services that can explain their proper use.

In emergency situations, women who are breastfeeding should be given priority in all food and feeding programmes. Supplementary food, vitamins and minerals, especially important for HIV-positive women, should be made available for all women who are breastfeeding. Nationally and internationally, women living with HIV have joined forces and engaged in advocacy on a range of HIV/AIDS issues. Their expertise should be sought in developing policies and strategies for HIV-positive women in conflict situations.

Confronting the pandemic

Considerable, if belated, international attention was focused on the HIV/AIDS pandemic in 2000, and promises were made to dedicate greater resources to the struggle against the virus. Yet it is important that efforts to challenge the pandemic do not place even greater burdens on countries struggling with it. In 1998, an estimated $3 billion – $1.5 billion for prevention activities and $1.5 billion for basic care, excluding antiretroviral drugs – was needed,[21] but only $300 million was spent in developing countries.

In July 2000 the World Bank announced that there was no ceiling to the amount it would make available to combat the spread of HIV/AIDS, but its initial pledge was only $500 million for the whole of Africa. That money, to be allocated within a Multi-Country HIV/AIDS Program (MAP) for Africa, was made available in the form of soft loans. A number of countries refused the offer on the grounds that they can ill afford to increase their debt burden. In December 2000, the African Development Forum (ADF) Consensus document declared that "foreign donors and international financial institutions must greatly increase their financial commitments to HIV/AIDS and development programmes," adding that "this assistance, wherever possible, should be in the form of grants, not loans."[22]

Meanwhile, the international community has begun to consolidate strategies and resources for the fight against AIDS in Africa. In 1999, for example, the International Partnership Against AIDS in Africa (IPAA), a collaboration among African governments, international donors, United Nations agencies, civil society and the private sector, called for increased support for fragile government structures in conflict-affected countries, to give priority to the development of comprehensive national AIDS programmes.

Since the beginning of 2001, UN Secretary-General Kofi Annan has renewed the United Nations effort to combat HIV/AIDS. The Secretary-General has called for political leaders to take urgent and decisive action to change the course of the pandemic. In an April 2001 meeting in Abuja (Nigeria), the Secretary-General called for the establishment of a "global war chest" worth $7 billion to $10 billion to combat the disease in Africa and prevent a catastrophic spread. The Group of Seven donor nations (G7) is currently negotiating the establishment of a Global Health Fund to finance initiatives to eradicate HIV/AIDS, as well as malaria and tuberculosis.

Within the United Nations, an Inter-Agency Standing Committee (IASC) subgroup on HIV/AIDS in complex emergencies was formed to draft policy and coordinate programmes in response to the HIV/AIDS pandemic in war-torn countries. And the United Nations Consolidated Appeals Process (CAP) has given prominence to HIV/AIDS prevention and care during emergencies. Donors are urged to respond.

Although some information has been gathered regarding HIV transmission and the effectiveness of treatment, pilot programmes have not been conducted in conflict areas. Nor have resources been allocated to assess the links among AIDS, conflict, children and gender. However, in December 2000, UNAIDS began a series of 12 assessments in conflict countries to improve data and knowledge on the impact of HIV. It is essential that children be at the centre of such assessments, an objective that can be achieved with the help of the UNAIDS Committee of Co-sponsoring Organisations (CCO).

The HIV/AIDS catastrophe can no longer be compared with any prior health disaster. It is the biggest challenge facing humankind today and must be confronted vigorously and resolutely. And yet so far the response has been tragically inadequate. Clearly, far more can be done to protect war-affected children from the ravages of HIV/AIDS. The United Nations General Assembly Special Session on HIV/AIDS in June 2001 confirmed support for the Secretary-General's call for a more urgent and concerted global response to the threat of HIV/AIDS. While the world now appears to be rallying, financially and practically, to meet the challenge of the pandemic, its toll of destruction to date cannot be minimised. Stephen Lewis, Special Envoy of the Secretary-General for HIV/AIDS in Africa, posed the ultimate challenge: "If we had the political will, there is no question that we have the money. Then why isn't it being done? And because it's not being done, why doesn't it amount to murder? Mass murder. Even if the vaults now open, the number of lives already lost is an example of unconscionable international neglect."[23]

Chapter 5

Ending sexual violence and exploitation

"After returning from Sudan, I was a wife to
one rebel commander, then another junior
commander and then two older rebel soldiers.
I had one child who died when he was a few days
old. I was a slave to the rebels for 19 months.
I do not think I will marry again."

— A girl, now 18, who had been abducted by the Lord's Resistance Army[1]

In armed conflict, girls and women are threatened continually by rape, mutilation, violence, sexual exploitation and abuse. The dangers lurk in all settings, whether at home, during flight or in camps for displaced persons. Sexual violence, including rape, is any act of a sexual nature committed under coercive circumstances. As such, sexual violence is not limited to physical invasion of the human body. It may include acts that do not involve physical contact, such as forcing women and girls to dance unclothed for the entertainment of others.

Although the perpetrators of sexual violence and exploitation are frequently partners or acquaintances, in conflict situations they are more apt to be members of armed forces or armed groups. Senior officers, though accountable both for their own behaviour and for those they supervise, are often of little help, turning a blind eye to the sexual crimes of those under their command.

Sexual violence has long been used to terrorise populations or to force civilians to flee, and the general breakdown of social order during armed conflict increases the likelihood of random and uncontrolled sexual attacks. In Bosnia and Herzegovina, Croatia and Rwanda, rape has been used as a form of "ethnic cleansing" to deliberately impregnate the perceived enemy.[2]

Sexual violence is also common during periods of civil unrest. During the riots in Indonesia that led to the downfall of President Suharto, ethnic Chinese women were singled out for rape and sexual assault.[3]

Sexual violence and exploitation can take the form of sexual slavery, including forced prostitution. During World War II, thousands of Korean women were forced to serve as military sexual slaves dubbed "comfort women".[4] Today, nearly all girls abducted into armed groups face similar threats.

Until recently, these forms of sexual attack and exploitation were dismissed as the inevitable side effects of armed conflict. A more accurate view is that sexual violence and particularly rape are used as systematically as any other form of torture and as a tactical weapon of war to undermine the morale of the enemy.

Girls and women at risk

Women of all ages may become victims of sexual violence and exploitation in conflict situations. Adolescent girls are especially vulnerable because they may be physically and emotionally less capable of defending themselves. In addition, aggressors may think that young girls are less likely to be carriers of sexually transmitted infections or HIV/AIDS. Women may also be singled out for attack or exploitation for reasons beyond gender, such as ethnic origin, class, religion or nationality.

Sexual crimes are also committed against boys, although the extent of the problem is harder to quantify because their experiences tend to be under-reported. Many young boys have been raped or forced into prostitution. During the conflict in Bosnia and Herzegovina, for instance, sons and fathers were forced to commit sexual atrocities against each other.[5]

The effects of such violence reverberate beyond the immediate victims. Children who have witnessed the rape of a family member can suffer profound emotional damage. Other children may be ostracised. Unaccompanied children, women and single female heads of households are at risk during conflict, but especially so in camps to which they have fled for safety. There, amid cramped and crowded conditions, the presence of many combatants and poor security can escalate women's and children's exposure to violence.

Almost every married Burundian woman interviewed for a report prepared by Human Rights Watch (HRW) had endured domestic violence since becoming a refugee. In its 1999 World Report, HRW asserted that both the Tanzanian Government and international humanitarian agencies created an atmosphere of impunity by failing to investigate and punish instances of sexual and domestic violence committed by refugees, by Tanzanians from neighbouring communities and by police officers.[6] The Report found that local or traditional criminal justice systems are usually inadequate to treat such offences, especially when they are in the hands of male refugee leaders who have little legal knowledge and few powers of enforcement. Even the most serious cases of assault may only result in minuscule fines or the suggestion of family counselling.

The effects of sexual violence and exploitation

Sexual violence and exploitation have a devastating impact on physical, psychological and social development. The most immediate dangers are sexually transmitted infections and HIV/AIDS, which rapidly damage health, jeopardise future sexual and reproductive well-being and may ultimately cause death.[7] In 1996, it was estimated that 60-70 per cent of Cambodian child victims of prostitution were HIV positive.[8] During the Rwandan genocide, men who were knowingly HIV positive sadistically raped Tutsi women in an attempt to transmit the virus to them and their families.[9]

Women and girls often suffer in silence after the trauma of sexual violence and exploitation, fearing reprisals from those who attacked them or rejection by their families. Such is their humiliation and anguish that many withdraw into a shell of pain and denial. The World Health Organization (WHO) has found that rape victims are at especially high risk for suicide.[10]

When women become pregnant as a result of rape, whether they carry the pregnancy to term depends on many local circumstances, including the availability of community support, the pervading religious or cultural mores, the safety of abortion and access to appropriate reproductive health services. Victims of sexual violence who give birth during conflict must, in addition, contend with the economic and emotional consequences of raising a child without adequate support systems. The deterioration of public health systems reduces access to reproductive health services, such as family planning, STI treatment and pre- and post-natal care.

Complications in pregnancy and delivery are especially likely for children who give birth. Because of their physical immaturity, many adolescents develop infections as a result of unsafe or incomplete abortions. Young girls who give birth in the absence of trained birth attendants and in unhygienic conditions also run a greater risk of the chronic pelvic inflammatory diseases and muscle injury that can result in incontinence. Victims of repeated rape are also gravely endangered. Without sensitive, timely and adequate medical care, many of these victims die – some as a result of suicide. Sexual violence can lead to the isolation or stigmatisation of children and women by their families and communities, which can undermine social and community networks.

Sexual exploitation and trafficking

Sexual exploitation takes many forms, including prostitution, pornography and trafficking or "selling" of children for sexual purposes. During armed conflicts, poverty, hunger, desperation and fear may drive women and girls to exchange sex for food, shelter, safe passage, identification papers or other necessities for themselves and their families. In Guatemala, for example, some parents among internally displaced communities were forced to prostitute their children. In Colombia, girls as young as 12 have submitted themselves to paramilitary forces to assure their families' safety.

Once forced into prostitution in one country, women and children are more susceptible to being trafficked to work in brothels in other countries. Young women and girls from the Kosovar refugee camps in Albania and in the former Yugoslav Republic of Macedonia were trafficked for sexual purposes to Western Europe by criminal gangs, and since the end of the war in Bosnia and Herzegovina, thousands of foreign women have been trafficked into forced prostitution. Little has been done about these abuses; indeed some officials appear to be participating in the trafficking or patronising the brothels.[11]

The arrival of peacekeeping troops has been correlated with rapid increases in child prostitution. In 6 out of 12 country studies prepared for the 1996 Machel report, the arrival of peacekeeping troops was associated with a rapid rise in child prostitution. Following the signing of a 1992 peace treaty in Mozambique, soldiers of the United Nations Peace-keeping Operation recruited girls between the ages of 12 and 18 into prostitution. After a commission of inquiry confirmed the allegations, the soldiers responsible were sent home. Information has not been available about any subsequent disciplinary measures taken.

Although the United Nations has taken some action to control the behaviour of peacekeeping personnel, the investigation and punishment of peacekeepers for such obvious and gross violations of their mandates has been the exception rather than the rule.[12] In Somalia, two generals resigned after an Italian commission of inquiry determined that acts of sexual violence committed against Somali women by Italian peacekeepers were criminal acts that were made possible by a "stretched line of command" and "complacency toward such atrocities by junior officers."[13]

One of the more enduring effects of sexual violence and exploitation during conflict is that the forms they take can become institutionalised even after the fighting ends. For example, children who have been forced into prostitution for armies may have no other option but to continue after the conflict has ceased. In Cambodia, the number of child victims of prostitution in Phnom Penh continued to rise after the civil war; approximately 100 children are sold into prostitution each month.

Although the commercial sexual exploitation of women and children is a well-recognised consequence of armed conflict, both the 1996 World Congress against Commercial Sexual Exploitation of Children, and the Optional Protocol to the Convention on the Rights of the Child on the sale of children, child prostitution and child pornography,[14] failed to recognise and address these links.

The growing trend in the trafficking and sexual exploitation of women and girls in conflict situations and in post-conflict areas is not well understood or documented. During conflicts, these violations may be exposed, but they are rarely monitored or followed up. Very little is known about the situation of women and their children born following rape and forced pregnancy in countries such as Guatemala, Liberia, Sierra Leone, Uganda and the former Yugoslavia.

Supporting survivors

Reproductive health care and psychosocial support are crucially important for women and girls subjected to gender-based violence. Humanitarian assistance during armed conflict must include community-based psychosocial and reproductive health pro-grammes that give high priority to the needs of women and children who have witnessed or been subjected to gender-based violence. Responses should reflect strengthened policy guidance on gender-based violence and sexual exploitation and should include systematic reporting.

Overall, support for survivors of sexual violence has been inadequate. UNHCR, however, has been trying to ensure that relief workers are equipped to meet the special needs of refugee victims of sexual violence. It has published guidelines on how to prevent and respond to sexual violence against refugees.

There have been some effective programmes. Following the large number of rapes committed by bandits and local security personnel in the Somali refugee camps of north-eastern Kenya in the 1990s, UNHCR initiated a Women Victims of Violence project. Similarly in Bosnia and Herzegovina, there have been a number of community-based programmes, such as Bosfam and Bospo, which have provided support for women, including victims of sexual violence, helping them regain control over their lives through small-scale income-generating activities.

If such initiatives are to succeed, the local community must be involved in their design and implementation. To be effective, they should also provide comprehensive services, including economic assistance and psychosocial support, and avoid overtly identifying women as victims.

Towards ending impunity

Many societies fail to denounce and prosecute wartime rape partly because it is misconstrued as a personal attack or as an assault against honour rather than as a crime against the victim's physical integrity. Historically, it has been difficult to apply international human rights and humanitarian law to rape – a result of weaknesses in the laws themselves and in their interpretation.

The perpetrators of sexual violence during armed conflict, as well as those who authorise such acts, are violating international

Justice for "comfort women"

"One day in June, at the age of 13, I had to prepare lunch for my parents, who were working in the field, and so I went to the village well to fetch water. A Japanese soldier surprised me there and took me away. I was taken to the police station in a truck where I was raped by several policemen. When I shouted, they put socks in my mouth and continued to rape me. The head of the police station hit me on the left eye because I was crying. I lost eyesight in the left eye.

"After ten days or so I was taken to the Japanese army garrison . . . . There were around 400 other Korean young girls with me and we had to serve over 5,000 Japanese soldiers as sex slaves every day. Each time I protested, they hit me or stuffed rags in my mouth. One held a matchstick to my private parts until I obeyed him. My private parts were oozing with blood."[16]

In February 1996, Radhika Coomaraswamy, the first United Nations Special Rapporteur on violence against women, recom-

humanitarian law. When they do so on a massive scale, or as a matter of orchestrated policy, they are committing a crime against humanity.

Rape can be a violation of the 1949 Geneva Conventions, the 1948 Genocide Convention, the 1984 Torture Convention, and a crime against humanity under the Nuremberg Charter.[15] The International Military Tribunal for the Far East convicted Japanese officers for allowing and encouraging rape in Nanking (China), although not for committing rape themselves.

In December 1999, the United Nations Subcommission on the Promotion and Protection of Human Rights declared that the Japanese Government should compensate women forced to serve as sex slaves during World War II. The Government has not responded to these calls and Japanese courts have rejected claims filed by "comfort women" of various countries.

mended that the Japanese Government accept legal responsibility for violations of international humanitarian laws with regard to Korean women forced into sexual slavery by the Japanese army during World War II. She recommended that the Government pay compensation, make a written public apology to individual victims and raise awareness of this issue by amending educational curricula to reflect the historical realities.

In March 1996, the International Labour Organization supported these recommendations by finding that Japan's wartime use of Asian women as prostitutes to serve its soldiers should be characterised as sexual slavery, a violation of the ILO's 1930 Forced Labour Convention. The Special Rapporteur on the right to compensation for gross violations of human rights reported to the UN Commission on Human Rights that victims of slavery have the right to demand direct reparations and compensation from the offending State, not only for the crime of slavery, but also for the failure of a State to meet its obligation to punish perpetrators after a war.

Outraged by the glaring impunity for these crimes, a five-day people's tribunal, the Women's International War Crimes Tribunal for the Trial of Japanese Military Sexual Slavery, was organised in December 2000. Although the Tribunal had no authority to impose punishments, it found that the wartime Prime Minister and other top Japanese military officials bore principal responsibility for the sufferings of "comfort women" enslaved by the Japanese military and that the Government had "incurred state responsibility for its establishment and maintenance of the comfort system."

Rape in Rwanda

In 1998, the International Criminal Tribunal for Rwanda convicted Jean-Paul Akayesu of sexual violence committed during Rwanda's 1994 genocide, including nine counts of genocide, crimes against humanity and war crimes. Witnesses spoke of women being gang-raped and murdered while the defendant stood by.

The verdict was historic in several respects. It was the first handed down by the Rwanda Tribunal, the first conviction for genocide by an international court, the first time an international court has punished sexual violence in a civil war and the first time that rape was found to be an act of genocide.

The Rwandan Tribunal's judgement against Akayesu articulated a broad definition of rape under international law, calling it a form of aggression. "Like torture," the Tribunal said, "rape is used for such purposes as intimidation, degradation, humiliation, discrimination, punishment, control or destruction of a person. Like torture, rape is a violation of personal dignity, and rape in fact constitutes torture when it is inflicted by or at the instigation of or with the consent or acquiescence of a public official or other person acting in an official capacity."

Recently, the International Criminal Tribunals for the former Yugoslavia (ICTY) and for Rwanda have highlighted the use of sexual violence during those conflicts and brought charges of genocide and crimes against humanity against the perpetrators. Even though the judgements cover a tiny fraction of cases, they represent historic precedents.

In February 2001 the ICTY handed down the landmark convictions of three Bosnian Serbs for crimes against humanity that included rape, torture and sexual enslavement. Despite the gravity of the crimes, the sentences meted out were between 12 and 28 years' imprisonment. The ICTY established criteria under which rape and other forms of sexual violence constitute torture under international law, including situations of armed conflict or circumstances where such acts are committed or instigated by a public official to punish, coerce or intimidate the victim. Although there were approximately 20,000 victims of sexual attack in the former Yugoslavia, only 27 initial indictments were brought by the ICTY for rape and sexual violence.

During the Rwandan genocide, thousands of women were targeted by Hutu militiamen and soldiers of the former Government of Rwanda.[17] Tutsi women were individually raped, gang-raped, raped with objects such as sharp sticks or gun barrels, held in sexual slavery or sexually mutilated. The International Criminal Tribunal for Rwanda established that genocide could include measures to prevent births, such as sexual mutilation, the practice of sterilisation, forced birth control, separation of the sexes and prohibition of marriages. Although additional indictments have been amended to include sexual violence charges, the Tribunal brought only two initial indictments for sexual violence and one indictment for murder that involved sexual violence. Following testimony by survivors, the International Panel of Eminent Personalities to Investigate the 1994 Genocide in Rwanda and the Surrounding Events has concluded that practically every female over the age of 12 who survived the genocide was raped.[18]

The Rome Statute establishing the International Criminal Court has the potential to protect and promote the human rights of women and girls. Once in force, the ICC will complement national jurisdiction and will have the power to punish genocide, crimes against humanity, war crimes and aggression.[19] The ICC recognises sexual violence as war crimes and crimes against humanity. The Statute addresses counselling, rehabilitation, reparations and compensation to the victims of war crimes. It will also have gender- and child-sensitive court procedures.

States are urged to join the campaign for the establishment of the ICC to help end impunity for crimes against women and girls. For the ICC to realise its full potential, all countries that have ratified the ICC Statute must ensure that their national laws provide the necessary support and assistance to the ICC by amending or implementing appropriate national legislation.[20]

Strengthening procedures and mechanisms to prosecute sexual violence

National and international law must codify rape as a crime against the physical integrity of the individual and address the substantive nature of the abuse, providing appropriate remedies. Governments are legally bound to hold those who commit rape accountable and to recognise the distinct harm resulting from forced pregnancy.

In prosecuting sexual violence, protection for survivors who report violations should be provided. And it is encouraging that some organisations are approaching issues of gender violence more systematically, by including qualified personnel in international operations for monitoring, investigating and verifying the status of human rights.

Legal and other procedures will be more effective if gender balance is considered when governments and international organisations are reviewing candidates for judicial and relevant international bodies. This should apply, for example, to the International Court of Justice and the future International Criminal Court, as well as bodies related to the peaceful settlement of disputes.

Overall procedures and mechanisms to investigate, report, prosecute and remedy sexual violence and exploitation should be reviewed and strengthened, ensuring the protection of victims who report violations. Medical and relief personnel, prosecutors, judges and other officials who respond to crimes of rape, forced impregnation and other forms of sexual violence and exploitation should be trained to work in a way that both protects and respects the dignity of survivors.

Obviously, no court judgement, international treaty or policy guidelines can remedy the suffering of wartime victims of rape, forced pregnancy and other sexual violence and exploitation. But judgements that have defined rape and sexual violence as "crimes against humanity" – and the elaboration of these crimes in the Statute of the International Criminal Court – are important first steps.

Training and policy formulation and implementation can help prevent gender-based violence. But ultimately, success will hinge on States mustering the political will to hold perpetrators and governments accountable and to mobilise the resources to seek justice for victims.

Chapter 6

The toll on children's health

"The situation in the camp is not nice . . . .
People are starving there, not to death,
but not enough for human life."

— Wuoi, southern Sudanese youth[1]

Thousands of children are killed every year as a direct result of fighting – from bullets, knife wounds, bombs and landmines. But many more children die from malnutrition and disease heightened by armed conflict. Wars – many of them in the world's most impoverished regions – disrupt food supplies and destroy crops and agricultural infrastructure. They wreck water and sanitation systems, along with health services. And wars displace whole populations, tearing families and communities apart.

All this takes an immense physical and emotional toll on children. Beset by malnutrition, common childhood diseases and opportunistic infections, children by the thousands fall into a fatal spiral of failing health. Some of the highest fatality rates occur among children who have been uprooted from their homes, including those languishing in camps for refugees and the internally displaced. The dangers are further compounded where relief aid is inadequate and unevenly distributed.

All children are at risk when conflicts break out, but by far the most vulnerable are those who are under the age of five and already malnourished. Of the 10 countries with the highest rates of under-five deaths, 7 are in the midst of or recovering from armed conflicts: Angola, Afghanistan, Democratic Republic of the Congo, Liberia,

Mozambique, Sierra Leone and Somalia.[2] In Angola and Sierra Leone, nearly 1 child in 3 dies before reaching the age of five.

Of the 15 countries where children are in the greatest danger, nearly all are torn by armed conflict, according to a child risk measure developed by UNICEF. The measure, which combines key factors affecting child survival and development, identified Angola as the most perilous place in the world to be a child. In the Democratic Republic of the Congo, the International Rescue Committee found that 2.5 million civilians died as a result of armed conflict in the eastern sector between August 1998 and April 2001. One-third of them were children under five.

For every child killed by armed conflicts, three are injured or permanently disabled. According to the World Health Organization (WHO), armed conflict and political violence are leading causes of injury, impairment and physical disability. Many of those killed and injured by landmines during and after conflicts are children. Only 5 per cent of children with disabilities in developing countries have access to social services, including rehabilitation of any kind, while prosthetics and other supports are only available to between 10 per cent and 20 per cent of those who need them.[3] According to the United Nations Educational, Scientific and Cultural Organization (UNESCO), less than 2 per cent of children with disabilities attend mainstream schools.[4]

During armed conflict these children with disabilities are even less likely to get support – a consequence partly of the lack of basic services and the destruction of health facilities. UNICEF and Handicap International, the International Committee of the Red Cross (ICRC) and a number of other NGOs support programmes addressing childhood disability in a number of war-affected countries, but the lack of resources and political commitment makes it impossible to fulfil the rights of most children with disabilities.

Communicable diseases

Since 1990, the most commonly reported causes of death among displaced children during the early influx phase in camps have been communicable diseases such as diarrhoeal ailments, acute respiratory

Conflict causes 2.5 million civilian deaths in eastern Democratic Republic of the Congo

Between August 1998 and April 2001, armed conflict in the eastern part of the Democratic Republic of the Congo caused at least 2.5 million civilian deaths, according to a recent study by the International Rescue Committee. One-third of those who died were children younger than five.

About 350,000 deaths, 14 per cent of the total, were caused directly by violence. The rest were due to disease and harsh conditions. The main causes of death among children under five were malaria, diarrhoeal diseases, malnutrition and respiratory infections.

Among the most disturbing findings is the disproportionate effect on young children. According to Les Roberts, an epidemiologist at Johns Hopkins University who headed the study, in some areas hardly any children under two years of age survived. "In two districts, Moba and Kalemie," Roberts said, "an estimated 75 per cent of children born during this war have died or will die before their second birthday."[5] The study found that as a result of the conflict the region had become "an unchecked incubation zone for disease."

"Men with guns come and wreak havoc on a very regular basis," said Roberts. "Those men cause more death by making people flee their homes than actually shooting them and slitting throats. People flee into the forest when a village is attacked, often at night. If they get a little sick and they are not eating, they often die. One girl told us how she fled her village at night with her family of eight. Five of the eight died as they hid in the forest."[6]

infections, measles, malaria and other infectious diseases.[7] Even in peacetime these are major child killers. The lethal effects are accentuated during conflicts partly because of the prevalence of malnutrition, which leaves children especially susceptible to disease. Globally, over 10 million children die each year from mainly preventable causes.

Diarrhoea is one of the most common communicable diseases. Its spread and impact are heightened by the absence of adequate sanitation and clean drinking water. These factors are usually behind virulent outbreaks of cholera that have swept through displaced persons camps in countries like Bangladesh, the Democratic Republic of the Congo, Kenya, Malawi, Nepal and Somalia. In some parts of Somalia in 1992, diarrhoeal diseases were responsible for up to half of all child deaths.[8]

Children are also vulnerable to pneumonia and other acute respiratory infections. In 1994, one-third of the children who died in six refugee centres in Goma in former Zaire were victims of respiratory infections.[9] Tuberculosis (TB) has re-emerged as a health threat in many parts of the world, aggravated by the growing HIV/AIDS crisis. TB spreads easily in the crowded conditions of most refugee camps, and WHO has estimated that half the world's refugees may be TB carriers.

Malaria is another major cause of death in tropical areas, with or without the complicating factor of conflict. Nearly a million children, 90 per cent of them in Africa, die from malaria every year. Malaria is a major killer among displaced people who move through or settle in malaria-endemic areas, often sleeping without shelter at night. In Sierra Leone, more people have died of malaria during the past eight years than from war-related injuries.[10]

Armed conflicts also dramatically increase the potential for spreading sexually transmitted infections, including HIV/AIDS. The likelihood and frequency of unprotected sexual activity increase during armed conflict. The transmission of HIV/AIDS in conflict can also be accelerated by the heightened vulnerability of women and girls to sexual violence and coercion. The risks increase with the breakdown of health services and the lack of screening of blood in transfusion services.

Reproductive health

Emergency responses usually give high priority to health and nutrition, shelter, sanitation and access to clean water. But traditionally, reproductive health has not been given the same attention. Girls and women in conflict situations face reproductive health emergencies, from complications in pregnancy and birth to the consequences of rape or unsafe sex. Between 25 per cent and 50 per cent of maternal deaths among refugees are the result of post-abortion complications.[11] Women and girls must also contend with longer-term issues relating to their sexual and reproductive health, which is closely linked to the health of their newborns and children. Yet even when health services are available, many women and girls, for cultural, legal or religious reasons, underutilise them.

WHO has urged that reproductive health information and services should be available in all situations. Such services should be designed, implemented and assessed with the active assistance of women and adolescents themselves, which will help in designing more relevant programmes and in building up people's capacities.

Several agencies have been active in this field. Since 1996, the United Nations Population Fund (UNFPA) has promoted reproductive health in conflict situations. It has developed a reproductive health kit, first used in the Great Lakes region of Africa, that provides the basic supplies needed to perform clean, safe deliveries. The agency also supplies health centre kits that can be used to stabilise women suffering from convulsions, bleeding or other precarious medical situations. During the Ethiopia-Eritrea war in 2000, UNFPA airlifted 10 tons of emergency safe motherhood and reproductive health supplies to help displaced Eritreans.

In collaboration with other partners, UNHCR provides reproductive health information to adolescents in refugee situations. In refugee camps in Ethiopia, Save the Children has operated a reproductive health programme that includes advocacy against female genital mutilation and domestic violence. Rädda Barnen carries out awareness-raising workshops on early marriages and teen pregnancy. And in 1995, a number of other NGOs – the American Refugee Committee, CARE, Columbia University Center for Population and

Family Health, the International Rescue Committee, JSI Research and Training Institute, Marie Stopes International, and the Women's Commission for Refugee Women and Children – founded the Reproductive Health for Refugees Consortium, which has implemented programmes for refugees in more than a dozen countries.

Despite these efforts, support for reproductive health in humanitarian assistance programmes remains inadequate. Even basic supplies like sanitary napkins are often unavailable. That is why governments of war-affected countries, international agencies, NGOs and donor countries must devote increased resources and a higher priority to protecting women and girls from sexual and gender-based violence and to supporting their reproductive health. Increasing the numbers of female health and protection professionals during emergencies is another critical priority.

Threat to health services and health workers

During conflicts, health facilities often come under attack – in direct violation of international humanitarian law. Since the beginning of the crisis in Burundi in 1993, one third of rural health centres have been destroyed.[12]

In those that still function, wounded combatants frequently receive priority medical attention, sometimes at the expense of children. Patient care is affected by wartime travel restrictions, which hamper the distribution of drugs and other medical supplies, and by frequent breakdowns in health systems.

Both physical infrastructure and staff may come under attack. During conflicts, health workers, facing imprisonment or death, may be forced to relocate or flee into exile. In Afghanistan, two decades of warfare left much of the health infrastructure in ruins and many health professionals dead or exiled. In Tajikistan, many health professionals left government service as a result of the civil war.

There are also risks for those working for international organisations. Since 1992, UN agencies have lost over 200 civilian staff to violence, including air crashes.[13] More than that number have been victims of kidnappings and hostage-takings since 1994, and UN convoys have been hijacked and drivers killed or beaten.

Stronger steps are needed to end impunity for such acts. Armed groups are obligated under international humanitarian law to respect health facilities as safe environments for the care of patients and as safe workplaces for health workers. They must also permit the delivery of medical assistance and other humanitarian aid. These principles have been reflected in the Rome Statute establishing the International Criminal Court.

During times of war, those working in health services should try to ensure continuity of care and long-term follow-up – linking emergency health relief with long-term development support and planning. This enhances survival and can also bring about long-lasting positive changes in children's lives.

Days of tranquillity and National Immunisation Days

For children, one of the most dangerous consequences of a breakdown in health infrastructure is the disruption of vaccination programmes. A number of countries affected by conflict are also among those with the lowest immunisation rates.[14] In the Democratic Republic of the Congo, only 15 per cent of children are immunised against measles, a major killer of young children in developing countries, and in Somalia, only 26 per cent. Other war-torn countries with rates of less than 50 per cent include Afghanistan, Angola, Burundi, Republic of the Congo, Liberia and Sierra Leone.

In the midst of conflicts, UNICEF, WHO and other partners have negotiated "days of tranquillity" during which warring parties agree to suspend hostilities so that children can be immunised. The first such days were arranged in 1985 in El Salvador, and since then similar truces for children have been arranged in other parts of the world. The Global Campaign to Eradicate Polio relies on the concept of national immunisation days to gain access to children in conflict areas. In some cases, however, warfare has continued, curbing immunisation efforts. Immunisation campaigns have brought gains for the protection of children's health during conflict, but gross denials of children's right to health care, including immunisation, continue.

- In *Afghanistan*, Taliban authorities and opposing forces upheld ceasefires in 2000 to allow 5.4 million children to be immunised in four rounds of National Immunisation Days (NIDs).[15]
- In *Angola*, the campaign for 2000 aimed to immunise 3 million children, but about 20 per cent were in areas outside government control and could not be reached. In June 2000, the first round of NIDs was marred by the murder of the chief nurse of Belize Municipal Hospital.[16]
- In *the Democratic Republic of the Congo* in 1999, 8.7 million children were immunised. Fighting in eastern areas disrupted preparations in the region for NIDs in July 2000, but a door-to-door outreach campaign immunised an additional 1 million children.[17]
- In *Sudan*, UN agencies helped negotiate days of tranquillity to immunise children in the Nuba Mountains in February 2000 – the first time in 19 years that UN agencies were able to provide humanitarian assistance to the region. However, the second round of immunisation was postponed in March due to failure to secure a ceasefire.[18]
- In *Somalia*, conflicts prevented health workers from immunising children against polio during NIDs in 1999 in Mogadishu. In 2000, however, warlords and militias in the capital city agreed to arrange access. During four days, more than 300 immunisation teams went from house to house and were able to immunise 200,000 children.[19]

Disruption of food production and supply

Food production and supply are often disrupted during conflict. Landmines and the threat of attacks force farmers – often women and older children – to stop working on plots of land too far from their homes. Irrigation and flood control systems may be destroyed, and restrictions on movement limit farmers' access to such necessities as seeds and fertilisers, and keep them from taking their produce to market.

Sometimes the damage to food systems is an accidental result of fighting; sometimes it is deliberate. Armed groups use food as a weapon of war, stealing or destroying food stocks and burning fields. By starving children, they seek to punish communities or apply political pressure. Armed groups or governments also manipulate or prevent the distribution of relief. Contravening humanitarian law, warring parties frequently block relief supplies, divert them for their own use or attack feeding centres for children and vulnerable groups. The perpetrators of these crimes against humanity are rarely brought to justice.

During conflicts unemployment increases and families have less cash to purchase food supplies. In desperation, people may resort to looting to feed their families, thus escalating the violence.

The international community has responded to such crises in vastly different ways, as the cases of Kosovo and Angola demonstrate. According to the 2000 United Nations' 4th Report on the World Nutrition Situation, at the peak of the Kosovo emergency, about 800,000 refugees were forced from the province. In Angola, an estimated 900,000 people were displaced, with many fleeing to cities in the highland provinces. Both groups became virtually dependent on food assistance during the summer of 1999.

The humanitarian response to the Kosovo emergency prevented an increase in malnutrition among children ranging in age from six months to four years. This was not the case for the displaced children in Angola, where the level of wasting (low weight in relation to height) in besieged cities reached 20 per cent, and severe wasting 7 per cent.

"Many explanations for the difference can be given," the Report says. "The most important of these was the huge imbalance in assistance given."[20]

The two cases show how disparities in humanitarian assistance cost the lives of children, and why donors and international agencies must override the shifting political priorities that underlie these inconsistencies.

Malnutrition

For the youngest children, health problems during armed conflicts are generally linked to malnutrition. Children under five in developing countries, including those not caught up in conflict, are twice as likely to die if they are even mildly malnourished. Moderate malnutrition increases the risk of death by more than four times, and for children under five who are severely malnourished, the risk is more than eight times that of children who are adequately nourished.[21]

In 1998 in four provinces of Burundi, UNICEF found that between 15 per cent and 24 per cent of children under five were malnourished.[22] In Angola in 2000, nearly 30 per cent of under-five children in Ganda, Benguela province, were acutely malnourished.[23] And south Sudan has one of the world's highest levels of malnutrition.

Malnourished children are less able to resist attacks of common childhood diseases or infections from contaminated food. As a result, the course and outcome of these diseases are more severe, and they are more often fatal. Malnutrition also hampers children's cognitive development.

In addition to these nutritional hazards, armed conflicts greatly increase exposure to environmental hazards, particularly those related to water and sanitation. Poor sanitation and inadequate or contaminated water supplies aggravate the vicious circle of malnutrition and infection.

Many children suffer from deficiencies in specific micronutrients, such as vitamin A and iodine. Vitamin A deficiency is the leading cause of blindness among children in developing countries. It also significantly heightens children's risk of dying from such common illnesses as measles and diarrhoeal diseases.

National Immunisation Days have been used widely as opportunities to distribute vitamin A supplements. Several war-affected countries achieved supplementation coverage of 80 per cent or more during NIDs, including the Republic of the Congo, Eritrea, Somalia, Sudan and Uganda.[24]

Iodine deficiency disorders (IDD), the world's single greatest cause of mental retardation, affect 740 million people. They are linked to brain disorders, cretinism, miscarriages and goitre. A global campaign to eliminate IDD through iodisation of table salt made great strides during the 1990s.[25] But progress has been slower in a number of war-torn countries in recent years. In Ethiopia and Sudan there is no iodised salt at all; in Cambodia, only 7 per cent of households use iodised salt; in Angola, only 10 per cent. In

Sri Lanka and Tajikistan less than half of all households were found to consume iodised salt.

Adequate nourishment also depends on the availability of food and how it is prepared. Without clean water and sanitation, even the most basic hygienic practices, like hand washing, cooking or cleaning food, become almost impossible tasks. Moreover, armed conflict forces mothers and other members of the family to spend more time outside the home, searching for water, food or work, and when the whole family has to flee, there is little opportunity to give children the close attention and affection they need. Where conflicts compromise a child's care, malnutrition is an immediate risk.

The importance of breastfeeding

Breastmilk is the only continuously reliable food resource in an emergency. And it is one of the best nutritional defences for infants. Breastfeeding provides ideal food for infants, reduces the incidence and severity of infectious diseases and contributes to women's health. Children who are not breastfed are more likely to incur potentially fatal bouts of diarrhoea, pneumonia and other infections. Infants should be breastfed exclusively for about six months and should continue to be breastfed with adequate complementary food for two years or beyond.

During conflict, breastfeeding is often interrupted. Children may become separated from their mothers, and mothers are less likely to receive the information and support they need to breastfeed. Even when families remain together, mothers who are themselves hungry, exhausted or traumatised may feel less able to care for their children. They can also lose confidence in their ability to produce milk. Unless they are severely malnourished, however, most mothers, even under great stress, can continue to breastfeed adequately. Stress may temporarily make their milk flow less easily, but with skilled help and reassurance, these difficulties can be quickly overcome.

Amid food shortages, special efforts are needed to ensure that breastfeeding women get the nourishment they need to breastfeed their children and sustain or restore their own well-being. Donors often fail to support breastfeeding, instead providing infant formula or feeding bottles. This is particularly dangerous in war zones, refugee camps and other crisis-affected areas, where the health risks linked to artificial feeding are magnified by overcrowding, poor sanitation and absence of health care services, including a lack of access to clean water, fuel and reliable supplies of breastmilk substitutes.

Breastmilk substitutes lack the antibodies and enzymes that help protect an infant against illness. Additional risks are introduced through feeding bottles, which, unlike open cups, are difficult to clean properly. Parents who rely on infant formula can become so desperate when supplies are interrupted that they are tempted to over-dilute the feeds while they search for a new supply.

A major issue for breastfeeding mothers who are HIV positive is the risk of passing on the virus. A child whose mother is HIV positive and does not receive antiretroviral treatment runs an estimated 15 per cent risk – about 1 in 7 – of contracting the virus through breastfeeding, in addition to the 1 in 3 risk of HIV infection during pregnancy or delivery. Women who do not know their HIV status should be supported in breastfeeding, while learning how to protect themselves from HIV infection.

Protecting food security

During armed conflicts the nutritional quality of available food can deteriorate, and families may not know how, or be able, to maintain a balanced diet, especially for their youngest members. This is why governments and relief agencies should ensure that available food supplies have a high concentration of energy and nutrients. But food relief should not be seen as a solution in itself; rather it should be part of a wider strategy aimed at building good nutrition and improving general health. In southern Sudan, households given food also received support for agriculture, livestock and fisheries. In many cases, however, recourse to outside food assistance is unavoidable.

The primary objective of food assistance should be to meet the basic nutritional needs of families. In too many situations, organisations have treated child-feeding issues separately from the whole family, creating child-specific feeding programmes without considering other, more effective ways to improve children's nutritional status, such as improving overall household food security and basic care.[26] In any case WHO surveys suggest that less than 50 per cent of mothers bring malnourished children to feeding centres. Some families express feelings of shame about using the centres. Mothers may not have the time, resources or support to take a malnourished child to a feeding centre that may be a long distance away. In fact, when centres are overcrowded and lack basic sanitation, hygiene and water supplies, they can actually enhance the spread of disease. In recent years, the implementation of WHO guidelines on nutritional rehabilitation has led to significant improvements in the way emergency feeding centres respond to children's nutritional needs.

The World Food Programme (WFP) has sought to give women more control over food aid, encouraging them to participate in designing, implementing and monitoring systems of food distribution.[27] In Sudan, where about 3 million people are receiving food assistance, WFP and its NGO partners strive to ensure that women have a greater role in allocating and distributing food. Women are elected to take part in "relief committees" that decide, at the community level, how and to whom the food is distributed. This gives many women their first opportunity to participate in decision-making.[28] Another programme in the displaced persons camps of Sudan, Women Knocking on Women's Doors, trains women in family health and nutrition and in the effective use of rations and encourages them to educate others.

WFP has found that women were less likely to be caught up in local political problems that can affect the distribution of aid – and are more likely to put the immediate needs of families first. Men tend to control most community administrative structures, yet assistance given to men may not reach women and children. Worse, men may trade food supplies for weapons.

Such efforts can, however, provoke resistance from men. In Afghanistan, WFP supported 350 women-operated bakeries that provided bread for approximately 7,000 families headed by war widows. The project was closed down in June 2000 by the Taliban authorities, who objected to women working outside their homes.[29]

Even when conflict is over, it may take a long time to return to normal diets. In Mozambique, for example, some young couples returning from refugee camps did not know how to prepare foods other than the maize, beans and oil that had been distributed to them as rations.[30] They were not familiar with traditional foods or feeding practices and did not know which local foods to use when introducing complementary foods for their breastfeeding babies. And where parents or grandparents had been lost, there was no one to teach them.

Chapter 7

Promoting psychosocial recovery

**"It is very difficult to live in war.
You just wait for the moment you will die."**

– Sanel, age 12, who lost an arm to a shell in Mostar (Bosnia and Herzegovina)[1]

Children who survive armed conflict have to deal with the horrors they have witnessed. War undermines the very foundations of children's lives, destroying their homes, splintering their communities and shattering their trust in adults. Children spared the direct experience of violence in armed conflict still suffer deep emotional distress in the face of the death or the separation of family members and the loss of friends.

In Rwanda, a survey in 1996 found that 96 per cent of children interviewed had witnessed violence; 80 per cent lost a family member; and 70 per cent had seen someone killed or injured.[2] These experiences can destroy a child's world and leave emotional scars that last a lifetime.

War affects every aspect of a child's development – physical, emotional, intellectual, social and spiritual. Children who have lived through conflict need psychosocial support. Article 39 of the Convention on the Rights of the Child guarantees the right of children to psychosocial recovery and social reintegration following armed conflict or other abusive experiences.[3]

The term "psychosocial" underlines the dynamic relationship between psychological and social effects, each of which continually influences the other. Psychological effects are those that affect emotion, behaviour, thoughts, memory, learning ability, perceptions and understanding. Social effects refer to relationships altered by death, separation, estrangement and other losses; family and community breakdown; damage to social values and customary practices; and the destruction of social facilities and services. They also extend to the economic dimension, for war leaves many individuals and families destitute, destroying their capacity to support themselves and maintain their standing in society.[4]

Psychosocial programming can cover a range of activities and must be integrated into all aspects of emergency and post-conflict reconstruction programming for children. These are best developed and implemented in partnership with children, parents and responsible authorities. Activities should aim to support the psychological and social aspects of child development while mitigating the effects of armed conflict.

There has been a tendency to view psychosocial assistance in terms of individually focused counselling programmes. Yet children's social development – and the ways in which children understand their world – is the product of continuous interaction among the child, the family and the community. This is why pyschosocial interventions must be rooted within the community and avoid the institutionalisation of children. The effectiveness of psychosocial recovery programmes depends also to a large extent on an understanding and respect for local cultures, knowledge and traditions. Spirituality, for example, plays an important role in many cultures and, where appropriate, should be incorporated into psychosocial support strategies.

All programmes in emergency situations and their aftermath have the potential to promote or to undermine the psychosocial well-being of children and families. Humanitarian and development personnel must be conscious of the psychosocial implications of their work or they may miss opportunities to protect children – or even needlessly cause harm.

Coping with the effects of conflict

All children are affected by armed conflict, but not in the same way or to the same extent. A child's ability to cope with and positively adapt to adverse circumstances depends on a variety of factors: age, stage of development, sex, personality, cultural background, experience, resilience, the availability of social support and the nature and frequency of violent events in the child's life. The way children cope with the effects of conflict may also be influenced by the prevailing cultural belief system.

The way children express anxiety and depression may change during the course of their development. The capacity of younger schoolchildren to concentrate and learn may be affected adversely, especially when compounded by malnutrition and poor learning environments. Small children may cling excessively to caregivers while adolescents may exhibit antisocial behaviour, suicidal tendencies or eating disorders.

Exposure to armed conflict also contributes to a child's internalisation of the culture of violence. Children take cues from their adult caregivers, so when they witness situations in which the anxiety and vulnerability of their parents is exposed, they tend to become more fearful and insecure themselves. Children can also have difficulty understanding erratic, overly protective or authoritarian attitudes in adults.

The events surrounding the loss of a close relationship are among the most significant factors in the development of lifelong emotional scars. Children who have been attacked or abused by neighbours or friends, as happened in Rwanda and the former Yugoslavia, lose their ability to trust and tolerate others.[5] A Bosnian boy described a wartime encounter with a friend with whom he had spent much of his childhood. "I saw him," the boy recalled, "and hoped that he would save my life. But he was ready to kill me."[6]

It is easy to generalise about the incidence of long-term or permanently disabling psychosocial damage to children in conflict situations. But it is important not to overlook the fact that many children display remarkable resilience in the face of adversity.[7] Resilience refers to the capacity to overcome and deal with adversity. It is a fluid notion, dependent on individual characteristics and environmental factors. Psychosocial support programmes should build on these innate capacities.

In the early 1990s, a large group of unaccompanied boys

embarked on a long and harrowing journey on foot from southern Sudan to Ethiopia. These boys had been trained from an early age to live in harsh conditions away from home in nomadic cattle camps. Their survival skills helped them to recuperate more quickly when they reached the relative safety of refugee camps.

When children have supportive families and feel secure in their communities, they have a greater capacity to overcome the negative effects of armed conflict.[8]

Adolescents

Adolescents are often overlooked in psychosocial support programmes. While their increasing maturity endows them with greater awareness and more highly developed reasoning skills, they have not had sufficient time to develop adult coping mechanisms.[9] War affects the psychological and social well-being of adolescents at a time of life when they are deeply focused on establishing their identity. In the aftermath of war, many adolescents have great difficulty imagining a future that holds a meaningful place for them. Having lost their role models and other sources of positive guidance, they may fall into serious depression and, in the worst of circumstances, commit suicide.

During armed conflict, adolescents often find themselves saddled with more weighty responsibilities than they are prepared for. Those who become heads of households – the majority are girls – must cope with adult hardships of supporting younger siblings. The psychosocial well-being of girls can be profoundly damaged by the lack of access to education and appropriate health services, by gender discrimination and by sexual violence and exploitation. Sexual taboos in communities can make it especially difficult for girls who have been sexually abused to return to their communities. Adolescent girls with young children face even greater obstacles, and their children are often stigmatised, carrying the effects of abuse across generations. The high risk of sexual assault and violence, against boys as well as girls, must be addressed as a priority in relief programmes. Special measures should be put in place to ensure equality of access to all services.

Guiding principles

The following principles for assisting war-affected children are increasingly used in the design and application of psychosocial programmes by UN agencies, NGOs and others. They were developed as part of a 1998 inter-agency workshop led by UNICEF.

Human rights: All child-focused programmes in emergencies must be designed and implemented to promote respect for child rights, consistent with the Convention on the Rights of the Child (CRC).

Non-discrimination: Programmes should be provided to all children without discrimination of any kind, while ensuring inclusion of girls and children of especially disadvantaged, oppressed or persecuted groups.

Best interests of the child: In all decisions affecting the psychological and social well-being of the child, primary consideration should be given to the child's healthy development, consistent with the CRC and the Convention on the Elimination of All Forms of Discrimination against Women (CEDAW).

Values and culture: Psychosocial programmes should be based on a situational assessment that includes information about the culture and values of the community into which the child is being reintegrated.

Child participation: Programmes must be based on an understanding of principles that promote healing, well-being and development, and ensure that children participate in their own recovery. Participation includes the right to join together in groups, to express opinions and views and to have access to information and knowledge.

Family and community-oriented approach: Programmes should increase the capacity of communities to respond to the needs of children for cultural identity, economic security and physical safety. All programmes should incorporate positive local care practices and promote the strengthening of families and communities.

Family and community-based approach: Participation of families and communities will contribute to the long-term recovery of children and help prevent further violations of their rights. Programmes should promote community ownership of psychosocial recovery processes to ensure sustainable services.

Well-being and prevention: Psychosocial programmes should re-establish a state of well-being necessary for the healthy development of children, while protecting them from further harm. This includes educating the public about the psychological and social effects of violence on children, and training parents and other caregivers to recognise these. Fundamental to a preventive approach is the recognition of healing as a long-term process.

Situation analysis and assessment: Programmes should be based on detailed situational analyses, including human security, economic issues and the particular needs of children, their families, caregivers and other community members.

Long-term commitment and continuity: To ensure continuity of care, capacity-building strategies must be incorporated into all phases of programming.

Partnership: Civil society, agencies and national and local government should work in partnership to support children's recovery from war and to prevent further disruption to their physical, mental and emotional development. A consultative process should be established to coordinate integration of internationally agreed principles for rights-based programme development and implementation.

There is limited and conflicting information on what constitutes appropriate psychosocial interventions for adolescents.[10] While some programmes take an individual approach, a growing number of others emphasise the resiliency of adolescents, their creative coping skills and the need for community-based interventions.[11] It is now a recognised general principle of good practice that adolescents with special needs, such as demobilised combatants or young people with disabilities, should receive psychosocial support within broader programmes for all war-affected children. If programmes are developed in close cooperation with a community, its members can identify any additional support that may be needed for adolescents with special needs.

Best practices for psychosocial support[12]

All humanitarian relief programmes have psychosocial implications. Psychosocial support for the child, the child's family and the community should be provided in tandem with health, education and economic development activities[13] and must be a front-line intervention in emergencies. Interventions should be flexible enough to adapt to changing circumstances.[14] Storytelling, drama, art, play and sports have been used to encourage healing.

This is what occurred in Kosovo, where psychosocial programmes were given increased priority by donors in response to the emergency conditions in the province. In Burundi in 1999 and 2000, the framework for humanitarian action in response to regroupment camps gave priority to restoration of basic education that integrated psychosocial support.

Humanitarian workers, journalists and other practitioners should protect children from the pain that may result from inappropriate interventions, "trauma therapies" or interviews that lead children to recount or relive their worst moments. These can open up old wounds and tear down a child's defences, especially in the absence of continuing support or follow-up. The same dangers exist for children in contexts such as testimony to truth commissions, war crime tribunals and other justice mechanisms.

Building on the work of the International Save the Children

Alliance (ISCA), UNICEF convened a series of workshops in 1997 and 1998 to develop a consensus on a set of guiding principles for psychosocial programming. These principles emphasise respect for local culture, community-based approaches, recovery and children's participation. They are reflected increasingly in humanitarian responses in conflict-affected countries and in training packages developed by the Office of the United Nations High Commissioner for Refugees (UNHCR) and by ISCA.

Respecting local culture

The ways in which individuals and communities cope with stressful events can vary markedly from one culture to another. How people express pain, shock and distress depends largely on social, cultural, political and economic factors. The rites and ceremonies related to growing up and becoming an adult, as well as those associated with death, burial and mourning, are especially important. What children are customarily told about death and how they are expected to behave in response to loss and grief vary across different cultures.

Traditional practices can be useful in promoting children's psychosocial recovery, especially where the elimination of a culture was an element of the armed conflict. Cleansing ceremonies and rituals to drive away troublesome spirits have been used to alleviate stress and to reconnect children with their communities. In their eagerness to support these traditional approaches, humanitarian organisations have offered to subsidise them with cash payments. This can inadvertently commercialise traditional practices, distorting their original intention and ultimate impact.

Many healing traditions attribute forces of nature to the presence of spirits and ancestors. In Angola, children believe that if they conduct a proper burial ritual, they will be blessed by their parent's spirit, but if they fail to do so, they may be punished.

Some cultural mores can exacerbate a child's injury. It is not uncommon for child victims of sexual abuse to be imprisoned or sent to remand homes. In some cultures, a girl who has been raped may be forced to marry the rapist to save the honour of her family.

In some situations, individual psychotherapeutic approaches that emphasise emotional expression may be harmful. For example, it may seem counter-intuitive for a therapist to avoid asking a child to describe his or her feelings and experiences. But Angolan rituals used to "cleanse" former child soldiers hold that bad spirits may revisit children if they speak about what happened to them during the war.

In other cases, opportunities to explore feelings can aid a child's process of recovery. Ideally, these should take place in a stable, supportive environment with caregivers who have a continuing relationship with the child, such as family and friends. Gloria, a 16-year-old from Colombia, put it this way: "Every child has the ability to express opinions but they don't always do it in the same way. Some prefer to show their ideas by painting pictures. Some are good at making speeches. I like to tell stories. I go to different schools in Bogotá and tell stories about the war so that children can understand what it is like. It doesn't matter how children express themselves. They can use any method they want. They just need to be appreciated."[15]

Mobilising the existing care system

Stable and nurturing relationships with adults are an important factor in a child's psychosocial recovery. All of those who are a part of children's daily lives have a role in the healing process, but parents and primary caregivers are best positioned to help children rebuild their trust in others by playing with them, listening to and supporting them – and keeping promises.

To do this, families and communities must feel secure and confident themselves. Programmes should therefore help parents and teachers communicate with children on difficult issues. In Rwanda, radio messages, videos and pamphlets were used to introduce trauma sensitisation at the community level.

Governments, donors and relief organisations should work actively to prevent the institutionalisation of children. And institutionalising specific groups of children, such as child soldiers, orphans or separated children, may stigmatise them and encourage their withdrawal and isolation.[16] Institutional care is also expensive to maintain, can be of uneven quality and in times of armed conflict is often unregulated.

Rather than create special centres, the existing social care system should be strengthened to provide psychosocial support. A 1998 evaluation of Rwanda trauma recovery programmes recommended training for health professionals in hospitals where most traumatised children and their families had sought help.

Recovery

Organisations such as the International Save the Children Alliance, the International Rescue Committee (IRC), the Christian Children's Fund and others have developed programmes to help children establish some sense of normalcy through daily routines of family and community life such as going to school, preparing food, washing clothes and working in the fields. Intellectual and emotional stimulation is offered through structured group activities including sports, drawing and drama.

In 1999, immediately following the mass population displacement, Save the Children organised open-air schools for 40,000 to 60,000 Kosovar children in 20 refugee camps and community centres in Albania.[17] Teachers and social workers from the refugee community were provided with educational materials such as blackboards, chalk, paper and pencils. In Rwanda, more than 25,000 social workers including schoolteachers, trauma advisers and clinical staff have received training in areas relating to psychosocial well-being. An evaluation of the programme reported that in school classes where the teacher had received training, pupil attendance was higher and children achieved better grades.[18]

Accelerated or catch-up educational and skills training can foster a child's sense of purpose, self-esteem and identity. These programmes should be integrated within the national education system and linked realistically to the needs of the local labour market. Young people should not be given a few months of vocational or skills training and then sent out with a mistaken belief that they have a marketable skill. To this end, analysis of local markets and links to economic policy are needed to identify the most appropriate form of apprenticeships or economic development approaches. In Sierra Leone, agencies are placing older children, formerly associated with the fighting forces, in workshops within the community, where they work as apprentices for up to three years.[19]

Children's participation

A key principle of psychosocial programmes is that children should be actively engaged in the planning of all community-based relief, recovery and reconstruction activities.[20] This increases the relevance and sustainability of these programmes, helps children rebuild working relationships with adults and strengthens their sense of identity and self-worth. Programmes should ensure wide-ranging participation by local authorities, communities, parents and by children themselves.

The involvement of adolescents in the design of psychosocial programmes can increase their relevance and effectiveness. One way in which programmes have succeeded in giving adolescents a sense of meaning and purpose is by involving them in child-to-child approaches. Since 1994, the International Rescue Committee's programmes in Rwanda have included youth development activities designed to promote responsibility and community participation through culture and sports, non-formal education and income-generating projects. Adolescents conduct activities such as playgroups, sports, dance and theatre for younger children and receive support for their own activities as well.

Monitoring and evaluation

Little is known about the long-term psychosocial effects of war. But certainly children who lose parents and other close family members will bear the effects of the loss for the rest of their lives. The longevity of such feelings was underscored on a global scale during the 50th anniversary of World War II as survivors described how their painful childhood experiences continued to affect them.

Humanitarian agencies should work with government and

communities to help them monitor and provide for children in need of special protection. In Rwanda, it has been recommended that data collection on psychosocial effects be linked to the national epidemiological system and that mental health be integrated into primary health care policy.[21] In 1999, Save the Children (US) formed an International Psychosocial Measurement Committee in an effort to improve quantitative and qualitative methodologies in this area and to document best practices.[22]

Chapter 8

Education for survival and development

"For six years, my school has been a railroad car. It is difficult to learn. There is no glass in the windows. During summer it's impossible to stay cool and during winter it's impossible to stay warm.... I don't have any gloves, so it's terrible to write. After one or two lessons in the cold, the teachers usually let us leave."

– Isa, age 17, Azerbaijan[1]

During the chaos of conflict, education can create a zone of security for children. Initially, education can be as simple as organised play. Recreational activities such as sports, drawing and music can help children cope with the trauma of conflict. Informal classes or play sessions help re-establish daily routines and give children more confidence in themselves, their families and their community. Through education, children can enjoy the company and support of their friends while benefiting from regular contact with teachers who can monitor their physical and psychological health. Education gives children opportunities to develop life-saving knowledge and skills and brings shape and structure to their lives.

Education is, in short, a life-affirming activity. It is vitally important that it continue even in the midst of conflict, or that it be resumed as quickly as possible when fighting ends. "Our hopes are for our children," said a war widow in Rwanda with five children. "If we can keep them in school, then they will grow up and have a future."[2]

A recent study by the World Bank found that increases in school enrolment contribute to the safety of the community and reduce the probability of civil war.[3] Education can promote respect for human rights and improve prospects for peace. It helps bind communities by bringing together children, parents, educators and local officials with a shared purpose. Communities that have schools feel they have something durable and worth protecting. During war or in its aftermath, the resumption of schooling offers reassurance by signalling a degree of stability. When schooling continues even in the most difficult circumstances, communities are asserting confidence in the future.

Schools in the firing line

Schools are high-profile targets in conflict situations. In rural areas, the school building may be the only substantial permanent structure, making it highly susceptible to shelling or looting. In Mozambique, some 45 per cent of primary school networks were destroyed during the civil war.[4] UNICEF has reported that in Sudan, near the border with Chad, out of 153 schools, only 17 are open.[5]

Teachers are vulnerable to attack because they are important community members and tend to be more than usually politicised. During the genocidal violence in Rwanda, more than two-thirds of teachers either fled or were killed.[6] In Sri Lanka in July 2000, guerrillas reportedly targeted teachers who had tried to protect schoolchildren from forced recruitment and abduction.[7] In Turkey, teachers in Kurdish areas were threatened by non-state forces for using the Turkish curriculum.

Fear and disruption make it difficult to maintain an atmosphere conducive to learning, and this can take a grievous toll on school morale. In Palestinian schools, surveys found many teachers and students had trouble concentrating, particularly if they had witnessed or experienced violence or had family members in prison or in hiding.[8] And because formal education requires consistent funding and administrative support, it is difficult to sustain amid political instability. During intense conflict, governments are far more likely to fund defence budgets than those for education or health.

However, in the midst of low-intensity conflicts, such as in Sri Lanka, education has continued. And where fighting is intermittent, schooling can carry on during periodic lulls, although in such circumstances, precautions are necessary to shield children from attack or recruitment by armed groups.

Establishing alternative sites for classrooms or changing venues regularly are possible solutions. In the villages of northern Ethiopia, near the border with Eritrea, children climbed a steep path to a classroom in a cave under the rock cliffs out of the range of shelling.[9] During the height of the fighting in the former Yugoslavia, classes were held in the cellars of people's homes, often by candlelight. Parents in Bosnia and Herzegovina and in Croatia were adamant that schooling continue despite the difficult circumstances.[10]

Education is increasingly recognised as the "fourth pillar" of humanitarian aid, along with food and water, shelter and health care. The Norwegian Refugee Council has been an active and influential advocate for education in emergencies. Yet, although the UN now requests funds for education in their humanitarian appeals, in 2000 only 34 per cent of funds requested were raised.[11]

Education for displaced children

During armed conflict most education programmes have been directed to refugee children. The reasons are in part practical. Children grouped together in camps are more accessible; there are economies of scale, and it is generally easier to approximate a classroom. In addition some donors are constrained by their mandate to work only with refugees. Others steer clear of national education systems, preferring to operate self-contained programmes.

But overall, funding for refugee education is glaringly inadequate – less than one-third of all refugee education is supported by international donors.[12] Many refugee communities organise schooling without waiting for international aid, using any means available to set up classrooms and begin instruction. A project in Guinea offers a particularly striking example. There, teachers within the refugee population from Liberia and Sierra Leone worked together to develop a curriculum and set up a school programme.

They later received support from UNHCR and soon had 12,000 refugee students. The International Rescue Committee (IRC) agreed to train and pay teachers and put roofs on the classrooms. Eventually, the programme grew to include more than 75,000 students in 135 schools, with more than 1,800 teachers.[13] Its success was tempered by the fact that, even with the programme in full swing, nearly a third of the children in the camps – almost 150,000 children – were still receiving no education.[14]

Providing even minimal compensation for teachers can create tension. For example, the monthly incentive paid to Liberian and Sierra Leonean refugee teachers in Guinea was perceived as a factor in discouraging their return home. In West Timor, compensation was provided for East Timorese refugee teachers. But this created resentment among the West Timorese since, in the midst of instability throughout the region, local teachers were not being paid at all.

Refugee children can sometimes attend mainstream schools in host countries, although such opportunities are usually open only to a very few. When this is possible, refugee children are likely to need special programmes to help them fill knowledge gaps and to learn the local language. But even when language is not a barrier, children may still suffer harassment, discrimination or bullying at school.

Most developing countries that host refugees have yet to achieve universal primary education for their own children. Some host governments are loath to provide educational activity for refugee children, fearing that this will encourage refugees to remain permanently in their territory. They may object to the relative advantages that international assistance may bring to refugees and in some cases refuse to allow humanitarian agencies to establish education programmes. The denial of education clearly contravenes both article 22 of the 1951 Convention Relating to the Status of Refugees and article 28 of the Convention on the Rights of the Child, which obligate States parties to treat refugee children in the same way as nationals with regard to elementary-level education.

In western Tanzania, for example, the Government initially resisted the idea of primary schools for Burundian refugees. Instead it established Children's Activity Centres, which were off-limits to international agency support. This had one beneficial effect. The refugee community took full ownership of the Centres, determined to provide education for children within the camps. After about a year, the Tanzanian authorities agreed to allow the camps to establish primary schools with the intention of preparing children to return home to Burundi.[15] Teachers and educators from among the Burundian refugees were able to quick-start the curriculum they had left behind. More than 270,000 children benefited. Cooperation between the two Governments enabled Burundian textbooks to be printed in Tanzania. The same grade six examination papers have been used across the border to keep refugee children on course and allow a smooth transition back into the Burundi school system. Two years later more Burundian children were attending school in Tanzania than in Burundi. This showed that a strong community-based approach from the outset can create an effective education programme in emergencies. But paradoxically, it may have also created better educational access for Burundian children living in refugee camps than for those living in Burundi.[16]

Internally displaced children face different obstacles than their refugee counterparts. Continued fighting and frequent dislocation complicate their access to education. In Azerbaijan, about 1 million Azeris were displaced outside the town of Terter. The same abandoned railway cars used to house 4,000 internally displaced people also serve as classrooms. Despite a shortage of books and supplies, teachers and students show up each day in railway cars that lack heat and glass in the windows. In the capital city of Baku, where displaced families occupy abandoned hospitals and other public buildings, schools for displaced children function without electricity and blackboards. Some classes are held in buildings with walls that have collapsed.[17]

Where government schools are available, internally displaced children may be prohibited from attending because they lack the identification documents needed to enrol. In Colombia, families driven off their land by paramilitary or guerrilla groups have been forced to keep their identities hidden for fear of being targeted. As a result, their children have no access to health care or state services, including school.[18] In 1997, the Sri Lankan Ministry of

Education allowed children without birth certificates to attend school but refused to allow them to sit for examinations or participate in sports.[19]

Education for adolescents

The paltry donor support for secondary education testifies to the seeming invisibility of adolescents within war-affected communities. Donors are now quicker to recognise the need to assure primary schooling for younger children during emergencies but have not made significant support available for adolescent education. The results are predictable. Without educational or vocational training opportunities, frustrated young people may be enticed or forced to join armies. Others may be exposed to sexual abuse and exploitation.

Many adolescents in impoverished, war-torn countries have not mastered basic literacy and numeracy skills and need accelerated learning programmes to help them catch up with the class level of their age group. In Georgia, a remedial learning programme prepares displaced adolescents to re-enter classes at grade levels five, seven or nine.[20] More typically though, there are no secondary schools for adolescents.

In Rwanda, children who fled the country before finishing primary school are now heading households and caring for younger siblings or orphans. Most lack basic educational skills. If they want to return to school they must study with much younger children. The humiliation of struggling to keep up in a classroom with younger children can discourage adolescents from re-entering the school system. Yet they have little prospect of alternative vocational training.[21]

Among those Rwandan children who have completed basic primary education, few can afford secondary school, which tends to take place in boarding schools that require payments for tuition, food and board. The Kigali Model Secondary School takes a different approach by enrolling adolescent girls from around the country who would not otherwise be able to attend secondary school. Built by UNHCR in 1996 and operated by the Forum for African Women Educationalists (FAWE), the school housed 160 students and four teachers in 2000. At last count, the school library had 25 books. But the headmistress, Emeritha Nzaramba, was looking ahead. "My dream is to have a textbook for every five students in every class," she said.[22]

Girls' education

Globally, two-thirds of all children not in school are girls and during conflict, gender imbalances are heightened. Parents may fear for their security in and on the way to school. In many cases, refugee girls have not been educated in their home countries, so parents may see no advantage in sending them to school in refugee camps. Globally, it has been estimated that only 1 in 10 school-age refugee girls attend class.[23]

During armed conflict, girls' need for education and vocational training is especially great. Many find themselves heading households at a very early age, making literacy, numeracy and accelerated training in life skills all the more essential.

Even when girls do gain access to schooling, they frequently suffer further discrimination as a result of gender bias in the curriculum and in the attitudes of teachers, administrators and fellow students. Among the Sudanese refugees in Uganda, for example, UNHCR found that school attendance for girls in East Moyo was significantly lower than for boys and dropped steadily for older girls. In lower primary schools, 35 per cent of the refugee children were girls, a proportion that fell to 13 per cent in secondary schools. The reasons were all too familiar. Cultural beliefs and early marriage often discouraged their enrolment. Families were unable to pay school fees or afford proper clothing for children. In some cases, it was simply that girls having reached the age of menstruation did not have sanitary supplies. Temporary classrooms set up during emergencies may not be equipped with separate bathrooms for boys and girls.[24] And often girls and their concerns are not represented in textbooks and classroom lessons and therefore girls may not see the relevance of school to their lives.

Some parents do not want girls and boys to attend school together after a certain age. In Afghanistan, the Taliban authorities have severely limited and at times denied girls' access to education. In protest, a number of organisations have withdrawn support for state schools in affected areas until both girls and boys are given the opportunity to attend school.

Education in emergencies can provide opportunities to address discrimination against girls. A programme supported by the IRC has developed a health education curriculum that addresses reproductive health and is designed to promote self-esteem among Liberian and Sierra Leonean refugee girls living in Guinea. Since September 1998, IRC has provided community education and counsellor training to support a programme that addresses sexual and gender-based violence. Girls expelled from school because of pregnancy have been readmitted to prevent further discrimination, with young women's social clubs and mentoring programmes providing emotional support and guidance.[25]

In 1991, a programme to promote girls' education was started in the Afghan refugee community in Pakistan. The programme has grown from its first year with 1,000 students to some 21,000 students in the year 2001. Over 70 per cent of students are girls. Altogether more than 2,000 teachers, the majority of them women, have been trained since 1991.[26]

Children with disabilities

During conflict, great numbers of children are disabled by landmines and other weapons. In Sierra Leone, thousands of children were mutilated during the conflict. Yet children with disabilities have very limited access to education in conflict situations.

For years, separate educational facilities have been the norm, but these have led generally to neglect, discrimination and greater isolation for disabled children. Approaches have changed and now many educational organisations encourage the inclusion of children with disabilities in mainstream classes. It is estimated that about 70 per cent of children with disabilities are able to integrate successfully in mainstream educational programmes. The remaining 30 per cent, including those with severe mental impairment or multiple disabilities, need special care and attention.[27]

In the Karagwe camps for Rwandan refugees in Tanzania, most children with disabilities attend mainstream classes, receiving special attention and instruction as needed, while an additional class in the same school is held for children with mental disabilities. The programme does not require much additional funding but, even so, resources are severely limited.[28] In most cases, local NGOs rely on the willingness of communities to assist in providing for the needs of disabled students.

New curricula and teaching methods

Where school facilities have been destroyed and teachers lost, communities may be more receptive to alternative methods of teaching. Emergency education kits have been developed to supply essentials such as chalk, blackboard, pens, pencils, paper and exercise books. Children can also be taught in home-based schools and through distance learning. These cost-effective systems allow children to study at home or in groups, using pre-packaged teaching materials complemented by broadcast and recorded media. This option is particularly valuable for girls whose parents are reluctant to have them travel far from home. In Afghanistan and Pakistan, UNHCR and Save the Children (US) and a number of other NGOs have established home-based schools for displaced children. The majority of the 1,100 Afghan girls in Baluchistan who attend these schools have had no previous education and have no other means of receiving classroom instruction.[29]

During emergencies, communities may be more receptive to changes in the curricula. Although non-competitive, learner-centred approaches can help foster self-confidence in children and develop a wide range of skills, these methods are unfamiliar in many countries and should be introduced sensitively, taking care not to disempower local teachers or confuse pupils.

In conflict situations, life-skills training can form the beginning of more structured schooling. Such programmes can promote psychosocial recovery and teach landmine awareness, youth health, HIV/AIDS prevention and vocational skills. They can also be a catalyst, promoting social justice and human rights. But in most war-torn

School-in-a-box

Education in refugee camps can be started with the simplest materials. The Teacher's Emergency Pack (TEP) and "edu-kits" are recent innovations. These packs contain very basic items, including a brush and paint for a blackboard, chalk, paper, exercise books, pens and pencils. The TEP is intended to cover the first few months of emergency schooling; longer-term initiatives require the development of more targeted materials.

The TEP was used to develop educational programmes for Somali and Rwandan refugee children and was used subsequently in Angola, from 1996 to 1998. In Angola the Norwegian Refugee Council worked with UNESCO and UNICEF to come up with emergency education kits for children, youth and adults that focused on basic literacy and numeracy. To qualify, communities were required to build the walls for a school in their village; the Norwegian Refugee Council then put on the roof. By 1998 approximately 6,000 children were enrolled in classes. More than 100 village schools were built or rehabilitated and 400 teachers were trained. Unfortunately progress was cut short when fighting broke out again in 1998.

Education kits provide essential teaching materials in times of emergency but they should allow for flexibility and local input. A danger of the education kit approach is "kit-mania" – when donors focus on the production and deployment of kits rather than on support for more comprehensive education programmes in emergencies.

As soon as possible, standardised kits should be replaced with locally selected and procured supplies. In fact, local production of educational supplies can provide business opportunities. When using kits to quick-start education in emergencies, it is important to keep in mind that the kits do not provide education but rather serve as a catalyst to bring together the elements of successful learning – community support, teachers, appropriate shelter and the development of a relevant curriculum.

communities, education tends to reflect the dynamics of the conflict. In the east of former Zaire, many refugee schools left unassisted by the international community came under the control of the ousted Rwandan Government that had been responsible for the 1994 genocide. They used the opportunity to teach Hutu youth a curriculum intended to prolong the ethnic divide.[30] If schools are to counter rather than perpetuate conflict, it is crucial that injustices and stereotypes previously validated in the classroom·are dismantled and that tolerance is encouraged.

Teachers in emergency settings must receive adequate support and training to ensure their full understanding of and support for changes in the curricula. Wider community support for cultural and social changes introduced in the classroom should also be sought. And gender balance should be promoted in both recruitment and training.

One of the best ways to support educational change is to ensure that teachers, parents, communities and children play an active role in the design, content and implementation of curricula and methodologies. Engaging parents in educational programmes and gaining their acceptance and support is a key factor both in the short-term and long-term success of education in emergencies. If parents are satisfied with the schooling that is offered, they are more likely to encourage their children to attend. And if the school is serving the families of the community, it can help promote reconstruction and reconciliation.

Faced with the practical and political challenges of negotiating new curricula, governments and specialised agencies have focused instead on the physical reconstruction of schools. Less support has been available for teacher training and the development of new curricula and teaching methods. Even where the political will to invest in education has been present, education systems often suffer from a persistent shortage of funds.

Education for peace

The groundwork for creating peaceful societies can be undertaken in schools, where education can promote peace, tolerance, social justice and respect for human rights. This was reaffirmed at the April 2000 World Education Forum, held in Dakar, where schools were heralded as the place for teaching children, especially war-affected children, negotiation, problem solving, critical thinking and communication skills.

In Burundi, the Let's Build Peace project is now a permanent feature in nearly all schools and literacy centres. Between 1994 and 1998, more than 5,000 teachers were trained in peace education and 7,000 more will participate in workshops run by local directors who have been trained as trainers.[31] In Sudan, a Life Skills Programme addressing peace, conflict resolution and human rights is being developed for adolescents in the south. Curriculum modules addressing the causes and consequences of wars and of family, village and ethnic conflicts were being distributed to schools by the end of 2000.[32] In Rwanda, a different approach is used. Conflict resolution and reconciliation have been brought into schools through the sports and games curriculum.[33] In Croatia, the school-based Trauma Healing and Peaceful Problem Solving Programme was started in three primary schools in 1996. Two years later, another 24 schools joined the programme.[34]

In the Jaba Rone IDP camp outside Khartoum, the NGO Fellowship for African Relief sponsors a programme that combines feeding for malnourished children with health education and conflict resolution. Games, songs and drama are used to raise awareness about the effects of war on children and families and the need for tolerance and peace. The children, in turn, bring ideas about health and human rights home to their parents and community.[35]

Education: The bridge between survival and development

To succeed, education programmes must bridge emergency relief and long-term development. If they are terminated when a conflict subsides, the hard-earned investment in training and capacity is lost.

Financing education presents complex challenges. Some donors may be reluctant to use emergency funds for what they interpret as long-term development activities. USAID-supported humanitarian assistance does not include primary or secondary education, but it has a Displaced Children and Orphans Fund that provides development assistance support for education-related interventions in war-affected countries. The European Community Humanitarian Office (ECHO) excludes education and income-generating projects from its emergency funding, which is limited to such areas as food, clothing and shelter.

Educational initiatives developed for conflict situations should be designed to integrate easily into education policy and planning in the post-conflict period. This is key when an armed struggle goes on for years. Continuity will require improved collaboration among relevant international agencies, governments and NGOs.

Chapter 9

Threats to life and limb: Landmines and unexploded ordnance

"We were playing. We were playing."
— Khaliq, age 14, after losing his leg to a landmine near Kandahar (Afghanistan)[1]

Of all the threats that war poses to children, few are more insidious than landmines and unexploded ordnance. They maim and kill not only in the midst of armed conflict, but for decades after. Children in some 80 countries live with the threat of uncleared anti-personnel and anti-tank landmines. Unexploded ordnance (UXOs) are an added danger: bombs, shells and grenades that fail to detonate on impact but can still be set off – causing injury or death – years later.

Landmines have been used in most conflicts since World War II and particularly in civil wars. One of the worst-affected countries is Afghanistan, where landmines and UXOs claimed 5 to 10 casualties a day in 1999.[2] Cambodia is similarly afflicted; in 1999, eight years after the civil war ended, mines and UXOs caused more than 1,000 casualties.[3] African children live on the continent most plagued by landmines; at least 26 countries in sub-Saharan Africa are affected by landmines.[4]

Cluster bombs, which have been used extensively over the past four decades, pose a similar threat. In the Lao People's Democratic Republic, there were at least 9 million unexploded cluster bomblets at the end of the war, causing at least one serious casualty every two days.[5] In its effort to stop the expulsion of ethnic Albanians from Kosovo in 1999, NATO dropped over 1,600 cluster munitions containing nearly 300,000 bomblets.[6] With "dud" rates estimated at 5 per cent to 30 per cent, as many as 60,000 unexploded bomblets threaten former refugees who have returned to the province. In Chechnya, Russian forces dropped large numbers of cluster munitions.[7] And Médecins Sans Frontières found that the Government of Sudan had carried out aerial bombardments of cluster bombs in the country's southern province of Equatoria.[8] The toll of unexploded cluster munitions on civilians, and especially children, has focused growing public attention on the immediate and long-term humanitarian consequences of these weapons – and the need for a worldwide moratorium on their use.

Threat to children

Children are more vulnerable to the danger of landmines and UXOs than adults are because they may not recognise or be able to read warning signs. Many mines are hidden or are not readily visible. But even if they are aware of mines, small children may be less able than adults to spot them: a mine laid in the grass and clearly visible to an adult may be less so to a small child, whose perspective is two or three feet lower. But even those that are visible are a threat, since children are naturally curious and likely to pick up strange objects they encounter. Devices like the "butterfly" mines, once used extensively in Afghanistan, come in several colours and have a "wing." Although they were not designed to look like toys, such devices still hold a deadly attraction for children.

Similarly, the unexploded, brightly coloured, shuttlecock-shaped cluster bombs used by NATO in Kosovo in 1999 contributed to over 100 deaths from mine and bomb accidents between June 1999 and April 2000, after most refugees had returned home. "Cluster bombs almost always cause multiple casualties, and it is nearly always young people who get injured," said John Flanagan, Programme Manager of the UN Mine Action Coordination Centre in Pristina, Kosovo. "We did not anticipate the number of them used and their attractiveness to kids."[9]

The survivors of mines and unexploded ordnance tend to be concentrated among the poor who are exposed when cultivating their fields, herding their animals or searching for firewood. In Viet Nam, for example, young children look after the family's water buffalo, which often roam freely in areas that have been mined or contain unexploded bombs and shells. Some poor children also work as scavengers and gather these devices to sell as scrap metal in the local market.

Young people who work in fields and forests and who fetch water are among those most at risk of mines. Children are endangered when their play areas, sports facilities and cultural centres are contaminated by landmines and UXOs.

The risk to children is compounded by the way in which mines and UXOs become incorporated into daily life – a familiarity that dulls awareness of the dangers. In Cambodia, civilians use mines and other devices to fish, to guard property and, in some cases, in acts of domestic violence. As a result, children may become so familiar with mines and other devices that they are less mindful of the danger these lethal weapons pose. Cambodian children have been seen playing "boulcs" with B40 devices and some have even started their own collections of landmines. In northern Iraq, children have been known to use mine casings as wheels for toy trucks.

Unexploded cluster bombs are even more lethal to children. Unlike some landmines which may be designed to inflict injuries, these devices are designed to kill. A study of cluster munitions in the Lao People's Democratic Republic found that "one of the most startling and disturbing facts to emerge from this data collection is the extraordinarily high proportion of children affected." Forty-three per cent of those injured or killed are age 15 or younger, the study reports, a far higher rate than in Cambodia, where landmines are the primary problem.[10]

Even when children themselves are not the victims, landmines and UXOs have an overwhelming impact on their lives. Landmine incidents devastate the livelihoods of families who already live on the edge of survival. Surveys in Cambodia found that more than half of the families with a mine victim to support were in debt because of the accident.[11] A field survey in Afghanistan reported that unemployment for adult males rose from 6 per cent to 52 per cent as a result of landmine accidents.[12] When parents fall victim to mines, they are frequently unable to work and are thus less able to support and protect their children.

On a broader scale, these indiscriminate weapons strike at a country's reconstruction and development. When strewn in roads and footpaths, landmines prevent refugees and displaced families from returning to their homes and inhibit the circulation of goods and services. When seeded across agricultural land, landmines and UXOs prevent rural people from growing food or earning a living.

No more soccer

On 23 October 1999, Yusup Magomedov begged his mother to let him go outside to play soccer in the Chechen village of Novi Sharoi following days of confinement because of the war. A few minutes after Yusup left his house, an unexploded Russian cluster bomblet detonated and shredded his legs. Seven children died in the explosion, and at least 15 were injured. A week later, while bombs rained down as Yusup and his mother cowered in a cellar, doctors sharing their hiding place amputated his gangrenous legs above the knees with a kitchen knife.[13]

The Ottawa Convention

The humanitarian and socio-economic crises caused by anti-personnel mines stirred an international movement to rid the world of this scourge. The drive for a global ban on anti-personnel landmines was led by the International Campaign to Ban Landmines (ICBL), made up of more than 1,100 NGOs active in over 60 countries, together with like-minded governments, the

International Committee of the Red Cross and UN agencies.

The effort culminated in the opening for signature in Ottawa (Canada) of the 1997 Convention on the Prohibition of the Use, Stockpiling, Production and Transfer of Anti-Personnel Mines, and on their Destruction. In 1997, the ICBL and its then Coordinator, Jody Williams, were awarded the Nobel Peace Prize. In March 1999, having achieved the threshold of 40 ratifications, the Convention became international law. Governments ratifying the Convention are obliged to abide by the following:

• Never to use or assist in the use of anti-personnel landmines.
• Never to manufacture or develop anti-personnel landmines.
• Never to transfer or assist in the transfer of anti-personnel land-mines.
• To destroy stockpiled anti-personnel mines within four years.
• To remove emplaced mines within ten years.
• To report annually on their implementation of the Convention.

Since the Convention's entry into force, the global production of landmines has greatly decreased. Of the 12 biggest landmine-producing and exporting countries, 8 are now signatories to the Convention and have ceased production of anti-personnel land-mines. The total number of producing countries has dropped from 54 to 16.[14]

Exports, too, seem largely to have stopped, according to ICBL's *Landmine Monitor Report*. All 34 countries that once exported mines, with the exception of Iraq, have stated they are no longer doing so.

The actual use of anti-personnel landmines is on the wane, although continued or new use by Angola, Burundi and Sudan, all signatories to the Ottawa Convention, has been reported. The armed forces of Eritrea, Israel, Myanmar, Pakistan, the Russian Federation, Sri Lanka and the Federal Republic of Yugoslavia, which have not signed the Convention, have also used anti-personnel landmines in recent years, as have rebel groups in Afghanistan, Angola, Chechnya, Colombia, Lebanon, Myanmar, the Philippines, Sri Lanka and Uganda.

Mine clearance is under way in dozens of countries and the

number of mine casualties has dropped in some seriously affected countries, including Afghanistan, Bosnia and Herzegovina, Cambodia and Mozambique.[15] In Cambodia, recorded casualties dropped from 3,046 in 1996 to 1,012 in 1999.[16]

The Convention requires that signatories complete the destruction of their stockpiles within four years. Around 20 million landmines have been destroyed from the stockpiles of at least 50 nations in recent years. Even so, stockpiles remain high, with around 250 million anti-personnel landmines in at least 105 countries.

Countries that have not ratified or acceded to the Ottawa Convention must do so – and all must move quickly to ensure effective implementation. However, many countries that have ratified the Convention have not enacted national legislation to give its provisions the force of law, and national reporting on implementation has been slower than hoped. As of July 2000, 48 countries had filed reports, but 36 had missed reporting deadlines.[17]

Mine action

Protecting children and other civilians from landmines and unexploded ordnance requires action in four areas: surveys and assessments to determine mine contamination and impact; mine awareness to help children avoid mines and take safety precautions; mine clearance to remove mines; and survivor assistance to support children's rehabilitation. National mine programmes must give a central place to mine-affected communities and their children. In practical terms, this means ensuring that families will have safe access to their homes, to health services, water points, schools, farms and play areas. National mine action programmes must give mine-affected communities a voice in setting priorities.

Peace can never be fully achieved while landmines continue to threaten innocent civilians. Mine action is critically important to peacekeeping and peace-building operations. Practically, this means supporting both military and humanitarian priorities. Repatriation of refugees, which is fundamental to any peace process, cannot be conceived of, let alone enacted, without the

Landmines in 2000

Producers of anti-personnel landmines:
China, Cuba, Democratic People's Republic of Korea, Egypt, India, Iran, Iraq, Myanmar, Pakistan, Republic of Korea, Russian Federation, Singapore, Turkey, United States, Viet Nam, Federal Republic of Yugoslavia.[18]

Largest mine stockpiles (millions of mines):
China (110), Russian Federation (60), Belarus (10-15), United States (11), Ukraine (10*), Pakistan (6), India (4).[19]
* Being destroyed.

States that have yet to accede to the Ottawa Convention:
Afghanistan, Armenia, Azerbaijan, Bahrain, Belarus, Bhutan, Central African Republic, China, Comoros, Republic of the Congo, Cuba, Democratic People's Republic of Korea, Democratic Republic of the Congo, Egypt, Eritrea, Estonia, Finland, Georgia, India, Iran, Iraq, Israel, Kazakhstan, Kuwait, Kyrgyzstan, Lao People's Democratic Republic, Latvia, Lebanon, Libya, Micronesia, Mongolia, Morocco, Myanmar, Nepal, Nigeria, Oman, Pakistan, Palau, Papua New Guinea, Republic of Korea, Russian Federation, Saudi Arabia, Singapore, Somalia, Sri Lanka, Syria, Tonga, Turkey, Tuvalu, United Arab Emirates, United States, Uzbekistan, Viet Nam, Federal Republic of Yugoslavia.[20]

requisite resources and commitment to clearing minefields along repatriation routes and in destination areas. The hundreds of thousands of children and women returning home must have safe land to develop and safe areas for schools.

The importance of integrating humanitarian mine action into

peacekeeping was shown in Kosovo in 1999 when UNICEF, in coordination with the UN Mine Action Coordination Centre, secured the International Security Force in Kosovo's commitment to give priority to demining schools. In Kosovo, following the return of refugees in 1999, landmines and UXOs in and around schools were a major obstacle blocking children's return to school. Through the work of mine clearance by NGOs and other agencies, 776 schools and a number of play areas for children were demined and deemed safe by the end of November 2000.[21]

Formed in 1997, the United Nations Mine Action Service (UNMAS) has played an excellent coordinating role among UN agencies and works closely with UNICEF and other UN and NGO partners to ensure mine awareness, survivor assistance and rehabilitation for children and affected communities.

Surveys and assessments

The Global Landmine Survey is a cooperative effort by NGOs, the UN Mine Action Service and the Geneva International Centre for Humanitarian Demining, to coordinate national surveys and landmine assessments. These determine the extent of mine contamination and its socio-economic impact. Between 1997 and 2000, regional or national landmine assessments and surveys have been carried out or are under way in 24 countries and areas. In Yemen, a comprehensive national survey was due for completion in mid-2000, and similar surveys were under way or planned in Afghanistan, Angola, Cambodia, Chad, Eritrea, Ethiopia, northern Iraq, Kosovo province, Lebanon, Mozambique, Somaliland (in Somalia), Thailand and Western Sahara.[22]

Ideally, assessments and surveys should identify flows of refugees and displaced persons and camp locations, schools, health and cultural facilities, farms and play areas. In 2000, the devastating floods in Mozambique, affecting approximately 2 million people, have complicated mine action in some areas, washing away minefield markers and shifting mines into areas already cleared or considered mine-free.

War on children: A testimony

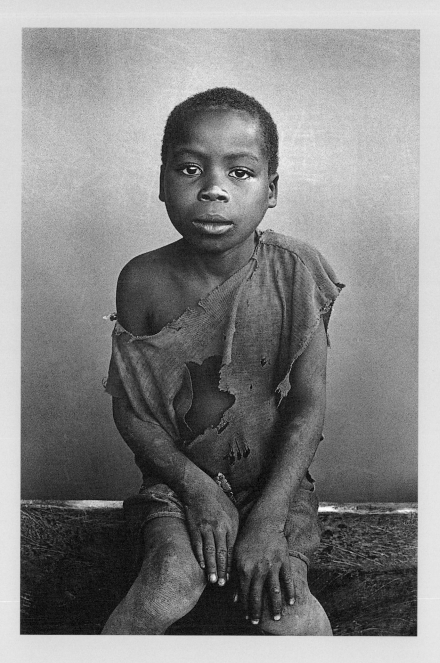

Mozambique, 1994.

Children and women are targets during an air attack.
Ethiopia, 1985.

A refugee behind a shattered window.
Federal Republic of Yugoslavia, 1995.

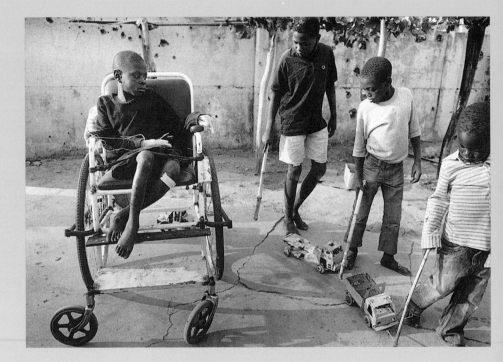

A child paralysed from a war accident.
Kuito, Angola, 1997.

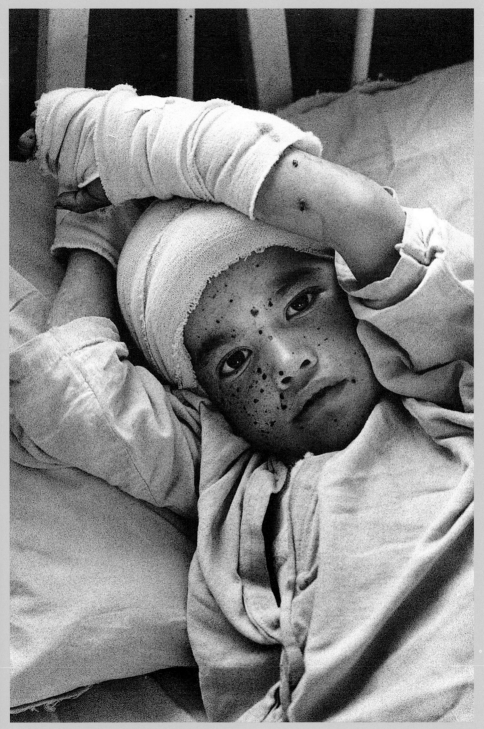

A shrapnel victim.
Kabul, Afghanistan, 1996.

A landmine survivor.
Siem Reap, Cambodia, 1990.

Tajik refugees in a class on landmines and unexploded ordnance.
Mazar-i-Sharif, Afghanistan, 1996.

Third generation Palestinian refugees continue to live
in restricted areas, after more than 50 years of exile.
Tripoli, Lebanon, 1998.

One of thousands of indigenous peasants displaced by conflict in the south.
Chiapas state, Mexico, 1998.

Refugee children, lost or separated from their parents during
the aftermath of Rwanda's genocidal civil conflict, await assistance.
Former Zaire, 1997.

Displaced by war, women care for their own children and for others who have lost their parents.
Milange, Mozambique, 1994.

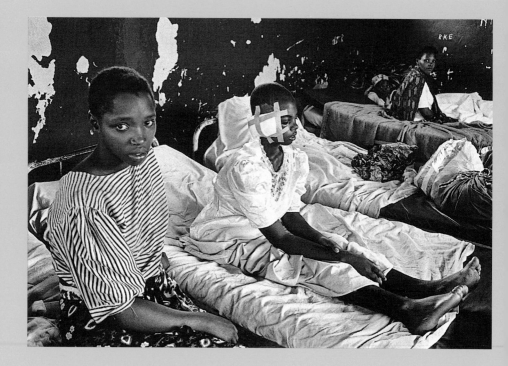

Women and girls recover from attacks they suffered during the genocide.
Kigali, Rwanda, 1994.

More than a decade after their husbands, fathers and sons were taken away,
displaced ethnic Kurd women and children continue to await their return.
Erbil, northern Iraq, 1997.

Thousands of Vietnamese refugee children have
spent their entire lives in this detention camp.
Hong Kong, 1995.

During war, children are often under threat of malnutrition and disease.
Kuito, Angola, 1997.

An outdoor class for refugee children from southern Sudan.
Kenya, 1993.

Mine awareness

Mine awareness helps people recognise and avoid landmines and suspected mined areas and take safety precautions when a mine is discovered or an incident occurs. Around half of the world's mine-affected countries have undertaken mine awareness programmes. Often, mine awareness teams simply enter a community, present information and leave – without addressing the daily life patterns that expose children and their families to injury and death. Using the media and participatory approaches, recent mine awareness programmes have involved communities in the learning process. And international donors are now more prepared to support such longer-term programmes.

In Kosovo, UXOs are a greater threat than landmines in some areas, and mine awareness messages need to reflect this. Mine awareness can be incorporated into school curricula using interactive techniques tailored to the needs of different age groups. In the Lao People's Democratic Republic, mine awareness is particularly crucial for children, since many of their daily activities put them in close contact with unexploded cluster bombs. In May 2000, a clearance project in Houa Phan province removed more than 300 cluster bomblets from a school courtyard.[23]

UNICEF, the lead UN agency for mine awareness, has developed international guidelines[24] and training materials, in cooperation with other partners. Though generic in nature, the guidelines highlight child-to-child techniques so that children educate and alert their friends. While games and role-playing exercises have helped children understand the risks, much more needs to be done to reach children with these messages.

In Angola, for example, UNICEF and its partner organisations supported mine awareness campaigns that in 1999 reached approximately 400,000 people through provincial theatre groups, posters, puppet shows, traditional songs, dances and plays.[25] In El Salvador, community-based mine awareness education has been a component of a mine action programme that has rid the country of the landmine threat following the end of the civil war in 1992. Mobile units used child-friendly material to develop teams of trainers in rural communities, including nearly 26,000 students, with messages reinforced by radio and television campaigns.[26]

In 1999, UNICEF played a lead role in coordinating mine awareness education for Kosovar refugees prior to their return home. While in refugee camps, teachers were trained and support was provided for mobile theatre groups and for radio and TV messages. More than 1 million posters and leaflets were distributed.

Mine clearance

Clearing landmines is a long, expensive and dangerous business. Each one takes 100 times longer to remove than to deploy, and a weapon that costs $3 or less to manufacture may eventually cost $1,000 to remove. Around the world, deminers risk their lives to clear these dangerous weapons. Demining is carried out with various priorities and objectives. These may include clearing strategic areas, such as airports or power stations; transport links such as roads and bridges; fields and pastures for food production; and homes, water sources, clinics, schools, footpaths and other areas essential for community life.

In Bosnia and Herzegovina, demining was hindered because no agreement could be reached on which of 18,000 minefields should be cleared first. In this case, contracts for demining projects were based on the size of each area cleared, so deminers focused on farmland and pastures rather than on urban areas. In the town of Vitez, for example, a commercial deminer cleared open land and avoided homes. In 1999, UNHCR supported a demining programme to clear homes for resettling refugees and cleared 70 houses in the town.[27]

A large minefield in a remote area may pose little immediate threat, while a small number of mines or UXOs in populated areas can imperil many lives and severely disrupt economic activity. There are more than 110,000 internally displaced people in Cambodia, for example, either waiting to resettle or who have recently returned to their home villages. Most of these villages are either mined or near areas suspected of being mined, and it is difficult to rehabilitate roads, schools and irrigation systems until the mine threat is removed.[28] In Mozambique, eight landmines prevented more than

20,000 people from returning to their villages in the Mahniça valley for seven years until they were cleared in 1996.[29]

Afghanistan has one of the world's largest mine clearing operations, but mines still claim many victims, an overwhelming number of them children. In the city of Kandahar, the poorest people have been building makeshift housing in the midst of a minefield that is still being cleared, and children play in the dangerous rubble.[30] Such situations point to the need for integrated mine programmes that link surveying, marking, mine awareness and survivor rehabilitation with the reconstruction of communities.

Assistance for child survivors

Clearing mines is expensive, but it is a small price to pay to prevent the devastating injuries they inflict. The majority of mine survivors are civilians, including women and children. Anti-personnel mines are designed to attack adults – not so much to kill them but to leave them maimed. For the slighter physique of a child, however, the explosion of even the smallest mine can be lethal. In Cambodia, around 20 per cent of all children injured by mines and UXOs die from their injuries.[31] For the children who survive, the medical problems related to amputation are often severe, as the limb of a child grows faster than the surrounding tissue and requires repeated amputation.

Assistance to mine survivors is mandated under the Ottawa Convention, and the Convention on the Rights of the Child requires ratifying countries to promote the physical and psychological recovery and social reintegration of children injured in armed conflicts. Comprehensive treatment and rehabilitation for a survivor can cost up to $1,000 in poor developing countries,[32] where the average GNP per person is only a few hundred dollars a year. The cost of prostheses varies from $35 to $250 or more. Lifelong care for an amputee can run into thousands of dollars.

Worldwide, there are some 300,000 landmine survivors.[33] In Angola, coping with existing amputees would require 5,000 new prostheses every year, more than twice the number currently being produced there. Landmine survivors often face prejudice and stigmatisation, even within their own families.

In a number of mine-affected countries, emergency medical care and prostheses are becoming increasingly available. But survivors are often left on their own to deal with the long-term consequences of being disabled. Prostheses are only one critically important element of assistance. The ICBL has set key priorities for child survivors of landmines, which include:[34]

a) ensuring that they attend and complete as much schooling as possible;

b) providing psychological support;

c) working with families to help them understand the physical and psychological impact of a traumatic disability so that they better support the child's recovery;

d) working at the family and community level to combat the stigma surrounding disability; and

e) advocating at the national and international levels to convince policy makers of the range of needs of landmine survivors and to assist them in setting and implementing national agendas to promote and protect the rights of landmine victims to physical care and rehabilitation, psychosocial counselling, education and vocational training, and reintegration into their communities.

International assistance has been slow to arrive for mine-related activities in general, but particularly for assistance to survivors. According to the United Nations Mine Action Service, eight donor countries and the European Commission provided $32 million between 1993 and 1999 for survivor assistance – a fraction of what is needed.[35]

To rally more support, in September 1998, the Berne Manifesto was adopted by the ICRC, UNICEF, WHO and the Government of Switzerland. Together, they called for improved care and rehabilitation for child survivors of landmines.

Resources for mine action

Despite the Ottawa Convention's call for international cooperation to end the landmine threat, aid has been slow to arrive. The United

One child, three surgical operations

A 10-year-old boy arrived at an ICRC first aid post in a taxi hired by his father. Ten hours earlier, he had stepped on a small, buried anti-personnel mine that shattered the whole of his left foot. The boy had a below-the-knee amputation under a general anaesthetic. Four days later he was taken back to the operating theatre to have the skin flaps of the amputation stitched together. Five days later, the dressing was taken off and the boy saw for the first time how his leg ended in a stitched stump. This was a great shock to him and he began to cry. His father also cried.

Over the next two weeks he had a lot of physiotherapy and learned to walk on crutches. After a month the boy was transferred to the ICRC limb-fitting centre where he received an artificial leg made out of a plastic material. Five months later he broke the limb when he was playing football with his friends. He and his father headed for the ICRC limb-fitting centre again and he was given a new leg. A year later he needed an operation to remove a piece of bone that was still growing in the stump. The stump was now a different shape and so he had to have yet another artificial limb fitted – his third in the 18 months since the mine blast.[36]

States proposed that $1 billion be raised annually, but although allocations have doubled since the signing of the Convention, only $211 million was provided by the 17 major donors in 1999.[37]

One of the main UN financing mechanisms is the Voluntary Trust Fund for Assistance in Mine Action. The Fund supports the coordination of UN mine action and the initiation of new mine action projects, but also bridges funding gaps in ongoing programmes. Over 40 countries and the European Union have provided funds, but they have not significantly increased support in recent years. A total of $8 million was donated in 1997, $11 million in 1998, $12 million in 1999 and $4 million in the first four months of 2000.

In 1999, the UN Office for the Coordination of Humanitarian Affairs (OCHA) issued a consolidated appeal for over $63 million for mine action activities in seven countries, but in the following 10 months only $10 million was received. Urgent and accelerated donor support is needed, both bilaterally and internationally, for mine action in affected countries.

Companies and countries that have used landmines and UXOs or profited from their sale should be identified and required to contribute resources for mine action. Leaders responsible for causing civilian deaths and injuries and economic damage through the use of landmines should be held accountable for their actions under international law.

The Ottawa Convention is now part of international law, and far fewer landmines are being produced and deployed since its entry into force in March 1999. Yet children continue to be killed and maimed by landmines each day, and resources for mine clearance and for the support and rehabilitation of survivors are inadequate. With sufficient determination and resources, countries should be able to eliminate all landmines in their territories within the 10-year time-frame set by the Ottawa Convention.

Chapter 10

Small arms, light weapons: Mass destruction

"I did learn some things when I was with the rebels. I learned how to shoot, how to lay anti-personnel mines and how to live on the run. I especially knew how to use an AK-47 twelve-inch, which I could dismantle in less than one minute. When I turned 12 they gave me an RPG, because I had proved myself in battle."

– Abducted child, now a 19-year-old soldier in northern Uganda[1]

The most widely used weapons of mass destruction are not nuclear or biological – they are the estimated 500 million small arms and light weapons that are fuelling bloodshed and mayhem around the world.[2] Inexpensive and easy to use, they are a major reason for an alarming rise in civilian casualties in armed conflict over the last decade[3] – and in the obscene transformation of hundreds of thousands of children into professionalised killers.

The ready availability of these weapons leads to vicious cycles of violence and insecurity, prolonging suffering and obstructing post-conflict reconstruction. Small arms circulate easily into communities at peace, where they are routinely used in acts of assault, robbery, rape and murder, sometimes on a mass scale. So light and simple to use, these weapons make it easy to exploit children as soldiers – some 300,000 children have participated in over 30 recent conflicts.

One pull of the trigger on an assault rifle can fire a burst of up to 30 rounds.[4] And while some sophisticated weapons require specialised training and sheer physical strength to wield, simpler and more lightweight weapons like hand grenades, handguns and AK-47 rifles can be used by small children with deadly effect. Even a 10-year-old can be taught to strip and reassemble an AK-47.

Small arms and light weapons take many different forms. Broadly speaking, small arms are designed for individual use. They include revolvers and self-loading pistols, assault rifles, sub-machine guns, grenades, anti-personnel landmines[5] and light machine guns. Light weapons are designed for use by several persons serving as a crew and include heavy machine guns, portable anti-aircraft guns and missiles, mortars and anti-tank missile and rocket systems.[6] Although designed for use by armed forces, the portability, size and price make small arms and light weapons advantageous for private armies and mercenaries. The growing privatisation of security and warfare also contributes to the rising trade in small arms.

The militarisation of daily life adds to general levels of instability, blurring the boundaries between warfare, crime and local disputes. In these environments, non-state actors are often better armed than the police. Fuelled by fear and oppression, individual citizens may acquire arms to defend themselves, their families and property.

The possession of weapons can also be a source of pride, a status symbol and, in some cases, a symbol of ethnic and cultural identity. By itself, this does not necessarily lead to a culture of violence. However, a culture of weapons may be transformed into a culture of violence when a State cannot guarantee the security of its citizens or control illicit activities that depend upon small arms. The breakdown of social codes and of traditional mechanisms for conflict resolution further undermines stability.

Consequences for children

Small arms and light weapons maim and kill thousands of children each year. Many children have witnessed or themselves suffered direct attacks by light weapons in their homes, schools and communities. In Lokichokio (Kenya), families kept their children at home after a primary school was attacked and 10 students were killed. In an effort to increase children's safety, schools moved into the vicinity of the UN compound.[7] And children are being dragged into the line of fire in the armed conflict between rebel groups and the Philippine Government. In camps, youngsters are brandishing M-16 and AK-47 assault rifles. "How does one know if the enemies are children," Jerome Pol-ang, a battle-tested Marine sergeant, said. "They have guns like us, they are in full uniform and they fight like any other soldier. But if you mean have I seen young dead enemies, most of the dead I saw were young. Perhaps 18 years or younger, 15 like my eldest son."[8]

And millions more children suffer indirectly from the emotional consequences of armed violence. "I work as a volunteer play therapist with children who have been forced to leave their homes because of war," said a 16-year-old Colombian boy. "Some of the children have seen terrible things, like seeing their father tortured and killed. They find it very difficult to understand what happened. We play together with the trucks and boats and rag dolls, and sometimes after that you can figure out what went on. Some of the children are very shy but I give them the parrot puppet and sometimes they tell him things. They often talk about the goats and chickens and cows they left behind when they left their homes. They worry about the animals."[9]

Children also pay a heavy price when their governments spend their countries' limited resources on defence budgets instead of on health, education and other programmes that are of direct benefit to children. In 1998, the UN Secretary-General called on African countries to agree to reduce their purchases of arms and munitions to below 1.5 per cent of GDP and to commit to a zero-growth policy for defence budgets for a 10-year period.[10] The most recent data available show that Burundi, for instance, spent 6 per cent of GDP on military expenditure, compared with less than 1 per cent on health and 4 per cent on education.[11]

Children suffer when small arms and light weapons obstruct emergency relief efforts. Humanitarian and peacekeeping personnel have increasingly come under fire. Since 1992, over 200 civilian national and international staff members have lost their lives in the service of the United Nations, the vast majority of them killed by small arms.[12] The growing presence of small arms in refugee and displaced persons camps led the Security Council to call on peace-keeping operations to protect the delivery of humanitarian assistance in such situations.[13] When the risks of delivering assistance and providing protection become too high, humanitarian organisations may be forced to suspend operations, which can put the lives and well-being of children at further peril. When several staff members of the International Committee of the Red Cross were abducted at gunpoint in Somalia, the ICRC suspended activities in that country. And after the fatal shooting of two UN staff members in Burundi in 1999, all humanitarian interventions slowed down considerably.[14]

Stemming the flow

The half-billion small arms and light weapons in circulation around the world are in part the product of a steady process of accumulation. Small arms and light weapons have been mass-produced for a half century or more and are very durable. More than 70 million AK-47 (Kalashnikov) assault rifles have been manufactured worldwide since the Soviet Army first introduced the weapon in 1947, and great numbers of them remain in circulation principally because they and similar weapons have few moving parts and are easy to maintain.[15]

When a war ends, the guns remain. And since small arms are exceptionally portable, they are easy to hide, hoard and trade. Weapons that the United States introduced into Central America in the 1970s are now in the hands of Colombian guerrillas. Guns that the former Soviet Union shipped into Afghanistan in the 1980s are now circulating throughout northern India and Pakistan. Weapons left by the US army in their withdrawal from Somalia in the 1990s have appeared in Kenya and other east African countries.[16]

The end of the Cold War has also resulted in many surplus stocks being shipped from Eastern Europe to Africa. Indeed, it is often cheaper to dump surplus weapons overseas than to destroy stockpiles.[17] As a result, these weapons are now extremely cheap and widely available. In a number of African countries, $5 or a bag of maize will buy a well-worn but serviceable weapon.

Small arms and light weapons continue to be produced in vast numbers. In early 2001 more than 600 companies in over 95 countries throughout the world were legally producing small arms.[18] Of those, at least 50 developing countries are producing small arms and 26 are exporting them.[19] Insurgent and opposition groups in several countries even have the capability of producing simple, small-calibre weapons of their own.

Ammunition for small arms and light weapons is also produced in ample quantities. Globally, over 150 major companies in 50 countries are involved in the manufacture of ammunition for military weaponry.[20] Ammunition production is centred in the West and the United States is the world's leading supplier. But since the end of the Cold War, the Russian Federation and parts of Eastern Europe have begun to emerge as important producers. In addition, developing countries including India, Kenya, Myanmar, Pakistan and South Africa are becoming increasingly involved in manufacturing ammunition for regional markets.[21]

Another worrying development is the growing reach and influence of private arms traders. In the recent past, most sales were made by large manufacturers or governments, which allowed for some controls over the trade. Increasingly, however, both governments and manufacturers are working through private dealers who will sell arms to anyone – and are accountable to no one. Private arms brokers often circumvent laws to supply arms to, and through, illegal and organised crime groups.

Small arms, light weapons and ammunition trading often escape the traditional boundaries of arms control. Many illegal weapons currently in circulation were at one point transferred legally by governments. And the trade is not confined to new weapons: a significant part consists of transfers from existing stockpiles, recycled from one conflict to another. The precise magnitude of the international small arms and light weapons trade is not known. In 2000, the legal trade was estimated to be worth at least $4 billion to $6 billion.[22] Illegal trade is even more difficult to gauge and has been estimated at up to $10 billion.[23]

The ability of governments to counter the uncontrolled spread of small arms can be strengthened in a number of ways. By drawing up binding international instruments and legislation, governments and arms producers can be held accountable for licit and illicit arms and ammunition flows, production and stockpiling. Regulations governing production, sales, export, import, re-export, transit, diversion, brokering and licensing are also necessary. These controls should relate to both civilian- and state-owned firearms, small arms, light weapons and ammunition. International norms and guidelines on marking and tracing weapons and ammunition need to be put in place.

If small arms and light weapons are to be controlled, there must be transparency on trade-related issues. In the absence of regulations, information of this kind is rarely made public. Information about small arms and ammunition flows can contribute greatly to early warning and conflict-prevention strategies. Like the UN Register on Conventional Arms, one instrument to channel information might consist of regional and national registers for small arms, light weapons and ammunition.

If enforced, weapons embargoes can deny both state and non-state actors the tools with which violent abuses are committed. The UN Secretary-General has called for arms embargoes to be imposed, monitored and enforced in situations where civilians are targeted, where widespread and systematic violations of humanitarian and human rights law are committed and where children are recruited as soldiers.[24] During the 1990s, the UN Security Council imposed weapons embargoes on 13 different parties. In the majority of the cases, the embargoes targeted government groups, but in the cases of Angola, Rwanda and Sierra Leone, the embargoes were also directed against non-state actors.

Embargo violations should be criminalised and violators prosecuted. Increased cooperation among affected States and the international community is necessary to monitor and enforce weapons embargoes and to ensure that countries or groups that commit such violations do not receive military assistance.

Collection and destruction of weapons

Without effective disarmament, sustainable peace is not possible. A critical opportunity to remove weapons is when armed groups are being disbanded. All peace agreements should include specific provisions for the collection and destruction of weapons and ammunition. In a peacekeeping environment, institutional arrangements to disarm soldiers, including child combatants, should be funded and given appropriate support. But taking weapons away from soldiers is only a part of the process, because they can easily acquire others. If former soldiers are not to return to violence, they need other survival options. It costs more to demobilise a child than an adult, but without this support, children are easily re-mobilised into the thick of conflict. That is why full-fledged disarmament, demobilisation and reintegration programmes must also provide former combatants with vocational alternatives. This is especially important for child soldiers, particularly girl combatants, who are often excluded from formal disarmament, demobilisation and reintegration programmes. In some cases demobilisation has been organised on the basis of "one man-one gun." Since children rarely own the guns they may have used, they may be disqualified from these demobilisation programmes. All such eligibility requirements for children should be waived.

Soldiers are not the only people with guns. Disarmament also has to involve civilians. Weapons-collection programmes can help, during conflict and after. "Buy-back" programmes have been used to collect and destroy weapons in exchange for cash. This option, however, can create a new demand for weapons and reward those who collect or deal in them.

Such problems can be avoided by offering something other than cash. In Nigeria, for example, the US Peace Corps has a "guns for food" programme. Guns can also be swapped for development aid. In Mozambique, since 1995, the Christian Council of Mozambique has organised a Tools for Arms Project that has collected around 75,000 weapons and other pieces of equipment. In exchange for weapons, the organisation offers such useful items as sewing machines, hoes, bicycles and construction materials.[25] Weapons can also be transformed into more useful objects. In Liberia, a project supported by UNICEF turns small arms into agricultural tools. In Mozambique, artists have transformed fragments of destroyed weapons into works of art symbolising peace.

Collection programmes have also attempted to offer community, rather than individual, benefits in exchange for surrendered weapons. The United Nations Development Programme (UNDP) and the UN Department for Disarmament Affairs (DDA) have been running a programme of this kind in Albania. In 1997, during social unrest surrounding the collapse of a rash of pyramid investment schemes, people stole 600,000 weapons from police or military stores. Following a government request, UNDP and DDA responded with a "weapons-for-development" programme. It was launched in 100 villages in the Gramsch district, where there were thought to be 10,000 illegal weapons.[26] There, in exchange for the voluntary surrender of weapons, UNDP organised the construction of a number of community facilities, including roads, street lighting and telecommunications, as well as facilities for health care and sanitation.

While such experimental programmes have effectively engaged communities in rebuilding their society, they have yet to develop a specific child focus. Nor have they amassed significant numbers of surrendered weapons or clarified institutional responsibilities for their storage and disposal. If people are to be motivated to give up their weapons, collection programmes must take cultural, development and security issues into account.

The collection and storage of weapons must be in the hands of technical or military personnel with the necessary specialist skills. This can forestall the involvement of humanitarian personnel, who, by handling weapons, risk compromising their neutrality. To prevent looting, weapons need to be stored under secure conditions. In Cambodia, for example, an extensive campaign resulted in the surrender of thousands of weapons, including AK-47s. But many of these weapons later reappeared on the black market.[27]

The process of collecting and destroying weapons should be open and transparent. In the majority of cases it is advisable to destroy the collected weapons and ammunition in public in order to bolster voluntary collection programmes. If, for safety reasons or environmental considerations, public destruction is not advisable, a publicised symbolic destruction would be an alternative. In 1996, 3,000 decommissioned weapons were destroyed in a bonfire in Mali dubbed the

"Flame of Peace." Similarly, "Operation Rachel," supported by the Governments of Mozambique and South Africa, destroyed on-site more than 12,000 firearms found in community caches.[28]

Reversing the culture of violence

International action to stem the flow of small arms is vital. The flow of small arms is a global problem that, by definition, transcends national boundaries, and governments must cooperate to develop lasting solutions.

The 2001 UN Conference on the Illicit Trafficking in Small Arms and Light Weapons in All its Aspects is the beginning of an international process to address the proliferation of small arms. As the process develops, attention needs to be given to child protection, humanitarian and development impacts and the control of legal transfers and state-to-state transfers.

In 2000 and 2001 the UN Secretary-General, the Security Council and the General Assembly have taken important steps to respond to the risks that small arms pose to international peace and security.[29] And under the auspices of the United Nations, the Commission on Crime Prevention and Criminal Justice negotiated a supplement to the Convention against Transnational Organised Crimes in the form of a "Firearms Protocol." However, this document is limited to transactions involving commercial weapons.

Several regional and subregional organisations, such as the Council of Europe, the Economic Community of West African States (ECOWAS), the Organization of American States (OAS), the Southern African Development Community (SADC) and the European Union, have taken initiatives to stem the flow of small arms, including developing codes of conduct. Recent meetings such as the ASEAN Seminar[30] in Jakarta have signalled a growing official willingness to address the problem at regional levels. In December 2000, OAU Ministers adopted the Bamako Declaration for the Great Lakes and the Horn of Africa on illicit trafficking controls, which takes a comprehensive approach to the problems of proliferation, circulation and trafficking of small arms and light weapons.

In November 2000, the Organization for Security and Cooperation in Europe (OSCE), comprising most of the world's major small arms exporters, adopted a comprehensive policy document on small arms as a part of its work on conflict prevention and post-conflict stabilisation. Initiated by the Government of Mali, the West African Moratorium on the Export, Import and Manufacture of Light Weapons brought together suppliers and recipients. It established a potential model for action for other regions.

Civil society's role is crucially important in the effort to halt the uncontrolled global spread of small arms and light weapons. Not only are civil society groups providing technical advice, advocacy and information sharing, they are also ensuring that decision makers hear the voices of those most affected by the problem of small arms and light weapons. More than 200 NGOs have established an International Action Network on Small Arms (IANSA) to promote NGO action against the proliferation and misuse of small arms.[31] In 1997, 15 recipients of the Nobel Peace Prize, led by former President Oscar Arias of Costa Rica, developed an International Code of Conduct on Arms Transfers that seeks to prevent the transfer and use of arms by parties to conflicts that have violated international human rights standards.

In a number of African countries, NGOs run public-education campaigns on the dangers of weapons while also working to reduce gun dependency. Campaign messages need to be tailored to reach children and adolescents. The media can contribute. On the one hand, they can stop glorifying violence; on the other, they can publicise local disarmament initiatives.

In Albania, NGOs, with UNICEF support, organised social activities for Albanian and Kosovar young people under the banner of "Don't Let Guns Kill Our Dreams." In Croatia, UNICEF's Mine and Weapons Awareness Education programme highlights the danger of having weapons kept at home within the reach of children. There has been similar activity in Latin America. In El Salvador, the long legacy of civil war, including the high murder rate, has led local communities, supported by UNDP, to engage in programmes designed to counter the culture of violence.

Efforts to curb the proliferation of small arms and light

weapons are being strengthened. Global support for the UN Conference on the Illicit Trafficking in Small Arms and Light Weapons in All its Aspects highlights the growing need for action at national, regional and international levels. But the scale of the problem is huge – and there are few signs of significant reductions in the availability of small arms, in the hands of children or anyone else.

Chapter 11

Protecting children from sanctions

"There is no use going to school because life is so hard. I'm going to help my father."

— Mohammed, age 13, Basra (southern Iraq)[1]

Economic sanctions have been seen as a non-violent and inexpensive alternative to war, but their effects can be just as devastating, especially for children and other vulnerable civilians. Economic sanctions are coercive measures taken against countries or political leaders through the deliberate withdrawal, or threat of withdrawal, of customary trade or financial relations. They can take the form of trade embargoes, restrictions on exports or imports, denial of foreign assistance, loans and investments, and constraints on foreign assets and economic transactions.

Sanctions have been used as the centrepiece of efforts to repel aggression, restore democracy, condemn human rights abuses and punish regimes harbouring terrorists and others charged with international crimes. Sanctions may be aimed at complete or partial interruption of economic relations, of travel, media and other means of communication, and the severance of diplomatic relations.

When sanctions are applied, the official targets tend to be governments or political leaders. But in practice, most economic sanctions affect the regular economic and social life of the country. And it is the civilian population that must contend with these effects. Shortages of food and medical supplies and the deterioration of infrastructure essential for clean water, adequate sanitation and electrical power have tragic results. Livelihoods are destroyed and families and children experience deprivation, malnutrition and poor health.

Since 1991, under Chapter VII, Article 41 of the Charter of the United Nations, the international community has collectively imposed sanctions on Angola, Eritrea, Ethiopia, Haiti, Iraq, Liberia, Libya, Rwanda, Sierra Leone, Somalia, Sudan and the Federal Republic of Yugoslavia. In other cases, countries have employed bilateral sanctions. Myanmar, for example, has been subject to trade embargoes imposed by a number of individual countries. Sanctions have traditionally been used against States, but in recent years, the Security Council has imposed sanctions against non-state actors, including the National Union for the Total Independence of Angola (UNITA) and the Taliban in Afghanistan.

Unintended impacts

The negative effects of sanctions tend to fall most heavily on children, the elderly and the poor. Children have less resistance than adults and cannot survive long periods of hardship and deprivation. Studies from Cuba, Haiti and Iraq following the imposition of sanctions have shown a rapid rise in the proportion of children who were malnourished. In Haiti from 1991 to 1993, for example, one study indicated that the price of staple foods increased fivefold and that, from 1991 to 1992, the proportion of malnourished children increased from 5 per cent to 23 per cent.[2]

At the same time, restricted access to foreign markets contributes to economic depression and escalates unemployment, inflation and the cost of living. As a result, disparities in wealth and poverty intensify.

In his follow-up report to *An Agenda for Peace*, former UN Secretary-General Boutros Boutros-Ghali recognised the ethical dilemmas raised by sanctions and questioned whether the suffering inflicted on vulnerable groups in target countries is a legitimate means of exerting pressure on political leaders.[3] Four years later, in 1999, the Security Council reaffirmed its readiness to consider the impact of sanctions on civilians, and especially on children, whenever it applies sanctions.[4]

Damage to children: The Iraqi experience

The longest-running and most severe comprehensive international sanctions are those imposed on Iraq in the years since 1990. The Security Council first introduced sanctions to force Iraq to withdraw from Kuwait. This objective was achieved rapidly through military action, but the sanctions were maintained in an effort to force the Government of Iraq to abandon its weapons of mass destruction. More than a decade later, there is still no indication of when the Security Council will lift the sanctions.

Sanctions have had a crippling effect on Iraq's economy and health care system. Unable to import spare parts, most factories cannot function effectively. Water is polluted and sewers have cracked open. Power shortages are the norm; telecommunications and transportation systems have virtually collapsed. Government workers are paid little more than $2.50 per month and often must take on additional jobs to survive.[5] Communicable diseases have become part of the endemic pattern of the precarious health situation.

To date, an estimated half million Iraqi children have died during the current sanctions regime.[6] The infant mortality rate rose from 47 per 1,000 live births, during the pre-sanctions period, to 108 per 1,000 live births in the period after sanctions were imposed.[7] UNICEF's Child and Maternal Mortality Survey of 1999 showed that children under five in the south/centre area of the country were dying at more than twice the rate of 10 years ago – before sanctions were imposed against Iraq. Sanctions also have a broader negative impact on surviving children, especially on their long-term development and psychological health. Only 53 per cent of Iraqi children enrol in school, as more families are forced to rely on children to earn part of household incomes.[8]

Almost from the outset of the sanctions regime against Iraq, the Security Council sought to apply humanitarian exemptions. In 1991, in order to mitigate some of the effects on health and nutrition, the Security Council allowed Iraq to export up to $1.6 billion in petroleum and petroleum products to purchase food and medicine. It stipulated that these supplies had to be purchased and distributed under the supervision of the United Nations.[9]

Because of objections by the Iraqi Government, it was not until 1996 that Iraq agreed to the "oil-for-food" programme. This programme allowed Iraq to export up to $2 billion in oil every six months and use 66 per cent of the proceeds to pay for humanitarian imports. This cap was raised in 1998 to $5.2 billion, and the ceiling on the value of oil exports was lifted altogether in 1999.[10] Even so, these resources are wholly insufficient to repair Iraq's badly deteriorated oil industry and to rebuild its social infrastructure.

In renewing his call to lift the sanctions against Iraq, the UN's former Coordinator of Humanitarian Affairs in Iraq, Denis Halliday, said, "The oil-for-food programme is meant to supplement human needs, but it is hardly sufficient [at] only $200 per person per year."[11] In fact, the programme was never intended to meet all of the humanitarian needs of the population and was only envisaged as a short-term emergency measure. But even 10 years later, the oil-for-food programme continues to be renewed every six months.

Although the oil-for-food programme has resulted in an overall decrease in chronic malnutrition levels from 27 per cent in 1997 to 21 per cent in 2000, the Food and Agriculture Organization of the United Nations (FAO) estimated that, in 2000, at least 800,000 children under the age of five were chronically malnourished.[12]

For its part, the Iraqi Government has not given first priority to children and has been accused of obstructing the oil-for-food programme. And there has also been general bureaucratic slowness on the part of the United Nations. The secretariat of the Iraq Sanctions Committee was seriously overloaded in the initial phase of the programme. In theory the Committee should have been able to deal rapidly with requests for routinely exempted items such as food and medicine. Yet the process was slowed by objections from a number of governments on the Committee, in particular the United Kingdom and the United States, which intervened to put a hold on certain items considered to be of "dual use," that is, for both humanitarian and military purposes.[13] Chlorine, for instance, which is critical for water purification, may also be used for military purposes.

In practice, humanitarian exemptions tend to be ambiguous and their interpretation arbitrary and inconsistent.[14] For example, the Sanctions Committee has denied as "non-essential" Iraqi requests for such items as pencils, textbooks and spare parts for ambulances.[15] The delay and denial of requests for essential humanitarian goods causes severe shortages and disruptions of food, pharmaceuticals and sanitation supplies. Out of a total of $24.8 billion worth of humanitarian goods ordered between December 1996 and December 1999, only about $6 billion actually arrived in Iraq.[16] Consequently, the capacity to maintain the quality of water, air and medicine has been reduced significantly.[17]

The Security Council and the Sanctions Committee have sought to expedite the approval process for humanitarian goods. Under Security Council Resolution 1284, the Committee adopted a list of spare parts, foodstuffs and basic health, agricultural and educational supplies that would no longer require pre-approval. Security Council Resolution 1302 directed the Committee to adopt a similar list for basic water and sanitation supplies and equipment. Yet only slightly more than half of the $21 billion in contracts approved by the Committee between December 1996 and March 2001 was administered.[18]

The fact is that comprehensive economic sanctions affect the poor, not the powerful. The conclusions from the Iraqi experience show irrefutably that comprehensive economic sanctions against Iraq have failed to achieve the intended political results and have caused immense human suffering.

Targeted sanctions

Faced with mounting evidence that comprehensive sanctions are more likely to harm civilians and children than deter dictators, the Security Council established an informal working group in April 2000 to review UN sanctions policy and to consider the effectiveness of targeted sanctions.

Targeted sanctions have the potential of mitigating the suffering that results from the imposition of comprehensive sanctions. In principle and in practice, sanctions should target precisely the vulnerabilities of those responsible for egregious crimes against civilians. This can be achieved by freezing assets, withholding credits and loans, prohibiting investments and suspending economic transactions. Other examples include arms embargoes and isolation through cultural, communication and specific economic boycotts.

Targeted sanctions can also be aimed at diplomats and supporters of the targeted regime. The Secretary-General's Report on the Protection of Civilians in Armed Conflict went further by recommending the imposition of targeted sanctions against non-state actors that exploit children as soldiers.[19] The report of the Secretary-General, 'We the Peoples: The Role of the United Nations in the 21st Century', outlines alternative strategies explored by a number of governments, including Germany and Switzerland, to make targeted financial sanctions more effective.

The Security Council adopted targeted sanctions against Angola and Sierra Leone in an effort to counter the financing of conflict through the diamond trade.[20] The sanctions against UNITA are a test case, and hope remains that Angola will become a model to demonstrate how targeted sanctions can throttle the profits of "war economies" and reduce arms expenditures by armed groups.

An end to sanctioned suffering

No sanctions regimes of any kind – comprehensive or targeted – should be imposed unless the Security Council is persuaded, by a rigorous assessment, that they will not have a negative impact on children. Obligatory and enforceable mechanisms should be used to monitor the impact of sanctions on children and other vulnerable groups before, during and after their imposition. All monitoring should include an assessment of the impact on regional neighbours and major trading partners.

Since many of the effects of sanctions only become manifest in the long term, no sanctions should be allowed to continue indefinitely. When sanctions are applied, the Security Council must set time limits and clearly define objectives and criteria. Sanctions should be lifted as soon as the objectives are satisfied.

The Committee on Economic, Social and Cultural Rights has recommended that international human rights and humanitarian

"Blood diamonds"

In July 2000, the United Nations Security Council imposed a global ban on the import of all rough diamonds from Sierra Leone until the Government set up a certification system and regained control of rebel-held mining areas.[21]

Aiming to curb UNITA's ability to wage war, the United Nations imposed fuel, arms and diamond embargoes against the rebel group in Angola, froze its bank accounts and banned its leaders from travel. Targeted sanctions against UNITA were imposed in 1998, after UNITA had earned $3 billion to $4 billion from gem sales. Recent initiatives by the UN Security Council, the Angola Sanctions Committee and its Panel of Experts have improved the enforcement of these targeted sanctions.

In March 2000, the Canadian Ambassador to the United Nations, Robert Fowler, issued a report to the UN Sanctions Committee naming governments and individuals that were allegedly in breach of these sanctions.[22] Subsequently, in April 2000, in coordination with private sector actors in the diamond industry, the Security Council set up a monitoring mechanism to investigate alleged violations of sanctions against UNITA.[23] Partly because of such efforts, the International Diamond Manufacturers' Association resolved in July 2000 to establish a system to halt the flow of diamonds from conflict areas, including Angola, the Democratic Republic of the Congo and Sierra Leone.[24] These diamonds that have been traded for arms have been dubbed "blood diamonds."

The Angolan example marks the first time that governments, industry and the UN joined to ensure that targeted sanctions achieved their political objectives effectively, while seeking to minimise the humanitarian consequences for women and children. Corporations and other private sector actors should contribute to the strict implementation of targeted sanctions legitimately established by the international community in full respect for human rights and the rights of the child.

standards be taken fully into account when sanctions are imposed.[25] The Convention on the Rights of the Child, the Convention on the Elimination of All Forms of Discrimination against Women and the Geneva Conventions are among the most important.

When the Security Council imposes sanctions, it should simultaneously provide resources to UN agencies and independent bodies to monitor the situation of children and other vulnerable groups. In January 1999, the President of the Security Council called for the sanctions committees to monitor the humanitarian impact of sanctions on vulnerable groups, including children.

A number of indicators for monitoring humanitarian impact have been proposed. These would measure the impact of sanctions on public health, the economy, access to education, population displacement, governance and civil society and humanitarian activities. Child-focused indicators need to address factors such as nutritional status and infant and maternal mortality.

But monitoring humanitarian impact will always be difficult. Data from the embargoed country may be scarce and uneven. And it may be difficult to distinguish the damage caused by sanctions from that caused by other events and processes, especially if the country has recently been engaged in a violent conflict.

"People have been harmed, not regimes," the Executive Office of the UN Secretary-General said of the effect – but not the intent – of many recent sanctions regimes.[26] In practice, the governments targeted by sanctions often pay scant attention to human rights and are usually so deeply entrenched and fortified by internal security systems that sanctions have little effect on them. Indeed, the government leaders who are targeted generally escape the most deleterious effects of sanctions, since they have privileged access to scarce resources. Unintentionally, comprehensive economic sanctions reinforce the power of an oppressive elite over the civilian population and support the emergence of illegal markets.

Sacrifices imposed on the population at large rarely force changes in policy. In 1998, an expert evaluation of the humanitarian impact of sanctions in Haiti, Iraq, South Africa and former Yugoslavia found no correlation between the level of suffering and the degree of political change.[27] Another assessment of 116 cases of economic sanctions, the majority imposed by the United States between 1914 and 1990, concluded that only one-third had been successful in achieving their political objectives.[28] Indeed, as recently as August 2000, an expert to the UN Subcommission on the Promotion and Protection of Human Rights concluded that economic sanctions aimed at changing government policy are usually ineffective and often illegal under international law.[29]

The evidence from impact assessments of comprehensive economic sanctions shows indisputable damage to children, yet debates on issues of causality and responsibility continue to undermine prompt and adequate humanitarian responses.

Children will always suffer when comprehensive sanctions are imposed. The conclusion is inescapable: The international community must cease to impose comprehensive economic sanctions.

Chapter 12

Raising standards for child protection

"Try to imagine, how could 29,000 people live in approximately two kilometres square with no yards, gardens or playgrounds."

– Dareen, Nahr el Bared refugee camp (Lebanon)[1]

In ratifying the Convention on the Rights of the Child, the international community proclaimed its political, legal and moral commitment to safeguard children's rights and to ensure their protection as "zones of peace." Under the Convention, States are obliged to protect children at all times, including in situations of armed conflict. Governments that have ratified the Convention are required to incorporate its principles and standards into national laws and to ensure enforcement of those laws. Violations and abuses of children's rights during armed conflict, by governments or other parties, must be seen by the international community for what they are: reprehensible and intolerable.

Over the past 50 years, human values and norms have been codified into a comprehensive international legal framework, of which the two main bodies are international humanitarian law and human rights law. The two have developed separately – but their complementarity has become increasingly apparent. In matters involving the protection of children in armed conflict, the most important bridge between these bodies is the Convention on the Rights of the Child.

Humanitarian and human rights law

Humanitarian law is intended to govern the conduct of warfare. It was conceived of and developed to limit the suffering of civilians, prisoners of war and wounded combatants. The 1949 Geneva Conventions and 1977 Additional Protocols are the major instruments of humanitarian law governing the protection of vulnerable groups. They are applicable to conflicts between States, to non-state entities and to armed conflicts within States. They emphasise the need to provide care and aid to children in internal armed conflicts, including education and family reunion. The Geneva Conventions and Additional Protocols also stipulate that children be given special respect and be protected against any form of indecent assault. They prohibit the evacuation of children to another country except when absolutely necessary.

In general, humanitarian law represents a compromise between military necessity and humanitarian considerations. Thus it is pragmatic: acknowledging that wars do occur, it obliges belligerents to minimise civilian suffering and requires them to protect children. But such protection is insufficient, particularly for children trapped in internal armed conflicts.

Human rights law establishes rights that every individual should enjoy at all times whether in peace or war. In addition to the Convention on the Rights of the Child, this body of law includes a number of specialised treaties that are particularly relevant to children's protection in armed conflict. The International Covenant on Civil and Political Rights recognises many rights, including the rights to life and to freedom from slavery, torture and arbitrary arrest. The International Covenant on Economic, Social and Cultural Rights recognises the rights to food, clothing, housing, health and education. In addition, there are treaties that deal with specific themes or groups of people, covering such issues as genocide, torture, refugees and racial discrimination. The Convention on the Elimination of All Forms of Discrimination against Women affirms gender-based violence as a form of discrimination and notes specifically women's right to equal protection during international or internal armed conflict.

The 1989 Convention on the Rights of the Child (CRC), ratified by 191 countries, provides the most comprehensive and specific protection for children during peacetime and war. Only two countries, Somalia and the United States, have not yet ratified this human rights treaty. The Convention establishes a legal framework in which children are the direct holders of rights and acknowledges their distinct legal personality. It recognises a comprehensive list of rights including the right to life; the right to a family environment; the right to essential care and assistance; the right to health, to food and to education; and the right to a name and nationality. The guarantees of special protection in situations of armed conflict, contained in articles 38 and 39 of the Convention, reflect the complementarity of humanitarian law and human rights law.

In formal legal terms, only States can be contracting parties to the CRC and other human rights treaties. They hold, therefore, the primary responsibility to ensure that these treaties are respected and implemented. Since human rights law was envisaged originally to protect citizens against violations by States, non-state actors have not traditionally been considered to be directly bound by them. This more restricted interpretation is being broadened slowly in light of the growing number of armed conflicts taking place within States and where non-state actors are at war with the government and/or with one another.[2]

In 1995 several combatant groups in Sudan became the first non-state entities to pledge to abide by the provisions of the Convention. Significantly, they also put in place systems for information, reporting and dealing with complaints.

Although human rights law applies at all times, many human rights treaties allow States to suspend the exercise of certain rights temporarily during a public emergency. But a number of absolute human rights can never be suspended: the right to life; the right to freedom from torture and other inhuman or degrading treatment; the right to freedom from slavery; and the right to freedom from retroactive penal laws. It is important to note that the Convention on the Rights of the Child has no general derogation clause. In light of this, the Committee on the Rights of the Child has stressed that the most positive interpretation should always prevail to ensure the widest possible respect for children's rights, particularly during war when they are most at risk.

Although States in conflict may assert their prerogative to suspend some rights, derogation is only allowed legally under very specific and strict conditions. However, States tend to disregard such prerequisites during conflict and may violate or ignore fundamental rights and freedoms. Legal recourse at the national, regional and international levels is not systematically available. It is for this reason that human rights violations in armed conflict are considered not only a question of national concern, but also a threat to international peace and security.

It is in this context that UN Secretary-General Kofi Annan proposed a radical new course of action in respect of national sovereignty and human rights. In calling on the Security Council to intervene to protect civilians threatened in war, he argued that survival in the 21st century depends on a broader definition of national interest — an interest that unequivocally supports human rights. "It often goes against political or other interests," he said, "but there are universal principles and values which supersede such interest, and the protection of civilians is one of them."[3]

The Convention Relating to the Status of Refugees

Armed conflicts force large numbers of people to flee persecution and violence. The kind of legal protection to which they are entitled depends on whether they cross a national border or are displaced within their own countries. A refugee is someone who crosses an international border and meets the criteria set out in the Convention Relating to the Status of Refugees of 1951. The Convention defines a refugee as a person who, "owing to well-founded fear of being persecuted for reasons of race, religion, nationality, membership in a particular social group, or political opinion, is outside the country of his nationality and is unable or, owing to such fear, is unwilling to avail himself of the protection of that country." Since 1951, this definition has been broadened in both official and informal ways. Notably, the Office of the United Nations High Commissioner for Refugees (UNHCR) has added rape to the list of crimes of persecution, and consequently, gender as a reason for fearing persecution.

The 1951 Convention, together with its Protocol of 1967, is the most important instrument for the protection of refugees in countries of asylum. These are complemented by regional refugee instruments, notably the 1969 Organization of African Unity Convention Governing the Specific Aspects of Refugee Problems in Africa and the 1984 Cartagena Declaration on Refugees.

States have the primary responsibility for ensuring the protection of refugees within their boundaries. UNHCR is mandated to provide protection for refugees and to find permanent solutions to refugee situations. However, internally displaced persons (IDPs) do not have rights as refugees. Although IDPs have legal rights as civilians under international humanitarian and human rights law, these are often wilfully disrespected. They have no single caretaking body because they are supposed to be protected by their own governments. Although not mandated to do so, UNHCR will provide assistance and protection to IDPs when requested by a government and the UN General Assembly. Historically, any assistance or protection that IDPs have received has been the result of actions, often uncoordinated, by several UN agencies and NGOs.[4]

Bringing war criminals to justice

In calling for the establishment of an International Criminal Court, the UN Secretary-General said, "Many thought that the horrors of the Second World War – the camps, the cruelty, the exterminations, the Holocaust – could never happen again. And yet they have. In Cambodia, in Bosnia and Herzegovina, in Rwanda." A historic step was taken to end impunity for such crimes in July 1998 when the Rome Statute of the International Criminal Court was adopted. Once the required number of 60 countries have ratified the Statute, the ICC will be the world's first permanent international criminal court to try individuals for acts of genocide, crimes against humanity and war crimes.

The ICC Statute includes a number of provisions that are particularly significant for children.[5] Conscripting or enlisting children under the age of 15 into national armed forces or organised groups, or using them to participate actively in hostilities, is punishable as a war crime. The ICC has no jurisdiction over children below 18 years of age, because they are not deemed to have the capacity to commit the extremely serious crimes with which the Court will be concerned. The Statute goes further by attaching criminal responsibility to the commanders and superiors who indoctrinate, manipulate and instrumentalise children into committing atrocities.

Sierra Leone: The question of impunity

Untold suffering was inflicted on the civilian population during the nine-year civil war in Sierra Leone. Thousands of children were mutilated, raped and killed either deliberately or indiscriminately. An estimated 5,400 children fought in the conflict, forcibly recruited by Revolutionary United Front (RUF) rebel troops or pro-government forces. Child combatants, themselves victims, took part in atrocities. Many were threatened with death or desensitised with drugs and alcohol.

When the Lomé agreement was signed in July 1999, it set a new precedent as the first peace accord to focus attention on the special needs of child soldiers in disarmament, demobilisation and reintegration processes. But the agreement traded peace for impunity. By granting blanket amnesty to the members of armed groups that had carried out a campaign of terror in plain view of the international community, the Lomé Accord left the people of Sierra Leone vulnerable to further attacks. Worse still, the agreement rewarded many of those who had terrorised civilians. Foday Sankoh, the leader of the RUF, was known to have committed some of the most violent atrocities. Under the Accord, he was appointed Chairman of the Commission that controls the diamond mines of Sierra Leone.

Within the ICC Statute, crimes against humanity include the trafficking of women and children. Rape, sexual slavery, enforced prostitution, forced pregnancy and forced sterilisation and any other form of sexual violence of comparable gravity are considered both war crimes and crimes against humanity. The Statute also defines as war crimes intentional, direct attacks against schools, hospitals, civilian populations, humanitarian assistance personnel and vehicles. The forcible transfer of the children of a threatened national, ethnic, racial or religious group to another

Founded on a false peace, the Lomé Accord proved unstable. The terms of the agreement were broken repeatedly and finally discarded when, in May 2000, the RUF took 500 UN peace-keepers hostage. The failure of the Lomé Accord was a failure of accountability.

In the aftermath of the Lomé Accord, the United Nations and the Government of Sierra Leone agreed to establish a Special Court for Sierra Leone to prosecute those bearing the greatest responsibility for serious international crimes. The Court has not yet been established because of insufficient funds. But the Court's jurisdiction has also been hotly contested. Some have argued that crimes committed by children should be included. But according to the Statute of the International Criminal Court (ICC), children under the age of 18 cannot be tried as war criminals. Similarly, the ad hoc Tribunals for Rwanda and the former Yugoslavia have deliberately not prosecuted juveniles. Further, child rights advocates argue that the children are not among those bearing the greatest responsibility for serious international crimes; rather it is those adults who exploit children as soldiers. For these reasons, the UN Security Council considers the prosecution of juveniles before the Special Court to be "extremely unlikely." The Council is of the view that the Truth and Reconciliation Commission is better suited as the primary body for addressing the accountability of children under 18.

group is classified as genocide.

The ICC Statute takes children's special needs into account during the course of the Court's investigations and prosecutions. It calls for the appointment of judges and legal advisers with expertise on child rights and on gender-based violence. The Statute calls for the establishment of a Victims and Witnesses Unit to protect the security, physical and psychological well-being, dignity and privacy of victims and witnesses in the Court's proceedings. When child victims or witnesses participate in the Court's proceedings, the Court can consider conducting part of the proceedings in private and by electronic or other means.

The International Criminal Tribunals established for the former Yugoslavia and for Rwanda have made great strides towards ending impunity for violations of children's and women's rights. These tribunals, established to address the egregious violations and abuses committed, share certain common elements including the same chief prosecutor and the same five-judge appellate chamber. And both have articulated principles of international law and set precedents for other international criminal tribunals and courts. Both tribunals have pioneered advocacy for victim-oriented, restitutive justice in international criminal tribunals, including legal guidance, psychological counselling and medical care.

Following their lead, in July 2000 Cambodia and the United Nations reached a tentative agreement on an international criminal tribunal to try Khmer Rouge leaders for genocide and other atrocities. The plan, which included both Cambodian and international prosecutors, is still awaiting approval by the Cambodian Parliament, whose reluctance may stem from many members' former associations with the Khmer Rouge.[6]

In August 2000, the United Nations Security Council approved the creation of a Special Court for Sierra Leone to try those with the greatest responsibility for atrocities committed during that country's civil war.[7] The jurisdiction of the special court includes crimes committed in Sierra Leone under that country's national law, crimes against humanity, war crimes and other serious violations of international humanitarian law.

Translating international standards into reality

Armed conflict puts every right of the child at risk. The urgent widespread ratification and enforcement of international standards will go a long way towards protecting children in armed conflict. Yet, they will only be effective if and when they are widely known, understood and implemented.

Human rights and humanitarian standards reflect fundamental human values that exist in all societies. They should be reflected in national legislation and translated into national and local languages. Popularising legislation through the media and the arts can help promote a culture of human rights. In Rwanda, for example, Save the Children Fund-US, Haguruka (a local NGO) and UNICEF supported the development of an official Kinyarwanda version of the CRC. This version has been adopted into Rwandan law and publicised through radio, drama and print materials.

Since 1996 there have been a number of important developments that have strengthened the protection of children's rights under international law. The most important of these are the Optional Protocol to the CRC on the involvement of children in armed conflicts; the Guiding Principles on Internal Displacement; the Convention on the Prohibition of the Use, Stockpiling, Production and Transfer of Anti-Personnel Mines, and on their Destruction; the International Labour Organization Convention No. 182 on the Immediate Elimination of the Worst Forms of Child Labour; and the Rome Statute of the International Criminal Court.

Monitoring the realisation of child rights

Flagrant violations of human rights are increasingly among the root causes of conflict and the resulting humanitarian crises. However, the procedures and mechanisms to monitor, report, prosecute and remedy such violations are woefully inadequate. An effective international system for protecting children's rights requires prompt, efficient and objective monitoring. Whenever children's rights are trampled and national authorities fail to act, the international community must hold governments and other actors accountable.

Within the United Nations, the principal responsibility for monitoring human rights violations rests in practice with the Commission on Human Rights. The Commission can receive information from any source and, through a system of independent rapporteurs and working groups, can take an active role in gathering data and promoting action. With this information, the Commission can publicise violations and attempt to persuade States to change their policies.

Another dimension of monitoring by international bodies relates to the supervision of treaty obligations. Each of the principal human rights treaties has a monitoring body that is composed of independent experts. The various UN committees and, in particular, the Committee on the Rights of the Child are in a unique position to undertake systematic monitoring and reporting of violations committed against children in conflict situations. In view of its close cooperation with UN bodies, specialised agencies and other competent bodies, the Committee on the Rights of the Child is well placed to review measures undertaken by these partners to promote awareness about international standards, to enhance capacity building among their staff and to develop child-impact assessments of their policies and strategies.

States parties to the CRC are responsible for all children within their territory without discrimination. By ratification, States parties have accepted the role of the Committee on the Rights of the Child in monitoring the implementation of the Convention and have recognised that the protection of children is not just a national issue, but a legitimate concern of the international community. This is especially important since many of the most serious violations of children's rights take place in situations of conflict where there may be no functioning national government, or where its capacity is too limited to ensure the protection of its children and prevent the violation of their rights.

Article 1 of the Geneva Conventions requires governments to undertake to respect and to ensure respect for the Conventions. As the custodian of international humanitarian law, the International Committee of the Red Cross (ICRC) has been mandated by the international community to monitor its application by the parties to conflict. In this capacity, the ICRC encourages States to take practical steps in peacetime to ensure that the rules of humanitarian law will be applied in the event of war.[8]

Where the protection of children in armed conflict is concerned, much broader participation by governments, NGOs and UN agencies in the monitoring and reporting of abuses is required. Often on the "front lines," humanitarian agencies are particularly well placed to monitor and report on child rights violations and abuses. But in reporting violations, humanitarian organisations may risk being expelled from the country concerned or having their operations severely curtailed.

Without such reports, the international community is limited in its ability to assess conflict situations and to develop appropriate responses. The UN Secretary-General has therefore highlighted the need to reconcile the delivery of humanitarian relief with the defence of human rights[9] and has called for the integration of human rights action in the context of humanitarian operations.[10]

Similarly, the Secretary-General has also called for human rights action to be integrated into early warning, peacemaking and peace-building efforts.[11] To this end, the Report of the Panel on United Nations Peacekeeping Operations recommended substantially enhancing the field mission planning and preparation capacity of the Office of the High Commissioner for Human Rights. The Panel also called for the Office to be more closely involved in planning and executing the elements of peace-building operations that address human rights.[12]

Appropriate public or confidential channels should be established nationally and internationally through which to report on matters of grave concern relating to children. The Office of the High Commissioner for Human Rights, national institutions and ombudspersons, international human rights organisations and professional associations should be actively utilised in this regard. Resources should be made available to strengthen the monitoring and reporting of child rights violations. This must also be accompanied by quicker, more transparent and more effective use of such information by the international bodies active in the field of children's rights.

Despite encouraging steps, the enormous potential of international standards to become a forceful tool with which to ensure that the lives of children are protected and respected has not been utilised. Children's rights continue to be violated in situations of armed conflict and an unacceptably high degree of impunity for such violations and abuses remains. The two tribunals established by the UN Security Council to address the egregious violations in Rwanda and the former Yugoslavia are important initiatives to end impunity. Yet, in effect, they are the result of the failure of the international community to save people in those countries from genocide. Implementing international standards to safeguard the rights of children requires preventive actions as well as redress. The standards exist – yet all too often the political will to enforce them is lacking.

Chapter 13

Women and the peace process

"The protection of children in war-affected countries cannot take place without involving women. Conflict affects women and girls differently from men and boys. It is impossible to talk about effective humanitarian responses or inclusive peace processes without understanding and taking into account these gender dimensions."

— Noeleen Heyzer, Executive Director, UNIFEM[1]

It has taken the United Nations more than 50 years to address the role of women in furthering international peace and security. In March 2000, the UN Security Council declared peace to be linked inextricably with equality between women and men.[2] Further, it resolved that gender equality is advanced when women are central to peace processes and when the impact of armed conflict on women is recognised fully and addressed.

It was the first time that the Council had ever issued a statement on the subject – and it set in motion a process that directly linked women's full participation in peace processes with the maintenance and promotion of international peace and security. In its October 2000 Resolution 1325 on women, peace and security,[3] the Council provided a political framework within which women's protection and their role in peace-building could be addressed. The resolution was a landmark in the drive to ensure that the gender dimensions of security, resettlement, reconciliation and governance are routinely addressed in peace negotiations.

The impact of armed conflict on women

Understanding the impact of armed conflict on women and girls is the first step towards ensuring that the peace process will guarantee women's protection, recovery and rehabilitation. Typically, political and humanitarian institutions, policies and programmes do not reflect an understanding of the gender dimensions of conflict. They often assume that women will automatically become beneficiaries of humanitarian assistance. But this will not happen unless specific strategies are put in place to reach women and to address their special needs. Appointing women guards in high-risk areas is one way to minimise the risks to women's security. Unless women are identified as a beneficiary group with special needs, emergency relief will never be designed to address their specific reproductive health, nutrition or psychosocial needs. One of the main reasons that women's protection is so glaringly inadequate is that surveys, reports and information on the humanitarian and human rights aspects of conflict fail to disaggregate and analyse data by sex and age.

In May 1999, humanitarian agencies made a priority commitment to ensure that gender issues are brought into the UN Consolidated Appeals Process (CAP), the process by which funds are raised for humanitarian emergencies. Although women have benefited from the consolidated appeals in general, their specific needs remain largely unaddressed. In 2001, "Women and War" was the thematic focus of the CAP launch and yet only 1.4 per cent of the total CAP was targeted exclusively to women and gender-specific projects. Women were included among beneficiaries in only 21 per cent of the appeals.[4] The Security Council's first debate on women, peace and security in October 2000 addressed this concern and resulted in the Council's call for an assessment of the current institutional arrangements in place to protect women.

A more credible peace process

The credibility of negotiations that exclude half of the population on the grounds of gender is rarely challenged in the same way as negotiations excluding segments of the population on the basis of ethnicity, religion or political affiliation. "Women are half of every community," challenged Dr. Theo-Ben Gurirab, Namibia's Minister of Foreign Affairs. "Are they, therefore, not also half of every solution?"[5]

The principles of gender equality and inclusion are fundamental building blocks for democracy and peace-building. Giving citizens a stake in the political system and a say over the decisions that affect their lives is the essence of a human rights approach. Women bring to the peace table their practical understanding of the issues confronting them and their communities. But even more so, women's participation in peace processes enhances their legitimacy and sustainability.

In Uganda, a 30 per cent quota for women in locally elected bodies provides a mechanism for women to participate in the political arena. "Seizing the opportunity, women showed themselves to be effective leaders who were able to change the political agenda," said Ugandan parliamentarian, Winnie Byanyima. "At one point, they held more than 50 per cent of the seats."[6]

Once in office, this new intake of Ugandan women demanded from their Councils basic services including water, improved seeds, maternal and child care services and education for orphans. "They are opposing bureaucratic expenditures and corruption that divert scarce resources," said Ms. Byanyima. "Women are also deeply involved in ensuring the security of their communities because they value a peaceful neighbourhood."[7]

During Uganda's peace negotiations, the concept of exclusion was addressed primarily in ethnic terms, but political parties learned quickly that a commitment to gender equality could yield rewards. They significantly expanded their constituencies by engaging those marginalised by the conflict on the basis of their gender, age and disability. Similarly, in Guatemala and Northern Ireland, having women at the negotiating table resulted in a more inclusive dialogue. Having more stakeholders at the earliest and most fragile stages of the peace process broadened the discourse of the negotiations.

Grass-roots peace-building

In conflict, women expand their regular responsibilities, assuming activist roles while holding together their communities. Yet they often have little control over public and formal decision-making. In spite of these constraints, women's strategies to build and sustain peace at the community level have yielded significant results. In the Philippines, women established "peace zones" to protect their children from being recruited by armed groups. Colombian women inspired collective action through their Peaceful Road of Women campaign that took them through the most violent regions of the country.

Early in 1999, the New Sudan Council of Churches was involved in facilitating a peace conference between the Dinka and Nuer of Upper West Nile. Through the principle of affirmative action, women were able to participate in the peace process, and they were able to ensure that the resolutions of the resulting world peace conference addressed women's concerns.[8]

Women activists have joined together within and across political, ethnic and religious divides. In Burundi, the United Nations Development Fund for Women (UNIFEM) and International Alert are working together to train women community leaders from different political constituencies in conflict resolution and peace-building skills. The Liberian Women's Initiative united women from a diverse range of organisations in pursuit of a peaceful resolution of the conflict in Liberia. They initiated negotiations among leaders of warring factions and successfully introduced humanitarian and social concerns into the formal political peace process. "We worked hard to be at the peace table," said Mary Brownell, a Liberian peace activist. "We were not invited, but we forced ourselves in. If there is any semblance of peace in Liberia, we the women can say we played a major role."[9]

For many women, the tradition of community activism becomes a training ground for future political work. Mu Sochua, the founding member of the first Cambodian NGO, Khemara, or Cambodian Women, eventually became her country's Minister for Women's and Veterans' Affairs.[10] The members of the women's movement in Bosnia and Herzegovina have gained greater access to the formal political arena since the conflict.[11]

The link between international and national women's networks can be mutually reinforcing. The number of international women's coalitions for peace has proliferated. Women Waging Peace, Women in Black and Women Building Peace are examples of how coalition-building has helped prevent isolation among women's organisations working on similar causes. It has also helped broaden their substantive, organisational and resource base. Networks can be fostered through the media, political affiliations or on specific themes such as human rights or trafficking. They can also help strengthen women's leadership capacity by supporting the development of technical, political, negotiation and management skills. International organisations and the donor community can support these linkages through advocacy and technical and financial assistance.

Ensuring women's participation

Women's participation is essential to any credible peace process and is in itself a substantive issue to be placed on any peace agenda. Multiple strategies are required to ensure that women activists at the community level make it to the negotiating table. Whether as delegates within their negotiating parties or as independent interest groups, women must participate at all stages of negotiations as well as in the monitoring and implementation mechanisms created by a peace process. Women are making it clear that they will no longer take responsibility for supporting their families and communities, serve at the forefront of peace movements or fight alongside male combatants without an equal opportunity to voice their ideas in official peace negotiations.[12]

It is essential that the political parties, the facilitators and the international and regional bodies supporting a peace process be sensitised to the importance of gender issues and women's participation. This is one of the most effective guarantees of women's eventual entry into political life. In Burundi, women's participation in the peace process was enhanced when the Mwalimu Nyerere Foundation, under whose auspices the peace talks took place, invited UNIFEM to brief the negotiating parties and facilitation team on gender issues relating to the peace accord.

In Somalia, women delegates to the July 2000 Somali National Reconciliation Conference, with the support of the President of Djibouti, secured 25 seats for women in the 225-member Transitional National Assembly.

Establishing a women's platform is a long and difficult process.

Women's centrality to a new Burundi

In July 2000, more than 50 Burundian women presented a common vision for peace and reconciliation to former South African President Nelson Mandela, Chief Facilitator of the Burundi peace negotiations.

"We request that our rights be explicitly included in the final agreement. Through our efforts and sweat we have sustained Burundian communities and our contributions to the economy of Burundi should be acknowledged, rewarded and supported," the delegates stated. "It pains us very much that we and our daughters have suffered war crimes such as rape, sexual violence, prostitution and domestic violence that have gone unrecognised and unpunished. We ask that this agreement put an end to this impunity."

Key recommendations made by the women included the establishment of mechanisms to punish and put an end to war crimes such as rape and sexual violence; guarantees for women's rights to property, land and inheritance; measures to ensure women's security and safe return; and guarantees that girls enjoy the same rights as boys to all levels of education.

In a historic move, all 19 negotiating parties accepted the majority of proposals crafted by Burundian women during the first All Party Burundi Women's Peace Conference, making the peace agreement one of the strongest in recognising the centrality of women's rights and opportunities to democracy, governance, peace, security and reconstruction.

Women's participation in peace negotiations may not necessarily result in coalitions across political, ethnic and religious affiliation. It took more than a decade for women to form a strong cross-party coalition bridging the Palestinian-Israeli divide.

A tradition of women's activism and civil society organisations can make a difference. In the years leading up to the 1994 elections in South Africa, activists and academics formed a Women's National Coalition (WNC) that cut across racial, social and polit-ical lines. The WNC united women from political parties within the Multi-Party Negotiation Process (MPNP) that produced South Africa's interim constitution. While political parties divided women, the WNC provided a common forum outside of the for-mal negotiations.[13] Women worked with each other to achieve an agreement among all of the political parties requiring that one out of every two voting delegates had to be a woman.

After the negotiations, women's participation in the political process must be sustained. Women in Colombia and Georgia faced physical threats as a result of their activism after the negotiations were concluded. Women's participation in committees established by the peace process can help prevent such threats. Committees addressing truth and reconciliation, judicial reform, security and land tenure are especially important areas. The creation of a sepa-rate commission or women's machinery to follow up on commit-ments made to women during negotiations can help ensure their implementation.

Women's participation in implementation committees and in new structures of governance may make it easier to raise gender issues. However, participation alone will not ensure that gender issues are addressed substantively by these structures. For example, appointing a woman judge will not ensure that rape is addressed in a gender-responsive manner – instead this will depend on both the definition of the crime and its interpretation. Having women rep-resented in parliament will not necessarily guarantee the inclusion in the electoral law of a quota in favour of women. Naming a woman as force commander will not guarantee that the mandate of a peace-support operation will address women's protection.

Making women's participation and gender issues central to the mandates and structures of the peace process requires concerted sensitisation of key stakeholders and decision makers, both men and women. This should include party representatives, facilitators, judges and international and regional organisations. It also requires a full understanding of the gender dimensions of all of the substantive issues under discussion.

Gender justice in post-conflict peace-building

"After conflicts, resources are depleted, infrastructure is destroyed, and social, economic and political relationships are strained. Successful reconstruction depends upon the use of every available resource. Women, who have held social and economic fragments together, represent the most precious and underutilised of these resources," said Noeleen Heyzer, Executive Director of UNIFEM, in a statement to the United Nations Security Council in October 2000.[14]

Critical gender issues that arise in peace-building include the protection of and respect for the human rights of women and girls, particularly as they relate to the constitution, the electoral system and the judiciary.[15] In the context of repatriation, resettlement and rehabilitation, it is especially important to ensure women's rights to property and inheritance. Traditional and customary laws often prohibit women from inheriting land, or return land ownership to male family members when the father or husband dies. Women's right to ownership is therefore key to protecting their assets.

Unequal land rights leave women dependent on men, perpetuate poverty and can become a potential source of renewed conflict. For married women, dependency on their husbands in legal and economic terms can prevent them from obtaining credit if land ownership is required as collateral. The privatisation of land tenure further limits women's access to land, housing and property, since they lack the capital necessary to purchase or rent land.

The first step towards realising women's rights to land and property is to ensure that property rights, ownership and entitlement are enshrined in constitutional and statutory laws. This can begin to delegitimise customary practices that marginalise women.

Some progress has been made. In Rwanda, where genocide left

an estimated 65,000 households headed by children – 90 per cent of them girls, the law did not allow girls to inherit agricultural land. In November 1999, new legislation was enacted, giving girls and women the right to inherit farms and properties. Eritrea and Mozambique have also changed their inheritance laws, making it possible for girls and women to own land. In Liberia, the Association of Female Lawyers has been campaigning for women married under customary law to have the same right to inheritance that is enjoyed by women married under civil law. Similarly, in Guatemala, women successfully negotiated guarantees to equal access to land, credit, health care, education and training into their peace agreement. Mama Maquin, a Guatemalan refugee women's organisation, has established the right of married women and those living in common law unions to be co-owners, with their spouses, of land and property.

The Constitution

A nation's constitution should provide guiding principles for realising gender equality. It is the most important mechanism to guarantee human rights, including equal rights for women. Guaranteeing women's rights within a constitution can be achieved by integrating attention to gender throughout all relevant constitutional clauses. In South Africa, the right to gender equality is established within the Constitution's bill of rights. Including a Women's Charter as a distinct chapter within the constitution can complement this approach. The constitution should also incorporate the principles of international treaties and conventions supporting women's rights, including the Convention on the Elimination of All Forms of Discrimination against Women (CEDAW), the Convention on the Rights of the Child and the Beijing Platform for Action, adopted by the Fourth World Conference on Women, held in 1995.

Important constitutional principles include:
• The principle of non-discrimination, protecting women from discrimination on the basis of gender.
• The principle of equality, making it explicit that all women and men are equal before the law in all spheres of life.

- The principle of affirmative action to ensure women's representation at all levels of decision-making, including in political parties, committees, courts, judiciary and other government positions.
- The principle of freedom and security of the person, which includes the right to be free from all forms of violence from either public or private sources; the right to bodily and psychological integrity; the right to make decisions concerning reproduction; and the right to security in and control over one's body.

The constitution should be written with gender-sensitive rather than neutral language to avoid ambiguity and to ensure fairness and equality. Simple and clear language can make the constitution accessible to those without legal literacy. Popularising the document through translation into local languages can increase women's awareness of their rights.

The electoral system

The constitution and electoral laws must ensure women's right to vote and their right to stand for public office. An electoral system is a mechanism to convert votes into seats. Studies show that more women reach elected office under a system of proportional representation than in a constituency-based electoral system. In other words, women are more successful in a system in which voters focus on the party and its policies than one in which the focus is on a particular candidate.

Women's representation within the political process ensures that their voices and issues are heard and brought to public attention. The Beijing Platform for Action calls for nations to aim for a minimum of 30 per cent representation of women in the political process. This can be achieved most effectively by legislating quota systems in favour of women. Alternatively, it can be provided through processes within political parties. Quotas require that women constitute a certain number or percentage of the members of a body, whether it is a candidate list, a parliamentary assembly, a committee, or a government. Unless quotas are put in place until women's sufficient representation is secured, the barriers to women's entry into politics will remain entrenched. In Mozambique, a party quota introduced by

FRELIMO (the Front for the Liberation of Mozambique) resulted in the achievement of the 30 per cent target of representation by women in that country. Similarly, in South Africa, the African National Congress's commitment to a party quota has resulted in achieving 29 per cent representation of women in parliament.[16]

The socio-economic challenges facing women, including poverty and illiteracy, constrain their ability to participate in formal political systems. Capacity-building through the development of practical skills, awareness raising and economic support is critical for enhancing women's participation in elections, both as voters and candidates.

The judicial system

The delivery of justice to women must be without bias and discrimination. This is fundamental to women's ability to reconstruct their lives during and after conflict. Addressing gender bias within the judiciary – the very institution that determines how equality is achieved in society – is therefore essential. Although the function of making law rests with the legislature, in constitutional matters, judges play a more overtly political role, often striking down legislation or amending it to conform to a particular judicial interpretation of constitutional rights and freedoms. This interpretation often reflects gender bias. In criminal law, gender bias is found in many areas, but most notoriously in the judicial treatment of sexual assault.[17] Despite the fact that violence against women is a reality and is foreseeable, especially in conflict situations, women are often blamed and are rarely compensated for their injuries. Punishment of offenders rarely matches the serious nature of the crime.

Judges are not completely objective, disinterested or impartial because they reflect and represent their own subjective experiences. They must therefore be broadly representative of the population, reflecting race, gender, class and other demographic factors. Sensitising judges about women's human rights and about gender equality can also help mitigate doctrinal or perceived bias in the administration of justice. Gender training and information to increase gender awareness should be provided to judges, lawyers, law enforcement agencies, court personnel, law students and community leaders.

Women's inherent rights to dignity and equality must be protected when they are seeking justice. In practice, women's access to justice may be limited by their financial situation or their unfamiliarity with the judicial system. Support services and programmes should be provided to ensure the availability of legal aid and the fair treatment of women as witnesses and complainants. Such services can include counselling programmes for women and girls who have suffered violations of rights as well as special programmes for those committing crimes against women. The establishment of specially trained police units to investigate crimes against women and girls is important. Legal literacy programmes to raise awareness about the operation of courts and the judicial system must also be introduced.

Peace support operations

The Security Council's first resolution on women, peace and security issued an urgent call to incorporate a gender perspective into peacekeeping operations.[18] On the 10th anniversary of the United Nations Transitional Assistance Group, the Department of Peacekeeping Operations convened a meeting hosted by the Government of Namibia to consider strategies to mainstream a gender perspective in multidimensional peace support operations. The resulting Windhoek Declaration and the Namibia Plan of Action set out specific strategies to provide for women's protection within the mandates of preventive peace missions, peacekeeping and peace-building operations.[19] Two aspects were highlighted: the participation of women within peace operations; and the need to incorporate a gender perspective into all aspects and programmes of the operation.

With respect to the participation of women in peace operations, little progress has been made. Of the 58 Special and Personal Representatives and Envoys of the Secretary-General serving in peace support functions, not a single one is female.[20] The recent deployment of gender advisers in the UN peace operations for East Timor, Kosovo and Sierra Leone sets important precedents. But gender advisers and gender units have yet to be included systematically in all peace operations, and particularly within human rights verification and observer components.

It is also clear that gender expertise has not sufficiently informed the planning of peace operations, whether in assessment missions or in standard operating procedures. Appropriate budgetary support for field operations to protect and support the delivery of humanitarian assistance for women and girls, and especially for refugee and displaced women, is typically lacking. All functions supported by a peace operation – civilian police, disarmament, demobilisation and reintegration, electoral assistance or mediation – should support women's participation and develop strategies to address gender issues. All peace support operations should give priority to verifying gender-based violations and protecting women's human rights.

Regional organisations and arrangements have been called upon to support peace operations as conflicts take on increasingly regional dimensions. Some efforts have been made to address the gender dimensions at this level. Since 1992, UNIFEM has used regional approaches to improve women's protection and to support women's role in prevention and peace-building. UNIFEM's Africa Women in Crisis (AFWIC) programme supports women refugees in western and southern Africa. In 1998, it supported the establishment and work of the Federation of African Women for Peace. And in Latin America, UNIFEM is supporting regional networking among women's peace activists in Colombia, El Salvador, Guatemala, Nicaragua and Peru.

At the 4th High Level UN Regional Organisations Meeting in 2001, UNIFEM called on regional organisations to incorporate a gender perspective in six areas: 1) developing common indicators for early warning that take women and gender issues into account; 2) improving the flow of information about women's role in peace efforts and about gender-based violations; 3) strengthening linkages with civil society, and in particular women's organisations and networks; 4) bringing a gender perspective into regional peacekeeping training efforts; 5) increasing the participation of women in regional peace initiatives and negotiations; and 6) bringing a gender perspective into regional human rights instruments, compliance and advocacy.

Women in conflict situations have specific needs and important contributions to make to peace-building and conflict resolution. Recognising and supporting both of these aspects with equal vigour can help curtail the savageries of war.

Chapter 14

Media and communications

*"I want to go to school and become a journalist
so I can speak about my country and how useless
this war is."*

Information – and the media that transmits it – can be a force for positive change for children affected by conflict, while contributing to peace-building, reconciliation and reconstruction. From storytelling to the Internet, communication tools offer children and adults the possibility for self-expression and the ability to break down the barriers that separate communities and fuel conflict.

In the chaos and confusion of war, families and communities can protect themselves better when they are informed about political events and possible military strikes. Knowing how relief is organised, where emergency assistance is located or how they might speed up their search for family members that have been lost is essential for family survival. The media in all of its forms – including print, radio and television – provides tools that can enable communities to share vital, life-saving information. During armed conflict, the mass media may be the only way that information reaches isolated rural and displaced populations.

The media has immense power to shape attitudes and inspire action. Knowledge is still passed on through oral traditions, including music and storytelling. Trade routes, marketplaces and community gatherings are still centres where views and information are exchanged. But modern communications technologies are transforming radically the way in which information is shared. These tools, including radio, television, video and the Internet, have changed the way people give and receive messages. And in conflict situations, this transformation has the potential to entrench opposing views and deepen the divides among conflicting parties or to reconcile differences and build peace.

Media and conflict

Modern communications technologies, with their potential to reach vast numbers of people, can also be vectors of destruction. During the Rwanda genocide, Radio Télévision Libre des Mille Collines (RTLMC) used propaganda to fuel ethnic hatred and incite people to participate in the genocide. Media propaganda has also been used to foment violence in other conflict-affected areas, including Burundi and the Balkan States. This has caused concern among international media organisations and prompted steps to curb the negative manipulation of communications in conflict situations. The UN Security Council has condemned the use of media to incite hatred and its role in the commissioning of war crimes. As a countermeasure, it proposed that peacekeeping missions develop information strategies, broadcast human rights messages through UN radio stations and promote tolerance in local communities.[2]

National and international debate on media ethics has led to the development of codes of conduct and training materials on responsible journalism. Organisations such as the International Federation of Journalists have devised guidelines on child rights to help their members do their jobs as journalists without exploiting children caught in difficult circumstances.[3] A number of national and international NGOs have developed training for local media outlets on using media responsibly in situations of armed conflict. A variety of other organisations train journalists in conflict-resolution techniques, so that they can use their reporting to promote impartial information and advance peace-building rather than deliberately or inadvertently reinforce combative positions.

Journalists and other communications specialists often have

unique access to geographical areas, people and parties in conflict. They are well placed to use their professional training and skills to witness and report child rights violations and abuses. But this can put them at grave risk. In the year 2000 alone, 24 journalists were killed and more than 80 were imprisoned.[4]

New technologies can provide tools for early warning and make it easier to monitor, document and report violations and other transgressions. Organisations such as WITNESS, an NGO that reports on human rights violations, have been training human rights advocates throughout the world to document human rights violations through the use of modern communications technology. Independent information can be used to expose violations committed against children in conflict and to provide evidence in confronting the impunity that often exists for the perpetrators of such crimes.

Media can also be used effectively in a peacekeeping environment. Communications technologies including satellites, mobile telephones and radios can provide substantial security back-up for both the military and the civilian population. Through news and current affairs programmes, media can provide credible information about a mission's mandate and facilitate better interaction with local populations and with humanitarian organisations working in the country. UNICEF cooperated with the UN Department of Peace-keeping Operations in using communications to reach children and families more effectively with mine action messages. Schools were used as centres for community outreach.

Peacekeeping, peace-building and reconstruction can be enhanced by the active presence of strong, independent media that can provide reliable information about the conflict or about post-conflict activities. As early as 1989, the UN Transition Assistance Group in Namibia (UNTAG) used a variety of communication methods to inform Namibians about its activities and other issues affecting the country. In 1992, the UN Transitional Authority in Cambodia (UNTAC) established its own radio station and used television to inform the local population about its mission while supporting voter education and promoting human rights.[5] And in 1994, during the first democratic elections in South Africa, the media played a crucial role in voter education.

Communications for social change

Communications methods vary enormously and, when used imaginatively, they can increase the pace and enhance the outcome of programmes for war-affected children and communities. In Mozambique, Save the Children used photographs to assist family reunification activities, a particularly useful approach with very young children or illiterate adults. In the Great Lakes region, the ICRC, IFRC and IRC, in collaboration with UNICEF and UNHCR, used a combination of communications tools – ranging from pen and paper to photography and computer technology – to reunite thousands of families. In Colombia, schools and youth clubs are using a "peace-building kit" that makes innovative use of videos to train children in conflict resolution. In Tanzania, Radio Kwizera has offered 250,000 refugees and members of neighbouring communities a mix of educational, development and entertainment programming.[6] Developed with the participation of refugees, the station broadcasts 40 hours a week in Kirundi, Kiswahili, English and French on topics such as health and nutrition, children's issues, education and culture. In Kosovo, UNICEF used communications and cultural activities to facilitate dialogue and foster youth participation in community governance. In Burundi, Studio Ijambo, a Search for Common Ground (SCG) project, produces news items and a popular radio soap opera to stimulate community discussion about issues such as ethnicity, conflict and gender roles.

Like Radio Kwizera, Studio Ijambo was set up to counter the effect of "hate radio" such as RTLMC in Rwanda. In Liberia, Talking Drum Studio, another SCG project, produces and airs radio programmes that promote good governance and reconciliation. Through drama, news and current affairs and other programming, Talking Drum promotes dialogue in conflict-affected areas. Liberian journalists running the Studio have used the trust engendered by their roles to mediate conflicts in communities recovering from the country's years of armed conflict. In Albania, the BBC World Service and Radio Tirana used a soap opera to tackle communal issues such as violence against women and corruption.

Communications tools can be used to engage war-affected communities in interpreting and documenting their own experiences. Used in this way, they can enrich public and private dialogue, allowing people to tell their own stories to a wider audience, define their own agendas and negotiate change.

Radio, television and other types of communications programming can be an end in and of themselves, but their impact is far more powerful when integrated into broader social change strategies. In South Africa, for instance, the health communication initiative "Soul City" has relied on high quality, multimedia formats for its immensely popular print magazine, radio and television soap opera. But the success of this "edu-tainment" initiative hinges on its ability to integrate messages with wider national health and education strategies, such as on HIV/AIDS and sexual violence.

Media and communications hold a fascination for many young people. In South Africa, the community radio sector has engaged large numbers of young people in social and political debate. Once motivated and empowered by information that is relevant to their lives, young people can be more easily involved in decision-making and programme planning. They become essential resources for the community. Involving children in media production can help ensure that their voices and concerns are raised in public discussions and in decision-making fora. Indeed, media can be one of the few direct links between children and decision makers. Together with the Palestinian Broadcasting Corporation and UNICEF, Palestinian youth moderate a live television broadcast, "We Want Our Childhood." Volunteers from the Palestinian Youth Association for Leadership and Rights Activation (PYALARA) created the hugely successful series dealing with education, health and child rights.

Although resources for computer technology are still very limited in most of the world, and particularly among war-affected communities, some children do have access. UNICEF's *Voices of Youth* is an on-line Internet meeting place for children, with a special "room" for them to speak their mind about the effects of war on their lives. "So many more deaths have occurred [in Algeria] in the last eight years . . . many of the victims are young children. . . . Shame on the UN for practically ignoring Algeria," said one young Algerian adolescent in an on-line discussion.[7]

Protecting children from media exploitation

Humanitarian and advocacy groups must ensure that demands from the media and other organisations do not place war-affected children at further risk. There are far too many examples of development or humanitarian workers being complicit, sometimes unknowingly, in the exploitation of children for media purposes. In the effort to publicise a relief programme or organisation, or even to make a political point, ex-child soldiers have been identified publicly and asked to pose with guns. Survivors of sexual violence are named and photographed, or children are asked to relate horrific experiences solely for the benefit of cameras or microphones.

Humanitarian organisations have been known to comply with requests from film-makers and journalists to talk to "younger girls" who have been raped or to children with "more traumatic stories."[8] UNICEF has issued guidelines on how to conduct interviews with children in ways that allow them to tell their story without further exploiting their trauma or compromising their safety. It is vital that humanitarian organisations and advocacy groups ensure that children's rights are not further violated as a result of exploitative fundraising publicity or unscrupulous journalism.

And the media can distort information – deliberately or inadvertently. There is no doubt that the media has played a role in the conflict between the Occupied Palestinian Territories and Israel, on both sides. Children have been the focus of attention, portrayed both as victims of the war and as participants. Palestinian youth, in particular, have been shown as participants in the violent clashes. But according to a recent report, less than 1 per cent of the total Palestinian adolescent population is estimated to have taken part in the clashes. Most of the children killed or injured were mere bystanders, or in their homes or on their way to and from school.[9]

Although media organisations have guidelines on ethical journalism, self-monitoring has not often been successful. Organisations that facilitate access between children and the media must ensure that children are not put at further risk of exploitation. Humanitarian organisations need to ensure that their staff members understand such risks and are adequately trained to protect children in these situations.

Mass media

Although telecommunications are becoming cheaper and more accessible, countries in conflict often do not have ready access to modern technology. In Africa, few countries, even politically stable ones, have easy and wide access even to telephones. In 1998, the International Telecommunication Union estimated that 25 per cent of countries in the world have fewer than one telephone per 100 people.[10] In addition, the training, maintenance and local expertise needed to support telecommunications is often unavailable. During conflict, the situation is far worse, as communications infrastructures are often targeted or may have collapsed.

Even with such constraints, mass communication can still be effective. In many parts of the developing world, radio is the most far-reaching medium. Modern yet simplified technologies like the wind-up radio, for example, can bring life-saving information to war-affected communities even at the height of fighting. During conflict and after, they can be used for distance education, to support immunisation campaigns, to deliver crucial messages and to facilitate other development objectives.

In countries that are not experiencing armed conflict, the mass media has played an important part in publicising crises, shaping public opinion, and influencing humanitarian response and foreign policy development. Media imagery can be a powerful catalyst. The picture of a burning child running down a road in Viet Nam, a soldier dragged through the streets of Somalia, starving children in Biafra, massacres in Bosnia – these have the power to generate massive public action and resources.

However, such power can be dangerous. Communication is never neutral. Journalists, scriptwriters and producers interpret the information they receive, and there is the risk that this information may be accidentally or deliberately manipulated. And the mass media will use its own criteria in deciding which conflicts will be covered. These decisions can have a powerful influence on foreign policy. Indeed the news and other media have had such an impact on humanitarian response that it prompted UN Secretary-General Boutros Boutros-Ghali to call CNN "the 16th member of the Security Council."[11]

Chapter 15

A children's agenda for peace and security

"I wish that nothing was destroyed and that everybody could live like they lived before – without bombing and destroying houses."

— Jelena, age 9, Kosovo[1]

There is a growing international consensus that the safety and well-being of people is as important a gauge of global peace and security as the security of States. Maintaining global peace and security is the central concern of the international community and the main responsibility of the United Nations Security Council, which has increasingly acknowledged that efforts to prevent conflicts, end hostilities and reconstruct shattered societies must also lay the foundation for child protection and development.

Children's centrality to this agenda has only recently been recognised. The Security Council's first discussion about children in armed conflict took place in 1996 in the context of an informal briefing.[2] The Council recognised that more and more children caught in situations of armed conflict were being left in a vast security void. This paved the way, more generally, for increased Council action in support of humanitarian goals and the protection of human rights. The Special Representative of the Secretary-General for Children and Armed Conflict has played an active role in promoting children's issues within the peace and security agenda.

At the same time, the principle of human security was becoming more firmly rooted in UN policy. By linking humanitarian action and the protection of human rights with peacemaking, peacekeeping and peace-building, the pivotal UN policy statement, *An Agenda for Peace*, related aspects of UN peace operations to the protection of civilians. Since 1998, the Council has discussed children in armed conflict as a regular item on its agenda. But it was not until 1999 that any mandate referred specifically to children. The innovative first step was taken to deploy gender and child protection advisers within the UN peace operations for the Democratic Republic of the Congo and Sierra Leone.

As conflicts take on increasingly regional dimensions, regional and subregional arrangements have similarly expanded their focus on child protection. The Economic Community of West African States (ECOWAS), in 2000, set out a regional plan of action for the protection of children in situations of conflict and decided to establish a child protection unit. The Southern African Development Community (SADC) has established programmes for the armed forces of its member States in child rights, gender and protection issues. And discussions on the protection of children in conflict situations have taken place within the Organization for Security and Cooperation in Europe (OSCE), European Union, Organization of African Unity (OAU) and Organization of American States (OAS).

These and other recent international actions have given unprecedented legitimacy to child protection within international peace and security.[3] A number of recent Security Council actions have contributed to raising the standard for protecting children in conflict situations, namely those related to: the protection of civilians, conflicts in Africa, post-conflict peace-building, and disarmament, demobilisation and reintegration (DD&R). Collectively, these have provided a basis for action on behalf of children in the following areas:
• child-focused disarmament, demobilisation and reintegration;
• monitoring and reporting violations against children and women;
• child-focused mine clearance, mine awareness and victim assistance;
• post-conflict peace-building that includes women, supports the rule of law and safeguards child rights;
• protecting children from the effects of sanctions; and
• protecting humanitarian personnel and humanitarian assistance for children.

Together, these actions have also shown a new way for UN peace operations to leverage the strength of operational agencies present in the country before, during and after a conflict takes place. But caution must be exercised. The majority of peace operations function in extremely volatile environments, and safeguards are needed to ensure that humanitarian and human rights efforts are not compromised by military and political priorities.

As military and civilian personnel take on new functions, they have increased contact with local populations. Whether in the refugee camps they protect, the DD&R programmes they support, or in mine-action programmes, military and civilian peacekeeping personnel need to understand their responsibilities to women and children. The Security Council has recommended, therefore, that they be trained in international humanitarian, human rights and refugee law, child rights and gender, negotiation and communication skills, HIV/AIDS, cultural awareness and civilian-military coordination.[4]

Several UN bodies, the ICRC and NGOs such as Terre des Hommes and Rädda Barnen have begun to cooperate with national and regional peacekeeping training institutes and peace support operations to provide training in some of these areas. A number of countries, including Canada, Germany, Ghana, Norway and Sweden, already have begun to incorporate training on child rights and gender in their national military training programmes. An encouraging example is the joint United Kingdom-Canada initiative on gender training for peacekeeping personnel. Yet despite repeated calls for specialised training in the child and gender dimensions of conflict, there is no international consensus on the standards, policies and programme approaches on which to base the training. The absence of international consensus in these areas has meant that international humanitarian and peacekeeping personnel continue to be trained according to their respective national or institutional guidelines – be they from the government, the UN or an NGO.

Many such guidelines and the corresponding training materials lack an adequate focus on gender- and child-specific concerns. In view of these challenges, and as an interim measure, in-service training can be provided as soon as a mission is assembled. But training alone cannot guarantee the highest standards of conduct. The Secretary-General and the Security Council must be unrelenting in pursuit of the highest standards of conduct of peacekeeping

personnel. Urgent attention must be given to establishing disciplinary and oversight mechanisms in peace operations, in the form of
an ombudsperson, an Inspector General or an office created especially for that purpose. Where violations against women and children have been committed by UN peacekeeping personnel, States
must investigate and punish offences and make public the results
of such proceedings.

Peace processes, reconstruction and reconciliation

Until recently, children have not been recognised formally in peace
agreements. In July 1999, the Lomé Peace Agreement in Sierra Leone
included several provisions relating to children. Although the Lomé
Accord was seriously flawed in many ways, it remains a precedent in
recognising children's importance within the peace and reconstruction agenda. But the political recognition of child rights does not in
itself guarantee that during the transition to peace, resources for children's health, education and welfare will be provided. Profound
resource shortages and grave security risks frequently plague communities in transition and undermine reconstruction efforts.

   Every war-torn society faces a huge task of rebuilding – physical,
economic, political, cultural and psychosocial. Conflicts destroy more
than buildings and bridges; they rip apart the cultural fabric that
binds societies together. War shatters legal and moral norms, making
it more difficult for families to offer security to their children.
National rebuilding must therefore look beyond physical structures
and establish a culture of human rights that provides a safe, nurturing
environment for children and promotes social and economic policies
that protect them.

   During the aftermath of armed conflict, the Convention on the
Rights of the Child provides a strong framework for child-focused
reconstruction. In Guatemala, MINUGUA's (United Nations
Verification Mission in Guatemala) efforts to strengthen child rights
institutions led ultimately to the creation of a special government
office to promote child rights. This office is now responsible for investigating child rights violations, for monitoring public institutions
providing services for children and for ensuring the conformity of

national legislation with the Convention on the Rights of the Child. While virtually every country on earth has ratified the Convention, many have not taken the essential step of enacting national legislation to give its provisions the force of law. National commissions on the rights of the child can help guide this process.

Restoring basic public security institutions such as the police and the judiciary is an essential aspect of post-conflict peace-building. In several places in transition, including Cambodia, East Timor and Kosovo, the UN has supported local authorities in drafting and revising legislation on child rights to strengthen justice systems.[5] The first regulation issued by the UN administration in East Timor placed the Convention on the Rights of the Child among the core human rights instruments for implementation in the territory.

But these measures, important as they are, are only effective when accompanied by the political and financial support needed for their implementation. The process of reconstruction has barely started one year after the ransacking of East Timor by militias, which caused a quarter of the population to flee across the border and resulted in the destruction of 70 per cent of the buildings.[6] Faced with a scarcity of resources that has delayed the opening of schools and hospitals, and a court system that is only beginning to emerge, the struggle to rebuild is a slow and painful process. In such circumstances it is all the more crucial that commitment to children does not waver and that efforts are made to strengthen social infrastructure, in building towards a more secure and peaceful future.

Yet the challenges are enormous. Refugees may encounter problems during repatriation. Those who fled the country may be perceived as "disloyal," or their right to reclaim their land may be contested. In Bosnia and Herzegovina, ethnic tensions threatened resettlement. This led to a programme of "positive conditionality" in which communities agreeing to accept the return of minorities and guarantee their safety received support to rehabilitate schools, housing and health centres and for income-generating schemes.

Putting children at the centre of reconstruction also means involving them as a resource. Young people must not be seen as problems or victims, but rather as key contributors in planning and implementing long-term solutions. Civil society organisations are vital to ensuring this. The determination of such organisations was high-lighted by the Hague Appeal for Peace conference of May 1999, which drew thousands of youth participants. While international NGOs play a leading role in providing emergency support for children, governments and national NGOs wield the largest responsibility in the aftermath of war. Resources must be given to strengthen their capacity and broaden their scope.

Children's voices for peace

In 1996, in the heart of a war-torn region of Colombia, more than 5,000 children created a grand exhibit of pictures, poems and letters on the theme of peace. The Student Council drew up a declaration asking the warring factions for "peace in our homes, for them not to make orphans of children, to allow us to play freely in the streets and for no harm to come to our small brothers and sisters. . . ."[7]

This led to the creation of a national campaign – the Children's Movement for Peace. Within six months, a national children's referendum had been organised. Nearly 3 million children voted, making the rights to survival, to peace, to family and to freedom from abuse their highest priorities. The children's vote helped inspire a peace mandate that was later supported by more than 10 million citizens and made peace the focus of the subsequent presidential campaign.

While progress in peace talks has been slow, the Children's Movement for Peace has persevered in the face of great risks and has twice been nominated for the Nobel Peace Prize.

"Children are the seeds of a new Colombia," said 14-year-old Mayerly Sanchez, one of the organisation's leaders. "We are the seeds that will stop the war."[8]

Ending the fighting is only part of the transition from war to peace. The memories of atrocities, suffering and injustice live on, and unless they are specifically addressed through healing and reconciliation processes, their re-emergence can undermine the reconstruction process. To date, more than 15 countries in transition from conflict have organised truth and reconciliation commissions as a way to make public the transgressions that occur during war. These commissions help re-establish moral, legal and political accountability. However, only a few of these have focused attention on crimes against children. The International Commission of Inquiry on East Timor, for example, convened a special briefing, organised by UNICEF, on violations against children. In Guatemala, the Guatemalan Historical Clarification Commission noted the impact of the civil conflict on children. The United Nations Mission in Guatemala has worked with UNICEF to create a special commission that would locate children who disappeared during the conflict, as well as enacting legislation to nullify illegal adoptions. And in South Africa, a special day of hearings was dedicated to children.

The July 2000 OAU Report investigating the 1994 Rwandan genocide showed the challenges of achieving reconciliation. But despite difficulties in mustering political will, there must be no compromise in ending impunity for grave violations against children in conflict. Accountability is necessary, not only to punish those responsible for heinous crimes, but also to deter future violations and maintain the integrity of international law. The possibility of offering amnesty as a "quick fix" in peace negotiations can only lead to contempt for the law and the prospect of renewed cycles of violence.

Mobilising resources for war-affected children

Countries in transition face enormous economic challenges. Many communities have few resources for rebuilding. They may face the consequences of scorched-earth policies that have damaged the environment and infrastructure, or be unable to use roads or agricultural land because of landmines. The gains made during the short-term recovery period immediately following the end of hostilities may be forfeited when emergency funds dry up and international relief workers move on to the next crisis. The failure to support long-term recovery can destabilise a fragile peace and give rise to renewed conflict.

The Carnegie Commission on Preventing Deadly Conflict has estimated that the major conflicts of the 1990s, excluding Kosovo, cost the international community around $200 billion,[9] while the cost of NATO's military campaign in Kosovo and the amount spent in the first year towards rebuilding war-torn areas was an estimated $40 billion.[10] The social and economic costs to the countries at war have been far higher. A sustained flow of adequate resources is needed to prevent communities from sliding back into conflict. They must be managed in ways that stabilise communities and support local networks and infrastructure. Emergency assistance needs to be rooted in capacity-building efforts, in strengthening justice systems, training local authorities and leaders in child rights and developing new curricula that break down stereotypes of cultural, racial and ethnic discrimination.

Yet in far too many cases, donor assistance falls far short of the amounts requested. The disparities in resources mobilised for war-affected children across conflict situations have grown more pronounced since the end of the Cold War. Oxfam described the inconsistent responses by donors to humanitarian appeals as "one of the most brutal inequalities in the world today."[11] The only way to ensure that basic assistance will reach all war-affected children is to create a safety net. At a bare minimum, this requires fair criteria and guidelines for equitable distribution of donor funds.

In 1999, donors funded 72 per cent of the United Nations Consolidated Inter-Agency Humanitarian Appeals. Only 18 per cent of the appeal for the Democratic Republic of the Congo was funded, while donors came up with 84 per cent for south-eastern Europe, including Kosovo. The shortfalls and disparities in humanitarian relief reflect the patterns of official development assistance (ODA), which is vital for putting reconstruction on a firm foundation. Mozambique, struggling to rebuild after decades of war, received $61 per person in 1998, while Ethiopia, also rebuilding, received $11 per person. In contrast, 1998 ODA for Bosnia and Herzegovina reached $238 per person.

Poor countries with ongoing conflicts received much less: Burundi received $12 per person, Afghanistan $6 and the Democratic Republic of the Congo $3. Such inequities make it more difficult to give sufficient priority to children's welfare and, in many cases, have resulted in their neglect. Sub-Saharan Africa is the poorest region and the one suffering most from the impact of armed conflicts and from HIV/AIDS. ODA for this region plummeted by nearly 60 per cent between 1990 and 1999.[12] The region received $13.6 billion in ODA in 1998, only 27 per cent of the global total for the year.

Different funding criteria and processes for humanitarian relief, post-conflict and development assistance make coordination difficult. Funding decisions are often determined by political or strategic interests rather than on the basis of need. They are also influenced by public concern and by media attention. Conflicting priorities among international agencies, governments and affected communities often curtail coordination. Having lost skilled staff, governments in war-torn countries may find it difficult to carry out reconstruction programmes. These problems are compounded when fragile peace agreements are broken and conflicts drag on.

Programming and resource constraints during the transition between humanitarian relief operations and reconstruction and development must be addressed if children's rights are to be realised in countries rebuilding after war. UN agencies and offices are working to develop common strategies and to improve coordination among themselves and with other partners, including international NGOs and the World Bank, through the Inter-Agency Standing Committee (IASC) and with the Organisation for Economic Co-operation and Development/Development Assistance Committee (OECD/DAC).

Debt has also had a crippling impact: many war-torn countries are among the 41 heavily indebted poor countries (HIPC), including Angola, Republic of the Congo, Democratic Republic of the Congo, Ethiopia, Liberia, Mozambique, Nicaragua, Rwanda, Sierra Leone, Somalia and Uganda. But debt relief has been too slow and limited. Sub-Saharan Africa has been allocating an average of over

$12 billion annually over the past decade to service debt, more than double the spending on basic education.[13] This has devastating results for children. Cancelling the debts of heavily indebted poor countries is essential for children's future.

The 20/20 Initiative, which was endorsed by the 1995 World Summit for Social Development and the 1995 Fourth World Conference on Women, is a financial blueprint for supporting children's rights and achieving social goals. Yet studies have shown that developing countries and donors fall well short of the Initiative's benchmark allocations of 20 per cent of donor aid and of national budgets for basic social services. Support for 20/20 could, in fact, be generated by channelling savings from debt relief towards basic social services. That the international community has failed to take such steps to fight poverty and help fulfil children's basic human rights is shameful. And it sets the stage for deepening despair and conflict.

Preventing wars, resolving conflict

The best way to protect children from wars is to prevent conflict. The international community must shatter the political inertia that allows circumstances to escalate into armed conflict and destroy children's lives. This means addressing the root causes of violence and promoting sustainable and equitable patterns of human development. Such ideas have been eloquently expressed with analytic power in such texts as the report of the Carnegie Commission on *Preventing Deadly Conflict*, the report of the South Commission, *The Challenge to the South*, and the report of the Commission on Global Governance, *Our Global Neighbourhood*.

Once war erupts, all efforts to protect children can only mitigate, not prevent, children's suffering. At an international level, equitable and sustainable development is a precondition for preventing global conflict. Yet the international community has not been prepared to make the necessary investments. Today, 1.2 billion people live in absolute poverty, surviving on a dollar a day – and at least half of them are children.[14] Education has been heralded as the foundation for peaceful development, good governance and healthy economies. And yet more than 100 million children, 60 per cent of them girls, have no access to education.[15]

Governments bear the primary responsibility for protecting children from the scourge of war – by preventing war from occurring. Responsibility rests not only with warring governments, but also with governments whose citizens are indirectly responsible for inciting or prolonging conflicts for economic or political gain. Governments must lower the risk of armed conflict by demilitarising their societies, if for no other reason than to reduce the percentage of their GDP spent on military expenditures and to free those resources for human development. Tighter controls are essential, not only to halt the international flow of weapons, but to stop the illicit trafficking in diamonds, narcotics and other products that fuel so many conflicts.

There are always indicators that signal the potential onslaught of armed conflicts. Human rights violations are among the most important indicators and yet the most neglected. As the protection of children and women becomes increasingly central to peace and security, relevant and timely information about their situation should be made available. Both the UN Secretary-General and the Security Council have recognised the need to make use of the human rights information and analysis emanating from independent treaty body experts, mechanisms of the Commission on Human Rights and other reliable sources.[16] Operational agencies and NGOs have an important role to play.

But to be of any use, early warning must be linked to early action – and early action is inextricably linked to political will. The Rwandan genocide is a clear example of failure in both respects. Despite the warning signs, the lack of political will handcuffed the ability of the United Nations and the international community to prevent the conflict and the eventual genocide.

The commander of the small UN force in Rwanda at the time insisted that a well-equipped, modern force of 5,000 troops could have stopped most of the killings, a contention since confirmed in a study carried out by an Organization of African Unity (OAU) Panel of Eminent Personalities.[17] The Carnegie Commission on Preventing Deadly Conflicts concluded: "The problem is not that we do not know about incipient and large-scale violence; it is that we often do not act. Examples from 'hot spots' around the world illustrate that the potential for violence can be defused through the early, skilful and integrated application of political, diplomatic, economic and military measures."[18]

Preventing armed conflict and stabilising countries emerging from conflict lie at the heart of the mission of the United Nations and are central to the agenda of the Security Council and the General Assembly. Specialised political guidance, peacekeeping missions and technical assistance form a part of the preventive action of the United Nations. But throughout all of these actions, it has become clear that the international community is unwilling to invest adequate resources for prevention. Although many countries pay lip service to the potential of the United Nations, they are not prepared to give it the political or financial backing it needs to take decisive action. For every dollar the world's nations spend on military activities, less than half a cent goes towards United Nations peacekeeping.[19]

The flagrant violation of human rights is among the root causes of conflict and the resulting humanitarian crises. Human rights verification as part of early warning and preventive action can help deter and defuse situations leading to conflict. Yet the political will and the procedures to assess, report, monitor, prosecute and remedy such violations are woefully inadequate. In his plan for UN reform, the Secretary-General called for human rights to be incorporated in early warning activities, as a key element of peacemaking and peace-building efforts and in the context of humanitarian operations.[20] This is yet to be fully realised.

Conflict prevention and resolution will rely also on the efforts of civil society. NGOs and other civil groups have been behind many important anti-conflict campaigns, including the global ban on anti-personnel landmines, the global campaign to stop the use of child soldiers, the effort to curb small arms and light weapons and the promotion of the International Criminal Court.

Civil society groups play a key role in conflict resolution. Some specialise in this activity – helping to build relationships between warring parties and training participants in diplomacy and conflict resolution. In response to increasing conflict in the Great Lakes region, a group of 26 international NGOs, academics, UN agencies and governments, involved in conflict research, campaigning and policy development in Rwanda, formed the Forum on Early Warning and Early Response (FEWER).[21] The aim is to provide governments and international organisations with early warnings of conflict, as well as recommended forms of response.

Governments have the most important role to play in preventing conflicts and can lower the risk of violence by demilitarising their societies. The end of the Cold War has helped reduce defence budgets around the world, but progress has been uneven, and many countries continue to build massive arsenals. Many African countries that had reduced defence expenditure in the early 1990s subsequently increased it: since 1997 military expenditure in Africa has been rising steadily.[22] This may represent a small share of the world total, but it constitutes a heavy economic burden in countries that can ill afford it. In 1997, Eritrea, for example, spent 14 per cent of GDP on military expenditure, compared with around 2 per cent on education and 3 per cent on health.[23]

In 1998, the UN Secretary-General called on African countries to agree to reduce their purchases of arms and munitions to below 1.5 per cent of GDP and to commit to a zero-growth policy for defence budgets for a 10-year period.[24] The proliferation of armaments bolsters the power of militaries, skews economic priorities, perpetuates ethnic and territorial conflicts and threatens human rights. Governments worldwide should take uncompromising steps to demilitarise their societies by strictly limiting and controlling access to weapons.

Fair and equal access to the benefits of sustained human development is the best defence against violent conflict. All people need to feel that they have a fair share in decision-making, equal access to resources, the ability to participate fully in civil and political society and the freedom to affirm their own identities and fully express their aspirations. To achieve this, the international community must make a greater investment in social and economic development. The world has been spending more on dealing with the consequences of crises and emergencies, and less on preventing them.

The crippling burden of poverty has been compounded over the last five years by the impact of the HIV/AIDS pandemic, the greatest threat to social and economic stability in the developing world. The battle against HIV/AIDS cannot be separated from the battle against poverty. Both battles must be fought at once if children's rights are to be upheld. In fact, the fulfilment of children's rights will not be achieved without meeting the basic human rights of their families and their communities. By placing children first on the development agenda, society builds the best possible foundation for social and economic development.

Afterword

"We are the seeds that will stop the war."

— Mayerly Sanchez, age 14, Children's Movement for Peace (Colombia)[1]

There has been significant progress, both nationally and internationally, in the five years since the 1996 Report on the Impact of Armed Conflict on Children was presented to the United Nations General Assembly.

Landmark achievements can be noted. Children are now more central to the global peace and security agenda. Non-governmental organisations and civil society working together with governments and the United Nations have managed, step by step, to increase protection for children trapped in the madness of war. International laws protecting war-affected children have been strengthened and atrocities are being documented and reported more systematically. The deadly effects of comprehensive sanctions have been exposed; their end has been called for. The excessive proliferation of small arms and light weapons, one of the greatest threats to child survival, is being tackled at the highest political levels. Millions of stockpiled landmines have been destroyed. And the world has finally recognised the dire plight of children who are coping with the multiple effects of armed conflict and HIV/AIDS.

But even as the pillars of support for children – food, water, health care, education and shelter – are being strengthened, resources for development and humanitarian assistance plummet. And conflicts continue to rage. In the face of seemingly insurmountable difficulties, communities are trying to rebuild and children are playing an important part.

Despite all this, at least 20 million children have been uprooted from their homes. Children in 87 countries are growing up amid the lethal contamination of landmines and unexploded ordnance. Millions of children are scarred, physically and psychologically. And girls and women continue to be marginalised and excluded from mainstream humanitarian assistance and protection.

Humanitarian personnel are themselves being targeted and killed. Hundreds of thousands of children still die every year from disease and malnutrition in flight from conflict or in camps for displaced persons. An estimated 300,000 children are still being exploited as soldiers.

In tolerating this scourge of war against children, we ourselves are complicit in their suffering. No one – not the United Nations, not governments or civil society groups – has done nearly enough to counter the power, greed and political expediency with which adults countenance the criminal sacrifice of children in war.

The international community must address the plight of war-affected children and women with new urgency. Their protection is not a matter for negotiation. Those who wage, legitimise and support wars must be condemned and held to account as surely as children must be cherished and protected. Children cannot afford to wait.

Glossary of progress[*]

Protecting children's rights in armed conflict

October 1996 – September 2000

October 1996   Launch of Colombian Children's Movement for Peace, two-time Nobel Peace Prize nominee

November 1996   Graça Machel briefs UN Security Council (under the Arria Formula) on children in armed conflict

November 1996   Graça Machel's Report on the Impact of Armed Conflict on Children (A/51/306 and Add.1) presented to United Nations General Assembly

September 1997   Olara A. Otunnu appointed as Special Representative of the UN Secretary-General for Children and Armed Conflict

October 1997   The Office of the United Nations High Commissioner for Refugees (UNHCR) and Save the Children Alliance launch Action for the Rights of Children (ARC) training programme

October 1997   Nobel Peace Prize awarded to Jody Williams and the International Campaign to Ban Landmines

---

[*] Prepared for the International Conference on War-affected Children, held in Winnipeg (Canada) in September 2000.

March 1998	Rädda Barnen launches database on child soldiers
April 1998	Representative of the UN Secretary-General on Internally Displaced Persons introduces *Guiding Principles on Internal Displacement*
May 1998	Leading NGOs form the Coalition to Stop the Use of Child Soldiers
May 1998	Canada and Norway sign the Lysøen Declaration for human security, making a commitment to children's protection in armed conflict
July 1998	Adoption of the Rome Statute for an International Criminal Court, which includes crimes against humanity and war crimes against children and women
September 1998	The International Criminal Tribunal for Rwanda sets a precedent in prosecuting rape and sexual violence in civil war
October 1998	As an example for police and military forces worldwide, UN Secretary-General sets a minimum age requirement for UN peacekeepers: 25 for civilian police and military observers; for national contingents, preferably 21 but no less than 18
February 1999	The United Nations Children's Fund (UNICEF) launches a Children's Peace and Security Agenda

March 1999	Entry into force of the Ottawa Convention on the Prohibition of the Use, Stockpiling, Production and Transfer of Anti-Personnel Mines, and on their Destruction
May 1999	The International Action Network on Small Arms (IANSA) launches an international campaign against the accumulation, proliferation and misuse of small arms
June 1999	The International Labour Organization (ILO) Convention 182 defines child soldiering as one of the worst forms of child labour and sets 18 as the minimum age for forced or compulsory recruitment
July 1999	Special provisions for children included in the Lomé Peace Agreement for Sierra Leone
August 1999	Child protection officers included in the mandate of the UN Observer Mission for Sierra Leone (UNOMSIL)
August 1999	The UN Security Council adopts Resolution 1261 on children and armed conflict
September 1999	The UN Security Council adopts Resolution 1265 on the protection of civilians in armed conflict
October 1999	Nobel Peace Prize awarded to Médecins Sans Frontières
November 1999	Child protection included in the mandate of the UN Organization Mission in the Democratic Republic of the Congo (MONUC)

November 1999   Entry into force of the African Charter on the Rights and Welfare of the Child, the first regional treaty establishing 18 as a minimum age for all recruitment and participation in hostilities

November 1999   The Organization for Security and Cooperation in Europe (OSCE) Review Conference Declaration makes commitments to war-affected children

November 1999   International Alert and the United Nations Development Fund for Women (UNIFEM) launch an international Women Building Peace campaign

December 1999   The International Criminal Tribunal for the former Yugoslavia recognises rape as a violation of the laws or customs of war

December 1999   Rwanda adopts new law to support reconstruction, allowing girls and women to inherit land and other property

February 2000   The UN Secretary-General releases child-focused guidelines on the *Role of United Nations Peacekeeping in Disarmament, Demobilization and Reintegration*

March 2000   The UN Security Council issues its first statement (SC/6816) on women, peace and security, recognising women's role in conflict resolution, peacekeeping and peace-building

March 2000	The African, Caribbean and Pacific States and European Community Joint Assembly adopts a resolution against the use of child soldiers
April 2000	The Economic Community of West African States (ECOWAS) adopts the Accra Declaration and Plan of Action for war-affected children
May 2000	Adoption of an Optional Protocol to the Convention on the Rights of the Child establishing 18 as the minimum age for children's participation in hostilities
July 2000	The UN Security Council adopts Resolution 1308 on the HIV/AIDS pandemic worldwide and the severity of the crisis in Africa
August 2000	The UN Security Council adopts Resolution 1314 on children and armed conflict
August 2000	Special provisions for children and women are included in the Burundi peace agreement
September 2000	International Conference on War-affected Children, held in Winnipeg (Canada)

Summary of recommendations presented to the International Conference on War-affected Children*

Child soldiers

1. States must ratify without reservation, implement and incorporate in their national legislation the Optional Protocol to the Convention on the Rights of the Child on the involvement of children in armed conflict. Consistent with article 3 of the Protocol, they are encouraged to submit a binding declaration setting 18 as the standard minimum age for voluntary recruitment and participation in hostilities.

2. Programmes to disarm, demobilise and reintegrate child soldiers must be made a priority within and outside of a peacekeeping environment. These should include special measures to ensure children's protection from exploitation and re-recruitment and to address the special needs of girls and children with disabilities.

3. Governments and armed groups must prevent the recruitment of child soldiers and ensure their demobilisation and reintegration. To this end, birth registration should be promoted, especially among refugee and internally displaced children and children belonging to minorities.

---

* These recommendations, contained in a booklet entitled *The Machel Review 1996-2000: A Critical Analysis of Progress Made and Obstacles Encountered in Increasing Protection for War-affected Children,* were presented to the International Conference on War-affected Children, held in Winnipeg (Canada) in September 2000.

4. Child soldiers must be protected from retribution, summary execution, arbitrary detention, torture and other punitive measures, in accordance with the Convention on the Rights of the Child and international juvenile justice standards. Any judicial proceedings involving child soldiers must be within a framework of restorative justice that guarantees the physical, psychological and social rehabilitation of the child.

Children forced to flee

The following recommendations will be jeopardised if the international community does not increase its commitment to the care and protection of internally displaced children and women through the provision of adequate resources.

1. In every single situation where there are internally displaced persons, a lead agency should be identified. The agency most involved should be designated, and it follows logically that in the majority of cases this agency will be the Office of the United Nations High Commissioner for Refugees (UNHCR). In those instances where UNHCR is not already directly involved, the agency most engaged should be designated. It is expected that the lead agency will collaborate with all other agencies directly involved, e.g. the United Nations Children's Fund (UNICEF) and the World Food Programme (WFP). In all cases, UNICEF should be a major partner in the care and protection of internally displaced children.

2. States and other relevant actors should commit themselves to promote, disseminate, apply and integrate into national legislation and policy the *Guiding Principles on Internal Displacement*, with particular attention to the articles relating to children and women.

3. The international community is urged to provide increased financial and human resources to support the Representative of the United Nations Secretary-General (RSG) on Internally Displaced Persons, particularly in his efforts to: develop monitoring mechanisms to promote more effective compliance with the *Guiding Principles*; provide advice on obstacles encountered in the protec-

tion of internally displaced children and women; intervene in a timely manner; and mobilise effective international and regional responses. Specifically, UNICEF and UNHCR are encouraged to continue providing appropriate financial and human resources to foster closer collaboration with the RSG.

4. The survival and protection of unaccompanied and separated children must be ensured, giving priority consideration to family tracing. When family members cannot be identified, extended family and community care should be arranged.

5. Urgent attention must be given to meeting the special needs of displaced adolescents and involving them centrally in the planning, provision and management of services in camps.

Children under siege from HIV/AIDS

1. In the belief that care and services must be made available to all populations affected by AIDS, in peacetime and during war, governments, humanitarian and development agencies and NGOs are called upon to reframe their work and increase technical support and resources so that improved treatment, care and support are available for children affected by HIV/AIDS in conflict and in neighbouring communities.

2. On an urgent basis and during the tenure of the UNICEF Executive Director as Chair of the Committee of Co-sponsoring Organisations,* a full meeting should be devoted exclusively to issues of HIV/AIDS, children and conflict. UNHCR should be invited to this meeting. The discussion should address methods and standards for HIV/AIDS prevention, treatment and care for children affected by conflict, and for refugee, internally displaced and neighbouring communities. Specific reference should be made to the work of the International Partnership Against AIDS in Africa (IPAA).

3. Schools and educational systems should be the centrepiece for HIV/AIDS awareness, prevention and care during emergencies,

---

* The Committee of Co-sponsoring Organisations (CCO) is the implementing arm of the Joint United Nations Programme on HIV/AIDS (UNAIDS).

including expanded life-skills curricula that offer nutritional support, hygiene and other domestic survival skills.

4. Education and training on HIV/AIDS prevention should be made mandatory for all military and peacekeeping personnel, together with voluntary and confidential counselling, testing and treatment. Codes of conduct should be strictly enforced through disciplinary action, which can help lessen the incidence of sexual violence.

5. All relief organisations, and in particular NGOs, working in conflict-affected countries should ensure urgently the development and mainstreaming of HIV/AIDS approaches in their policy and practice.

6. More resources should be allocated to assess, including through data analysis, the links between AIDS, conflict and children, with particular reference to the gender dimensions of conflict and the pandemic.

Ending gender-based violence and sexual exploitation

1. A growing trend has been noted of the trafficking and sexual exploitation of women and girls in conflict situations, mainly through observation and anecdotal evidence. Data should be gathered and this trend documented systematically. Two specific assessments are recommended:

• A joint report on the trafficking of women and girls in conflict situations by the Special Rapporteur on the Sale of Children, Child Prostitution and Child Pornography and by the Special Rapporteur on the Eradication of All Forms of Violence Against Women;

• A second, multi-country study, 'Where are the babies?', to follow up the situation of women and the children born following rape and forced impregnation in countries including Guatemala, Liberia, Sierra Leone, Uganda and the former Yugoslavia.

2. States are urged to join the campaign for the establishment of the International Criminal Court (ICC) to help end the impunity for crimes against women and girls. In implementing the ICC Statute domestically, States should strengthen national laws to prevent and to prosecute gender-based and sexual crimes.

3. The UN Secretary-General and the Security Council must be unrelenting in their pursuit of the highest standards of conduct by peacekeeping personnel. Where violations against women and children have been committed by UN personnel, States must investigate and punish offences and make public the results of such proceedings. Urgent attention must be given to establishing disciplinary and oversight mechanisms in all peace support operations, in the form of an ombudsperson, an Inspector General or through an office created especially for that purpose.

4. All humanitarian responses in conflict situations must emphasise the special reproductive health needs of women and girls, include systematic reporting on sexual violence and reflect strengthened policy guidance on gender-based violence and sexual exploitation.

The toll from malnutrition and disease

1. Political pressure and other measures should be mobilised to ensure that warring parties provide access to health systems, clean water and adequate nutrition. "Days of tranquillity" and "corridors of peace," vital for securing emergency access, must be expanded to ensure respect for children's rights at all times during conflicts.

2. Donors and international agencies must work to end great disparities in international humanitarian assistance provided to different countries during armed conflicts. Shifts in media coverage, political priorities and other causes of "donor fatigue" must no longer cost children's lives in forgotten conflicts.

3. Upon ratification of the Convention on the Rights of the Child, States are required to allocate the maximum resources possible for children, including for health, sanitation, nutrition and water. This requirement is especially important in conflict situations and is reinforced by articles 4, 23, 24 and 28 of the Convention, which highlight the international community's special responsibility to make resources available to meet the needs of developing countries.

4. Governments of war-affected countries, international agencies, NGOs and donor countries must accord greater resources and a higher priority to protect women and girls from gender-based sexual violence and to support their reproductive health.

The psychosocial impact

1. Psychosocial support must be a central part of child protection in all phases of emergency and reconstruction.

2. Governments, donors and relief organisations should prevent the institutionalisation of children and prioritise the reunification of children with their families and communities. Arrangements such as foster care and peer group living need to be linked with appropriate community, social, cultural or religious networks that promote child protection.

3. Children with special needs, such as child soldiers, should receive support within the broader context of reintegration programmes for all war-affected children. Sensitivity to special protection issues affecting girls must be a priority for agencies and communities.

4. Psychosocial programmes should involve a range of players, including relevant government ministries, donors, UN agencies, NGOs, other civil society groups, teachers, health professionals, children and families.

Education for survival

1. Educational support should include life skills training, landmine awareness, HIV/AIDS prevention, human rights, peace education and psychosocial support in the core curriculum.

2. Inter-agency collaboration (UNICEF, UNESCO, UNHCR) and cooperation with governments and NGOs should be strengthened to consolidate immediate and long-term responses to education in emergencies.

3. Specialised accelerated learning programmes for adolescents should form a key part of the emergency educational response.

4. Parents, the community and young people should be involved in curriculum planning and development to ensure that teaching materials are locally relevant and also child-rights based, giving full attention to gender-sensitivity and ethnic and religious tolerance.

Landmines and unexploded ordnance

1. States that have not yet ratified or acceded to the Ottawa Convention must do so, and all ratifying countries must quickly ensure effective implementation, including through the enactment of national legislation and the inclusion of penal sanctions for violations.

2. Donor countries must provide far more support, both bilaterally and internationally, for mine action in affected countries, including through contributions to the United Nations Voluntary Trust Fund for Assistance in Mine Clearance.

3. The UN Security Council should hold an open debate on operational mine action in a peacekeeping environment, with a focus on integrating military and humanitarian priorities and with respect to specific operations, particularly in Africa.

4. The rights of children should hold a central place in surveys and assessments, planning and implementing mine action programmes. To develop policy and practice in this area, UNICEF and the United Nations Mine Action Service (UNMAS) should convene a technical workshop with relevant international agencies and NGOs.

5. Companies and countries that have used landmines and unexploded ordnance or profited from their sale should be identified and required to contribute funds for mine action. Leaders responsible for causing civilian deaths and injuries and economic damage through the use of landmines should be held accountable for their actions under international law.

6. A worldwide moratorium on the use of cluster munitions should be implemented and consideration given to the immediate and long-term humanitarian consequences of these weapons, especially for children.

Light weapons, mass destruction

1. Arms embargoes should be imposed, monitored and enforced in situations where civilians are targeted, where widespread and systematic violations of humanitarian and human rights

law are committed and where children are recruited as soldiers. Embargo violations should be criminalised and prosecuted.

2. Building on existing regional and subregional initiatives, governments and intergovernmental organisations should draw up binding international instruments and legislation to address legal and illegal arms flows, production and stockpiling.

3. All peace agreements should set clear provisions for disarming, demobilising and reintegrating soldiers, including child soldiers. Institutional arrangements for disarmament and the safe and timely disposal of arms and ammunition should be made explicit and be fully funded and supported.

4. States, UN bodies and civil society should promote a "culture of peace" through peace education programmes. Children and their families should be educated about the dangers of small arms and light weapons, and the popular entertainment culture that glorifies gun use should be challenged.

5. Civil society should be supported in playing an important role in arms prevention, reduction and awareness raising and in monitoring government policy.

Protecting children from sanctions

1. The international community should cease to impose comprehensive sanctions.

2. Sanctions must be selectively and thoughtfully targeted to avoid damage to vulnerable populations and especially women and children. No sanctions regime should be implemented unless the UN Security Council is persuaded, by a rigorous assessment, that such a regime will not have a negative impact on children.

3. When sanctions are applied, the Security Council must have clearly defined objectives and criteria for termination. Sanctions should be lifted gradually as the objectives are satisfied. Since many of the effects of sanctions, particularly the impact on health, may only become manifest in the long term, no sanctions regime should be allowed to continue indefinitely.

4. UNICEF, and other UN and NGO partners, should promote the identification of a set of agreed common indicators to

monitor the impact of sanctions on children before, during and after their imposition. All monitoring should include an assessment of the impact on regional neighbours and major trading partners.

5. The Security Council and its sanctions committees should improve their transparency and accountability through public reporting, debate, monitoring and periodic reviews.

6. Corporations should contribute to the strict implementation of sanctions legitimately established by the international community in full respect for human rights and the rights of the child.

Raising standards for child protection

1. Human rights treaty bodies should enhance their focus on child rights in conflict situations in reviewing government reports. Following its thematic discussion on children in armed conflict, the Committee on the Rights of the Child should undertake a comprehensive overview of measures undertaken by States parties and other relevant actors to promote children's rights in armed conflict, as well as of achievements made and challenges encountered in this endeavour.

2. The Office of the High Commissioner for Human Rights must be strengthened so that it can respond more effectively to violations of child rights. To improve child rights monitoring in armed conflict, all relevant agencies should promote the development of effective procedures for prompt, confidential and objective reporting.

3. States should sign and ratify the International Criminal Court Statute, the Optional Protocols to the Convention on the Rights of the Child and the International Labour Organization's Convention No. 182, and adopt national legislative and other relevant measures to ensure the fulfilment of children's rights.

4. The international community should examine the responsibility and culpability of external States that support non-state actors that commit gross violations of children's rights. This support should be considered a serious criminal offence.

5. Wherever gross violations of children's rights occur, the accountability of those who are directly or indirectly responsible should be established under relevant international or national pro-

visions. Where national legislation exists it should be implemented, and where it does not, States should enact relevant legislative measures and consider, whenever necessary, the conclusion of bilateral or multilateral agreements.

A children's agenda for peace and security

1. All operations to prevent conflict and build peace should include human rights monitoring and verification components. To this end, the Office of the High Commissioner for Human Rights should be strengthened to carry out such functions in conflict situations and especially in a peacekeeping environment.

2. The internal institutional arrangements of peace support operations must ensure that the humanitarian, human rights, gender and child protection components are able to safeguard the humanitarian principles of humanity, neutrality and impartiality in carrying out their work.

3. In reports and briefings to the UN Security Council, the Secretary-General should systematically elaborate on human rights and humanitarian concerns and provide relevant information and analysis on the situation of women and children. These reports should draw from a wide variety of sources, including from operational humanitarian and human rights agencies and NGOs.

4. Just as the Security Council hears regularly from the High Commissioner for Refugees, the Special Representative of the Secretary-General for Children and Armed Conflict, the Executive Director of UNICEF and the President of the ICRC, so it is desirable that the Security Council hear regularly from the High Commissioner for Human Rights on those matters relevant to her office and relating to children and armed conflict.

Reconstruction and reconciliation

1. The Development Assistance Committee (OECD/DAC), in consultation with the UN and NGOs, is urged to establish criteria and guidelines to reduce disparities in resource mobilisation for war-affected children and women across conflict situations and to

reduce the institutional, budgetary and functional barriers between relief assistance, reconstruction and development cooperation. These issues should be given priority consideration at the high-level consultation in 2001 on Financing for Development.

2. The UN Inter-Agency Standing Committee (IASC), together with representatives of developing countries and the NGO community, should ensure child-focused policy development, programme planning and implementation.

3. Those responsible for genocide, war crimes and crimes against humanity and against children must be brought to justice. Post-conflict assistance should prioritise truth and reconciliation initiatives and the rebuilding of justice systems, paying special attention to juvenile justice.

Women and the peace process

1. Two experts should be appointed to carry out parallel assessments of:
• The impact of armed conflict on women with a focus on institutional arrangements for women's protection and the delivery of humanitarian support. This should take into account recent developments, including the Beijing Platform for Action and progress made in the investigation and prosecution of war crimes against women;
• The second study should focus on women's role in peace-building and the gender dimensions of peace processes and conflict resolution. The United Nations Development Fund for Women (UNIFEM) should be called on to provide institutional support for this work, with financial support from the international community and, in particular, from the Development Assistance Committee (OECD/DAC) Working Party on Gender Equality.

2. Governments, the international community and civil society should provide financial, political and technical support for women's peace-building initiatives and networks.

3. Sex and age disaggregated data should be collected in all assessments, monitoring, reporting, evaluation and research. Mechanisms should be established to ensure appropriate informa-

tion flow on gender issues to inform the policy and planning process with respect to peace support operations.

Media and communication

1. UN agencies and civil society groups should explore ways in which modern communications technology can assist monitoring and verification of child rights violations in conflict situations.

2. Agencies and civil society groups should develop guidelines for their staff to assist interactions with the media that will not harm children in their charge.

3. Humanitarian agencies should develop programmes for adolescents to use new communications technology to promote community awareness in health, education and other vital areas for survival in conflict situations.

Preventing war

1. The UN Security Council, in cooperation with the rest of the UN system, must use all the tools at its disposal to prevent conflicts, including early warning, preventive diplomacy, preventive deployment of peacekeepers, preventive disarmament and post-conflict peace-building.

2. Regional approaches to preventing conflicts and promoting peace must be encouraged and strengthened, including through continued and improved collaboration with the United Nations, humanitarian organisations and NGOs, and increased attention to child rights, protection and gender.

3. While broad strategies to overcome poverty are needed, specific steps to fulfil children's rights to primary health care, adequate nutrition, clean water and sanitation, and quality basic education must be taken while ensuring rapid and deep debt relief for heavily indebted poor countries.

Endnotes

Preface

[1] Quoted in news feature, OneWorld news clearinghouse [www.oneworld.org].

Chapter 1: Wars against children

[1] Human Rights Watch (HRW), *The Scars of Death*, HRW, New York, 1997, Appendix A, pp. 86-87.

[2] Information was supplied by United Nations Children's Fund, Information and Data Management Section, Division of Evaluation, Policy and Planning, August 2000.

[3] Ibid.

[4] Brett, Rachel, 'Child Soldiering: Questions and Challenges for Health Professionals', draft, May 2000, a contribution to World Health Organization, *World Report on Violence and Health*, WHO, forthcoming in 2002.

[5] United Nations Office for the Coordination of Humanitarian Affairs (OCHA), United Nations Consolidated Inter-Agency Assistance Appeals, 1994-1999, summaries of requirements and contributions [www.reliefweb.int/ocha_ol/index.html].

[6] United Nations Report of the Independent Inquiry into the Actions of the United Nations During the 1994 Genocide in Rwanda, United Nations, New York, 15 December 1999 [www.un.org/News/ossg/rwanda_report.htm].

Chapter 2: Child soldiers

[1] Amnesty International Press Release, 'Sierra Leone: War crimes against children continue', AI Index AFR 51/038/2000, News Service No. 118, 16 June 2000 [www.amnesty.org].

[2] For names of countries where children are being used as soldiers, see the Coalition to Stop the Use of Child Soldiers website [www.child-soldiers.org].

[3] Brett, Rachel (Quaker United Nations Office, Geneva) and Margaret McCallin (International Catholic Child Bureau), *Children: The Invisible Soldiers*, Rädda Barnen, Sweden, 1998, p. 9.

[4] Brett, Rachel, 'Child Soldiering: Questions and Challenges for Health Professionals', draft, May 2000, p. 1; a contribution to World Health Organization, *World Report on Violence and Health*, WHO, forthcoming in 2002.

[5] Cited in Coalition to Stop the Use of Child Soldiers, *Asia Report: Myanmar*, May 2000 [www.child-soldiers.org].

[6] Minority Rights Group International (MRGI), *War: The Impact on Minority and Indigenous Children,* MRGI, 1997, p. 17.

[7] Ibid., pp. 24-25.

[8] Coalition to Stop the Use of Child Soldiers, *The Use of Children as Soldiers in Africa,* March 1999, pp. 14-17.

[9] Verhey, Beth, *The Prevention, Demobilization and Reintegration of Child Soldiers: Lessons learned from Angola,* forthcoming Working Paper, World Bank, 2001.

[10] United Nations Children's Fund (UNICEF), *The Progress of Nations 2000,* UNICEF, New York, 2000, p. 5.

[11] British Broadcasting Corporation (BBC), 'Row over Taliban soldier claim', 1 December 1999; 'Child soldiers for Taliban? Unlikely', *Christian Science Monitor,* 6 December 1999.

[12] Brett and McCallin, op. cit., pp. 50-52.

[13] United Nations, Optional Protocol to the Convention on the Rights of the Child on the involvement of children in armed conflict, A/RES/54/263, ratified by Sri Lanka on 8 September 2000.

[14] Coalition to Stop the Use of Child Soldiers, *Asia Report: Afghanistan,* May 2000 [www.child-soldiers.org].

[15] Ibid.

[16] The United Kingdom's minimum age for recruitment is 16 with parental consent; the United States permits the voluntary recruitment of 17-year-olds with parental permission.

[17] United Nations, Report of the Expert of the Secretary-General, Ms. Graça Machel, 'Impact of armed conflict on children', A/51/306, United Nations, New York, 26 August 1996, para. 41.

[18] McCauley, Una, Regional Adviser on Children and Armed Conflict in West Africa, Rädda Barnen, Sweden, in e-mail to UNICEF researcher Saudamini Siegrist, 11 August 2000.

[19] Coalition to Stop the Use of Child Soldiers, *The Use of Children as Soldiers in the Asia-Pacific Region,* draft, June 2000, p. 14.

[20] Coalition to Stop the Use of Child Soldiers, 'Africa Report: Executive Summary', March 1999 [www.child-soldiers.org].

[21] Timonera, Bobby, 'The Warrior Is a Girl Child', Philippine Human Rights Information Center, n.d.; reprinted in *Human Rights Forum,* vol. IX, no. 1, July-December 1999.

[22] Stavrou, Stavros and Robert Stewart with Amanda Stavrou, 'The Reintegration of Child Soldiers and Abducted Children: A Case Study of Palaro and Pabbo, Gulu District, Northern Uganda', Institute for Security Studies (ISS), Pretoria, 2000.

[23] Almquist, Kate, Robbie Muhumuza and David Westwood, *The Effects of Armed Conflict on Girls,* World Vision International, Geneva, July 1996.

[24] Brett and McCallin, op. cit., p. 98.

[25] Stavrou, S. and R. Stewart with A. Stavrou, op. cit.

[26] Amnesty International Press Release, 'Sierra Leone: War crimes against children continue', op. cit.

[27] 'Child Soldiers: Colombia attempts to rehabilitate ex-warriors', United Nations Foundation's *UN Wire,* 31 March 2000.

[28] United Nations, Report of the Secretary-General, 'The role of United Nations

peacekeeping in disarmament, demobilization and reintegration', S/2000/101, United Nations, New York, 11 February 2000.

[29] Verhey, op. cit.

[30] Ibid.

[31] Legrand, Jean-Claude, 'Lessons learned from UNICEF field programmes for the prevention of recruitment, demobilization and reintegration of child soldiers', UNICEF, New York, October 1999, p. 22.

[32] Ibid., p. 27.

[33] Ibid., p. 23.

[34] Brett, Rachel (Quaker United Nations Office, Geneva), reported in conversation with UNICEF researcher Saudamini Siegrist.

[35] Verhey, op. cit.

[36] Legrand, op. cit., p. 25.

[37] Youboty, James, *Satanic rampage: A graphic account of the Liberian civil war*, Modern World Enterprises, Philadelphia, 1993.

[38] Legrand, op. cit., p. 31.

[39] United Nations, Optional Protocol to the Convention on the Rights of the Child on the involvement of children in armed conflict, A/RES/54/263, United Nations, New York, 25 May 2000.

[40] Legrand, op. cit., p. 14.

[41] Both databases can be accessed through the Rädda Barnen website [http://www.rb.se].

[42] Legrand, op. cit., p. 13.

Chapter 3: Children forced to flee

[1] Women's Commission for Refugee Women and Children (WCRWC), *Looking Toward Home: Internally Displaced Adolescents in Azerbaijan,* WCRWC, New York, 1998, p. 10.

[2] The number of persons displaced as a result of conflicts and human rights violations is based on the number of internally displaced, estimated at 23 million by the Norwegian Refugee Council Global Survey; combined with the number of refugees and asylum seekers of concern to UNHCR, 12.8 million; and 3.2 million Palestinian refugees covered by a separate mandate of the UN Relief and Works Agency for Palestine Refugees in the Near East (UNRWA). That number does not include refugees who have acquired the citizenship of the asylum country. The estimated number of 40 million displaced persons is used by the Representative of the UN Secretary-General on Internally Displaced Persons.

[3] The *Guiding Principles on Internal Displacement,* prepared under the direction of Francis M. Deng, Representative of the Secretary-General on Internally Displaced Persons, and presented to the fifty-fourth session of the Commission on Human Rights, has developed the following working description of internally displaced persons: "Persons or groups of persons who have been forced or obliged to flee or to leave their homes or places of habitual residence, in particular as a result of or in order to avoid the effects of armed conflict, situations of generalised violence, violations of human rights or natural or human-made disasters, and who have not crossed an inter-

nationally recognised state border."

[4] Article 1A, paragraph 2, of the 1951 Convention Relating to the Status of Refugees defines a refugee as someone who, "owing to well-founded fear of being persecuted for reason of race, religion, nationality, membership of a particular social group or political opinion, is outside of the country of his nationality and is unable or, owing to such fear, is unwilling to avail himself of the protection of that country; or who, not having nationality and being outside of the country of his former habitual residence as a result of such events, is unable or, owing to such fear, is unwilling to return to it."

[5] "Unaccompanied children" are those who are separated from both parents and are not in the care of another adult who, by law or custom, has taken responsibility to do so. International agencies and NGOs use the term "separated children" or "separated minors" rather than "unaccompanied children" because adolescents may be overlooked in working with children and because relatively few children are actually unaccompanied. Separated children are those who are separated from both parents, or from their previous legal or customary primary caregiver, but not necessarily from other relatives; thus children who are accompanied by other adult family members are included. Office of the United Nations High Commissioner for Refugees (UNHCR), *Refugee Children: Guidelines on Protection and Care,* UNHCR, Geneva, 1994.

[6] Hague Conference on Private International Law, 'Recommendation Concerning the Application to Refugee Children and Other Internationally Displaced Children of the Hague Convention on Protection of Children and Co-operation in Respect of Intercountry Adoption', adopted on 21 October 1994.

[7] International Committe of the Red Cross, Persons unaccounted for in connection with Kosovo crisis, 2 Decemer 2000 [www.icrc.org]

[8] Organization of African Unity, International Panel of Eminent Personalities to Investigate the Genocide in Rwanda and the Surrounding Events, Executive Summary, OAU, Addis Ababa, July 2000, p. 6.

[9] International Committee of the Red Cross, *"Do you know this child?",* *Unaccompanied children in Rwanda and the Great Lakes region (1994-2000),* ICRC, July 2000, pp. 3 and 7.

[10] Ibid., p. 13.

[11] Ibid., p. 4.

[12] Ibid., p. 6.

[13] Ibid., p. 8.

[14] Ibid.

[15] Ibid., p. 13.

[16] United Nations Children's Fund, 'UNICEF Rwanda 1999 Country Annual Report' (internal publication).

[17] Ibid., pp. 6-8.

[18] United Nations High Commissioner for Refugees, 'Telecommunications in the Service of Humanitarian Assistance', speech by Sadako Ogata at the Telecom 99+ InterActive 99 Forum, Geneva, 14 October 1999.

[19] Relief Web, 'UNHCR and IOM announce technology partnership to set up system to register Kosovo refugees in Albania', 28 January 2000 [www.reliefweb.int].

[20] International Committee of the Red Cross, Persons unaccounted for in connection with Kosovo crisis, op. cit., p. 3.

[21] Office of the United Nations High Commissioner for Refugees, *Building partnerships through equality*, UNHCR, Geneva, May 2000, p. 19.

[22] Cohen, Roberta and Francis M. Deng, *Masses in Flight: The Global Crisis of Internal Displacement*, Brookings, 1998, p. 260.

[23] Office of the United Nations High Commissioner for Refugees, 'Refugee Children and Adolescents: A progress report', UNHCR, 7 February 2000.

[24] Ibid.

[25] Smith, Wendy, Education Technical Advisor, International Rescue Committee, Georgia trip report, August 2000.

[26] United Nations Children's Fund, 'West Bank and Gaza: Children contributing to peace', New York, 2000.

[27] Information supplied by Bo Viktor Nylund, Project Officer, Humanitarian Principles, Office of Emergency Programmes, UNICEF, New York, 2001.

[28] Minority Rights Group International (MRGI), *War: The Impact on Minority and Indigenous Children*, MRGI, London, November 1997, pp. 19-20.

[29] Office of the United Nations High Commissioner for Refugees, *The Impact of Armed Conflict on Children: The Refugee and Displaced Children Dimension*, UNHCR, Geneva, 1996, p. 53.

[30] Save the Children, *War brought us here: Protecting children displaced within their own countries by conflict*, Save the Children UK, London, 2000, p. 61.

[31] United Nations, *World Conference on Human Rights: Vienna Declaration and Programme of Action*, United Nations, New York, 1993, p. 40.

[32] Cohen, Roberta, '"Tough Nuts to Crack": Dealing with Difficult Situations of Internal Displacement', January 1999.

[33] United Nations Office for the Coordination of Humanitarian Affairs (OCHA), New York; Agence France Presse (AFP), 'Mandela says Burundians to be free from regroupment camps', Johannesburg, 7 June 2000.

[34] United Nations, S/RES/1314, S/RES/1261, S/RES/1265, New York, 1999.

[35] Cohen, Roberta and Francis M. Deng, *Masses in Flight,* op. cit. A second volume is: Cohen, Roberta and Francis M. Deng, eds., *The Forsaken People: Case Studies of the Internally Displaced*, Brookings, 1998.

[36] Inter-Agency Standing Committee, 'Protection of Internally Displaced Persons: Inter-Agency Standing Committee Policy Paper', IASC, December 1999.

[37] Office of the United Nations High Commissioner for Refugees, *Building partnerships through equality*, op. cit., p. 16.

[38] United Nations Children's Fund, *The Gender Dimensions of Internal Displacement,* UNICEF, New York, November 1998, p. 20.

[39] United Nations, 'Strengthening of the coordination of emergency humanitarian assistance of the United Nations: Report of the Secretary-General', A/55/82-E/2000/6, United Nations, New York, May 2000, p. 22.

[40] Office of the United Nations High Commissioner for Refugees, 'Summary update of Machel study follow-up activities', UNHCR, Geneva, May 1999, p. 2.

[41] United Nations Office for the Coordination of Humanitarian Affairs, *Manual on field practice in internal displacement,* OCHA, 1999, p. 71.

Chapter 4: Children under siege from HIV/AIDS

[1] Transcript of interview with Mary Phiri, Editor-in-Chief, *Trendsetters*, United Nations Children's Fund (UNICEF), New York, September 1999.

[2] United Nations, Press Release, SG/SM/7275 AFR/200 SC/6780, 6 January 2000.

[3] Joint United Nations Programme on HIV/AIDS (UNAIDS), *Report on the global HIV/AIDS epidemic June 2000*, Geneva, June 2000, p. 6.

[4] Joint United Nations Programme on HIV/AIDS, Press Release, 11 February 2000.

[5] Conclusion approved by Jan Vandemoortele, United Nations Development Programme (UNDP), United Nations, New York. Information gathered from UNICEF Operations Centre (OPSCEN); World Bank [www.worldbank.org].

[6] United Nations Development Programme (UNDP), *Human Development Report 2000*, Oxford University Press for UNDP, Oxford, 2000, pp. 214-217.

[7] Piot, Dr. Peter, Executive Director, Joint United Nations Programme on HIV/AIDS, Statement to the United Nations Security Council, United Nations, New York, 17 July 2000.

[8] Joint United Nations Programme on HIV/AIDS, 'AIDS and the Military', UNAIDS, Geneva, May 1998, p. 3.

[9] Ibid., p. 2.

[10] United Nations Children's Fund (UNICEF), *The Progress of Nations 2000*, UNICEF, New York, 2000, p. 7.

[11] Joint United Nations Programme on HIV/AIDS, Children and young people, Statement for the World Conference of Ministers Responsible for Youth, Lisbon, 8-12 August 1998.

[12] Jareg, Elizabeth (Redd Barna, Norway) and Lehnart Falk (Red Barnet, Denmark), 'Steps in the development of a monitoring and evaluation system for centre and community-based psychosocial work with war-affected children in northern Uganda', Report of a consultation with Gulu Support the Children Organisation, Gulu district, northern Uganda, 14 April-7 May 1999.

[13] Joint United Nations Programme on HIV/AIDS, 'A review of HIV transmission through breastfeeding', UNAIDS, Geneva, 1998.

[14] US Fund for UNICEF, 'Breastfeeding: Foundation for a healthy future', US Fund for UNICEF, New York, August 2000.

[15] United Nations Children's Fund, *The Progress of Nations 2000*, op. cit., p. 32.

[16] E-mail correspondence between Elizabeth Pisani (Senior Technical Officer, Surveillance and Evaluation – Asia, Family Health International) and UNICEF researcher Saudamini Siegrist, 13 April 2001; UNAIDS Discussion Document, 'AIDS – 5 years since ICPD: Emerging issues and challenges for women, young people and infants', UNAIDS, Geneva, February 1999.

[17] Donovan, Paula, 'The impact of HIV and AIDS on the rights of the child to education; discrimination and HIV/AIDS-related stigma and access to education – the response', SADC-EU seminar on the rights of the child in a world with HIV and AIDS, Harare, 23-25 October 2000.

[18] World Summit for Children, United Nations, New York, 29-30 September 1990; Dakar Framework for Action, 'Education For All: Meeting our collective com-

mitments', text adopted by the World Education Forum, Dakar, Senegal, 26-28 April 2000.

[19] United Nations, Press Release SC/6890, United Nations, New York, 17 July 2000.

[20] Joint United Nations Programme on HIV/AIDS, *Epidemiological Fact Sheet on HIV/AIDS and sexually transmitted infections, 2000 update, Uganda*, Geneva, June 2000, p. 3.

[21] Piot, Dr. Peter, Executive Director, Joint United Nations Programme on HIV/AIDS, Opening Statement to XIII International AIDS Conference, Durban, South Africa, 9 July 2000.

[22] African Development Forum 2000, 'The African consensus and plan of action: Leadership to overcome AIDS', Addis Ababa, 3-7 December 2000.

[23] Lewis, Stephen, *The Toronto Globe and Mail*, Canada, 26 January 2001; and subsequent conversation with author, May 2001.

Chapter 5: Ending sexual violence and exploitation

[1] Bennett, Elizabeth, Virginia Gamba and Deirdre van der Merwe, eds., *ACT against child soldiers in Africa: A reader*, Institute for Security Studies, Pretoria, 2000, p. 48.

[2] United Nations, Periodic Report submitted by Ms. Elisabeth Rehn, Special Rapporteur of the Commission on Human Rights, 'Situation of Human Rights in the Territory of the former Yugoslavia', E/CN.4/1996/63, UN Commission on Human Rights, Geneva, 22 October 1996.

[3] Human Rights Watch, *World Report 1999: Human Rights Developments: Violence Against Women* [www.hrw.org/hrw/worldreport99/women/women2.html].

[4] United Nations, 'Report on the mission to the Democratic People's Republic of Korea, the Republic of Korea and Japan on the issue of military sexual slavery in wartime', E/CN.4/1996/53/Add.1, UN Commission on Human Rights, Geneva, 4 January 1996.

[5] United Nations, Report of the Expert of the Secretary-General, Ms. Graça Machel, 'Impact of armed conflict on children', A/51/306, United Nations, New York, 26 August 1996, para. 93.

[6] Human Rights Watch, *World Report 1999: Human Rights Developments: Violence Against Women*, op. cit.

[7] United Nations Development Programme (UNDP), Social Development and Poverty Elimination Division, Bureau for Development Policy, *Dying of Sadness: Gender, sexual violence and the HIV epidemic*, UNDP, New York, 2000, p. 4.

[8] United Nations, Report of the Expert of the Secretary-General, Ms. Graça Machel, 'Impact of armed conflict on children', op. cit., para. 99.

[9] Organization of African Unity (OAU), *Rwanda: The Preventable Genocide*, Report of the International Panel of Eminent Personalities to Investigate the 1994 Genocide in Rwanda and the Surrounding Events, May 2000.

[10] Cited in United Nations, Report of the Expert of the Secretary-General, Ms. Graça Machel, 'Impact of armed conflict on children', op. cit.

[11] Ralph, Regan E., Executive Director, Women's Rights Division, Human Rights Watch (HRW), 'International Trafficking of Women and Children: Testimony before the Senate Committee on Foreign Relations Subcommittee on Near Eastern and South Asian Affairs', HRW, 22 February 2000 [www.hrw.org/backgrounder/wrd/trafficking.htm].

[12] United Nations, 'Report of the Special Rapporteur on violence against women, its causes and consequences', Ms. Radhika Coomaraswamy, submitted in accordance with UN Commission on Human Rights resolution 1997/44, E/CN.4/1998/54, United Nations, 26 January 1998.

[13] Grigg, William Norman, 'Beasts in Blue Berets: The Reality of the United Nations', *The New American*, September 1997.

[14] United Nations, Optional Protocol to the Convention on the Rights of the Child on the sale of children, child prostitution and child pornography, A/RES/54/263, United Nations, New York, 25 May 2000.

[15] Human Rights Watch, Press Release: 'Human Rights Watch applauds Rwanda Rape Verdict', HRW, September 1998 [www.hrw.org/hrw/press98/sept/rrape902.htm].

[16] United Nations, 'Report of the Special Rapporteur on violence against women, its causes and consequences', op. cit.; United Nations, 'Report on the mission to the Democratic People's Republic of Korea, the Republic of Korea and Japan on the issue of military sexual slavery in wartime', op. cit., para. 54.

[17] Human Rights Watch/Africa, Human Rights Watch Women's Rights Project, *Shattered Lives: Sexual Violence during the Rwandan Genocide and its Aftermath*, HRW, September 1996, p. 39.

[18] Organization of African Unity, *Rwanda: The Preventable Genocide*, op. cit.

[19] As of 28 May 2001, there were 139 signatories and 32 ratifications of the ICC Statute. For current information, see the website of the NGO Coalition for an International Criminal Court [www.iccnow.org].

[20] The Government of Canada funded two organisations – Rights and Democracy, and the International Centre for Criminal Law Reform and Criminal Justice Policy – to prepare a manual on implementing the ICC Statute. The manual highlights the obligations of countries that ratify the ICC Statute and suggests ways those countries might bring their domestic legislation into compliance with the ICC Statute's requirements. It is expected that the manual will be particularly helpful to countries that do not have extensive resources to support research and analysis on the implementation of the ICC Statute. The manual can be found at [www.icc.gc.ca] under 'Guide to Implementing the ICC' and 'Guide en vue de la mise en oeuvre de la CPI'.

Chapter 6: The toll on children's health

[1] United Nations Children's Fund (UNICEF) discussion website, *Voices of Youth*, 16 November 1999 [http://www.unicef.org/voy/chat/].

[2] United Nations Children's Fund, *The State of the World's Children 2001*, UNICEF, New York, 2000, p. 77.

[3] United Nations Children's Fund, 'Child disabilities: Global magnitude and basic facts', at [www.unicef.org/programme/cprotection].

[4] Cited in ibid.

[5] International Rescue Committee, 'IRC Study Points to Horrific Death Toll in Eastern Congo: 2.5 Million "Excess" Deaths in 33 Months of Unrest', 8 May 2001 [www.interescom.org/news/display.cfm].

[6] Crossette, Barbara, 'Death Toll in Congo's 2-Year War Is at Least 1.7 Million, Study Says', *The New York Times*, 9 June 2000.

[7] United Nations, Report of the Expert of the Secretary-General, Ms. Graça Machel, 'Impact of armed conflict on children', A/51/306, United Nations, New York, 26 August 1996, para. 140.

[8] United Nations, Report of the Expert of the Secretary-General, Ms. Graça Machel, 'Impact of armed conflict on children', op. cit.

[9] Ibid.

[10] World Health Organization, Press Release, 'Third of African malaria deaths due to conflict or natural disaster: Partnership plan to improve emergency response to prevent malaria', WHO/46, 30 June 2000.

[11] United Nations Population Fund, 'Working to Empower Women: UNFPA's Experience in Implementing the Beijing Platform for Action' [www.unfpa.org].

[12] United Nations Office for the Coordination of Humanitarian Affairs (OCHA), 'Consolidated Inter-Agency Appeal', New York, January-December 2000.

[13] Information supplied by United Nations Security Coordinator (UNSECO-ORD), United Nations, New York, April 2001.

[14] United Nations Children's Fund, *The State of the World's Children 2001,* op. cit., pp. 86-89.

[15] Information supplied by United Nations Children's Fund, Health Section, Programme Division, New York, April 2001.

[16] Ibid.

[17] United Nations Children's Fund, *The Progress of Nations 2000*, UNICEF, New York, 2000, p. 24.

[18] Information supplied by United Nations Children's Fund, Health Section, Programme Division, New York, April 2001.

[19] Ibid.

[20] United Nations, Administrative Committee on Coordination, Sub-Committee on Nutrition (ACC/SCN) in collaboration with International Food Policy Research Institute, *4th Report on the World Nutrition Situation*, Geneva, 2000, p. 71.

[21] Pelletier, D.L., et al., 'The effects of malnutrition on child mortality in developing countries', *WHO Bulletin*, vol. 73 (4), 1995, p. 444.

[22] Cited in United Nations, Administrative Committee on Coordination, Sub-Committee on Nutrition (ACC/SCN) in collaboration with International Food Policy Research Institute, *4th Report on the World Nutrition Situation*, op. cit., p. 76.

[23] United Nations Children's Fund Emergency Programme, Angola, Donor Update, 18 May 2000.

[24] United Nations Children's Fund, *The State of the World's Children 2001,* op. cit., pp. 82-85.

[25] United Nations Children's Fund, *The Progress of Nations 2000*, op. cit., p.16.

[26] United Nations, Report of the Expert of the Secretary-General, Ms. Graça Machel, 'Impact of armed conflict on children', op. cit., para. 164.

[27] World Food Programme (WFP), 'Commitments for Women', WFP, Geneva,

2000, pp. 1-3.

[28] Information supplied by Lindsey Davies, Information Officer, World Food Programme, Nairobi, 2001.

[29] United Nations Foundation, *UN Wire*, News item based on *Los Angeles Times*, 2 July 2000.

[30] United Nations, Report of the Expert of the Secretary-General, Ms. Graça Machel, 'Impact of armed conflict on children', op. cit., para. 161.

Chapter 7: Promoting psychosocial recovery

[1] Raymond, Alan and Susan, *Children in War*, TV Books, New York, 2000.

[2] Chauvin, Luc, James Mugaju and Patrick Jondoh Comlavi, 'Tackling new evaluation challenges: Rwanda Trauma Recovery Programme', Advocacy and Monitoring Section, UNICEF Rwanda, *PREviews: UNICEF newsletter on planning, research and evaluation*, Division of Evaluation, Policy and Planning, April 1998, vol. 2, no. 1.

[3] Convention on the Rights of the Child, 1989, article 39.

[4] UNICEF Workshop on Psychosocial Care and Protection, 1997.

[5] International Save the Children Alliance Working Group on Children Affected by Armed Conflict and Displacement, *Promoting Psychosocial Well-being Among Children Affected by Armed Conflict and Displacement: Principles and Approaches*, October 1996, International Save the Children Alliance joint contribution to the Report of the Expert of the Secretary-General, Ms. Graça Machel, 'Impact of armed conflict on children', op. cit.

[6] Interview conducted with a participant at a seminar on the Report of the Expert of the Secretary-General, Ms. Graça Machel, 'Impact of armed conflict on children', op. cit.

[7] International Save the Children Alliance Working Group on Children Affected by Armed Conflict and Displacement, *Promoting Psychosocial Well-being Among Children Affected by Armed Conflict and Displacement*, op. cit.

[8] Hiew, C., *Trauma and Resilience in Children*, University of New Brunswick, July 2000.

[9] Women's Commission for Refugee Women and Children (WCRWC), *Untapped Potential: Adolescents affected by armed conflict, A review of programs and policies*, WCRWC, New York, 2000.

[10] Ibid.; Lowicki, Jane, and Allison Pillsbury, 'Recognizing War-affected Adolescents: Frameworks for action', *Development*, vol. 43, no. 1, March 2000, pp. 76-77.

[11] Women's Commission for Refugee Women and Children, *Untapped Potential*, op. cit.

[12] International Save the Children Alliance Working Group on Children Affected by Armed Conflict and Displacement, *Promoting Psychosocial Well-Being Among Children Affected by Armed Conflict and Displacement*, op. cit.

[13] International Save the Children Alliance, contribution to the present report, 2000. Programmes have been implemented in Afghanistan, East Timor, Indonesia, Pakistan and Somaliland.

[14] International Save the Children Alliance Working Group on Children Affected by Armed Conflict and Displacement, *Promoting Psychosocial Well-Being Among Children Affected by Armed Conflict and Displacement*, op. cit.

[15] Cameron, Sara, ed., 'Voices of Colombian Children on War and Peace', *Development*, vol. 43, no. 1, March 2000, p. 26.

[16] Christian Children's Fund, contribution to the present report, 2000.

[17] International Save the Children Alliance members Norway, United Kingdom and United States, *Crisis in Kosovo*, 1999.

[18] Chauvin et al., op. cit.

[19] McCauley, Una, Rädda Barnen, Conference on War-Affected Children in West Africa, *Rehabilitating and Reintegrating War-Affected Children in West Africa*, 26-28 April 2000.

[20] Interregional Programming Workshop on Psychosocial Care and Protection, UNICEF Interregional Training Workshop, Nyeri, Kenya, 1-5 September 1998.

[21] Chauvin et al., op. cit.

[22] International Save the Children Alliance, contribution to the present report, op. cit.

Chapter 8: Education for survival and development

[1] Women's Commission for Refugee Women and Children (WCRWC), *Looking Toward Home: Internally Displaced Adolescents in Azerbaijan*, WCRWC, New York, 1998, p. 10.

[2] Women's Commission for Refugee Women and Children, *Rebuilding Rwanda: "A struggle men cannot do alone"*, WCRWC, New York, 2000, p. 10.

[3] Collier, Paul, 'Economic Causes of Civil Conflict and their Implications for Policy', World Bank, Washington, D.C., June 2000, p. 7.

[4] United Nations, Report of the Expert of the Secretary-General, Ms. Graça Machel, 'Impact of armed conflict on children', United Nations, New York, A/51/306, 1996, para. 186.

[5] Cited in Women's Commission for Refugee Women and Children, *Only Through Peace: Hope for Breaking the Cycle of Famine and War in Sudan*, WCRWC, New York, 1999, p. 1.

[6] United Nations, Report of the Expert of the Secretary-General, Ms. Graça Machel, 'Impact of armed conflict on children', op. cit., para. 186.

[7] Crossette, Barbara, 'Tamil Rebels Said to Recruit Child Soldiers', *The New York Times*, New York, 17 July 2000.

[8] United Nations, Report of the Expert of the Secretary-General, Ms. Graça Machel, 'Impact of armed conflict on children', op. cit., para. 188.

[9] United Nations Children's Fund (UNICEF), *The State of the World's Children 2000*, UNICEF, New York, 1999, p. 25.

[10] United Nations, Report of the Expert of the Secretary-General, Ms. Graça Machel, 'Impact of armed conflict on children', op. cit., para. 191.

[11] United Nations Office for the Coordination of Humanitarian Affairs (OCHA), '1999 and 2000 United Nations Consolidated Inter-Agency Appeal:

Education Sector', OCHA, December 2000.

[12] Sommers, Marc, 'Educating Children During Emergencies', Women's Commission for Refugee Women and Children, New York, March 1999, p. 11.

[13] International Rescue Committee (IRC), 'Program Report', IRC, New York, April 2000.

[14] Sommers, op. cit., p. 13.

[15] Bird, Lyndsay, 'The Tanzanian Experience', March 1999, pp. 1-3.

[16] Sommers, op. cit., pp. 14-18.

[17] Women's Commission for Refugee Women and Children, *Looking Toward Home: Internally Displaced Adolescents in Azerbaijan*, op. cit., pp. 8-9.

[18] Save the Children, *War brought us here: Protecting children displaced within their own countries by conflict*, Save the Children UK, London, 2000, pp. 59-61.

[19] Ibid., pp. 119-120.

[20] Smith, Wendy, Education Technical Advisor, International Rescue Committee, 'Georgia trip report' (internal), New York, August 2000.

[21] Women's Commission for Refugee Women and Children, *Rebuilding Rwanda*, op. cit., p. 13.

[22] Ibid., p. 12.

[23] Sommers, op. cit., p. 19.

[24] Office of the United Nations High Commissioner for Refugees (UNHCR), *Profile: Refugee education in northern Uganda*, UNHCR, Geneva, May 1998, pp. 15-17.

[25] Sommers, op. cit., pp. 12-13.

[26] International Rescue Committee, 'Program for Afghanistan: Progress Report, June 2000-March 2001', IRC, New York, 2001.

[27] Habibi, Gulbadan, 'UNICEF and Children with Disabilities', *Education Update*, UNICEF, vol. 2, issue 4, October 1999, p. 5.

[28] Bird, Lyndsay, 'Assisting the Most Vulnerable in Refugee Camps', *Education Update*, UNICEF, vol. 2, issue 4, October 1999, p. 20.

[29] Office of the United Nations High Commissioner for Refugees, *Building Partnerships through Equality*, UNHCR, Geneva, May 2000, pp. 30-33.

[30] Sommers, op. cit., p. 12.

[31] Office of the United Nations Children's Fund, 'Workshop on evaluation of peace education programmes', UNICEF, New York, May 2000, pp. 1-2.

[32] Ibid., pp. 13-14.

[33] Ibid., p. 16.

[34] Ibid., p. 4.

[35] Information supplied by Bo Viktor Nylund, Project Officer, Humanitarian Principles, Office of Emergency Programmes, UNICEF, New York, 2001.

Chapter 9: Threats to life and limb: Landmines and unexploded ordnance

[1] Bearak, Barry, 'Kandahar Journal: Every step is a risk in booby-trapped back-yards', *The New York Times*, 16 June 2000.

[2] International Campaign to Ban Landmines (ICBL), *Landmine Monitor Report 2000* [www.icbl.org/lm/].

[3] Ibid.

[4] Ibid, Executive Summary.

[5] McGrath, Rae, 'Cluster bombs: The military effectiveness and impact on civilians of cluster munitions', UK Working Group on Landmines, London, 2000; Monan, Jim, 'Curse of the bombies: A case study of Saravan Province, Laos', Oxfam, Hong Kong, 1998.

[6] Amnesty International, '"Collateral damage" or unlawful killings? Violations of the laws of war by NATO during Operation Allied Force', AI Index EUR 70/018/2000, Amnesty International, 6 June 2000 [www.amnesty.org]; McGrath, op. cit.; Peachey, Titus, and Virgil Wiebe, 'Cluster munitions in the US arsenal', chapter 1 in *Clusters of Death: Global Report on Cluster Bomb Production and Use*, Mennonite Central Committee, 2000 [www.mcc.org/clusterbomb/report/index.htm]; Human Rights Watch, 'Cluster bombs: Memorandum for Convention on Conventional Weapons (CCW) delegates', 16 December 1999 [www.hrw.org].

[7] Peachey and Wiebe, 'Cluster munitions use by Russian Federation forces in Chechnya', chapter 3 in *Clusters of Death*, op. cit.

[8] Peachey and Wiebe, 'Cluster bomb use in Sudan', chapter 4 in *Clusters of Death*, op. cit.; Médecins Sans Frontières, '"Living under aerial bombardments": Report of an investigation in the Province of Equatoria, Southern Sudan', 20 February 2000 [www. reliefweb.int/library/documents/sdbomrap.pdf].

[9] John Flanagan, Programme Manager, quoted in Gall, Carlotta, 'UN aide in Kosovo faults NATO on unexploded bombs', *The New York Times*, 23 May 2000.

[10] Peachey, Titus, 'Appendix 1: Laos', in Peachey and Wiebe, op. cit.; Lao National UXO Programme Workplan 1999 [http://uxo.apdip.net/workplan.htm]; Handicap International, 'National survey of the socio-economic impact of unexploded ordnance in Lao PDR', preliminary report of May 1997 and summary report of October 1997; Mennonite Central Committee / Mines Advisory Group, 'Unexploded Ordnance Removal Project – Xieng Khouang, Lao PDR', monthly report, 1 March – 30 April 1995.

[11] United Nations, Report of the Expert of the Secretary-General, Ms. Graça Machel, 'Impact of armed conflict on children', op. cit., para. 117.

[12] Ibid.

[13] Coker, Margaret, 'Tragedy in Chechnya', *Atlanta Journal and Constitution*, 6 February 2000, p. 7C, quoted in chapter 2 in Peachey and Wiebe, op. cit.

[14] International Campaign to Ban Landmines, *Landmine Monitor Report 2000*, op. cit.

[15] Ibid.

[16] Ibid.

[17] Ibid.

[18] Ibid.

[19] Ibid.

[20] Ibid.; United Nations, 'Multilateral treaties deposited with the Secretary-General' [www.untreaty.un.org], website update of 17 April 2001.

[21] North Atlantic Treaty Organization (NATO) Fact Sheet, NATO On-Line Library [www.nato.int/docu/facts/2000/kosovo-ff.htm].

[22] International Campaign to Ban Landmines, *Landmine Monitor Report 2000*, op. cit., Executive Summary, p. 15.

[23] Peachey, Titus, 'Appendix 1: Laos', in Peachey and Wiebe, op. cit.

[24] United Nations, *International guidelines for landmine and unexploded ordnance awareness education*, United Nations, New York, 1999.

[25] United Nations Children's Fund, 'A humanitarian appeal for children and women 2000 – Angola section', New York, UNICEF, 2000.

[26] United Nations Children's Fund, 'Anti-personnel landmines: Policies, strategies and programmes', UNICEF, New York, n.d.

[27] Eddy, Melissa, 'Bosnia still littered with land mines; corruption slows clearup process', Associated Press, 28 May 2000.

[28] International Campaign to Ban Landmines, *Landmine Monitor Report 1999*.

[29] Ibid.

[30] Bearak, op. cit.

[31] Williams, Jody, 'The Protection of Children Against Landmines and Unexploded Ordnance', UNICEF, New York, 1996, p. 2.

[32] Information supplied by United Nations Children's Fund, Child Protection Section.

[33] Landmine Survivors Network Database, 2000 [www.lsndatabase.org].

[34] Information supplied by the ICBL Working Group on Victim Assistance, 2000.

[35] United Nations Mine Action Service (UNMAS), Mine Action Investment Database, 29 August 2000 [www.un.org/dpko].

[36] International Committee of the Red Cross, 'Assistance for victims of anti-personnel mines: Needs, constraints and strategy', ICRC, Geneva, 1997.

[37] International Campaign to Ban Landmines, *Landmine Monitor Report 2000*, op. cit., Executive Summary, p. 31.

Chapter 10: Small arms, light weapons: Mass destruction

[1] Bennett, Elizabeth, Virginia Gamba and Deirdre van der Merwe, eds., *ACT against child soldiers in Africa: A reader*, Institute for Security Studies, Pretoria, 2000, p. 35. An RPG is an anti-tank weapon.

[2] Small Arms Survey project of the Graduate Institute of International Studies (Geneva) (abbreviated in subsequent references as Small Arms Survey project), 'Half a Billion and Still Counting...', chapter 2 in *Small Arms Survey 2001: Profiling the problem*, Oxford University Press, 2001.

[3] International Committee of the Red Cross (ICRC), 'Arms Availability and the Situation of Civilians in Armed Conflict', ICRC, June 1999.

[4] *Jane's Intelligence Review*, AK-47 Information Center [www.janes.com].

[5] Anti-personnel landmines are not included in this chapter but were addressed in chapter 9.

[6] United Nations, 'Report of the Panel on Governmental Experts on Small Arms', A/52/298, United Nations, New York, 27 August 1997.

[7] Muggah, Robert, and Eric Berman, 'Humanitarianism under threat: The humanitarian impacts of small arms and light weapons', draft, March 2001.

[8] Bengwayan, Michael A., 'Children forced onto front lines of conflict in Mindanao', *Earth Times News Service*, 4 January 2001 [www.earthtimes.org].

⁹ Cameron, Sara, ed., 'Voices of Colombian children on war and peace', *Development*, vol. 43, no. 1, March 2000, p. 26.

¹⁰ Cited in Stockholm International Peace Research Institute (SIPRI), *SIPRI Yearbook 2000*, Oxford University Press, Oxford [http://editors.sipri.se/pubs/yb00/ch5.html].

¹¹ United Nations Development Programme (UNDP), *Human Development Report 2000*, Oxford University Press for UNDP, 2000, table 16, p. 217.

¹² Information supplied by United Nations Security Coordinator (UNSECO-ORD), United Nations, New York, April 2001.

¹³ United Nations, 'Report of the Secretary-General to the Security Council on the protection of civilians in armed conflict', S/1999/957, 8 September 1999.

¹⁴ United Nations Children's Fund (UNICEF), 'Humanitarian Action Donor Update, Burundi Report', 1 March 2001.

¹⁵ Small Arms Survey project, 'Small Arms, Big Business', chapter 1 in *Small Arms Survey 2001*, op. cit.

¹⁶ Muggah and Berman, op. cit.

¹⁷ Small Arms Survey project, 'Fuelling the Flames', chapter 3 in *Small Arms Survey 2001*, op. cit.

¹⁸ Small Arms Survey project, 'Small Arms, Big Business', chapter 1 in *Small Arms Survey 2001*, op. cit.

¹⁹ Ibid.

²⁰ Stohl, Rachel, 'Deadly rounds: Ammunition and armed conflict', British/American Security Information Council (BASIC), London and Washington, D.C., May 1998, p. 9.

²¹ Ibid., p. 12.

²² Small Arms Survey project, 'Small Arms, Big Business', chapter 1 in *Small Arms Survey 2001*, op. cit.

²³ Renner, Michael, 'Arms Control Orphans', *The Bulletin of the Atomic Scientist*, Jan./Feb. 1999, vol. 55, no. 1 [www.bullatomsci.org]. In this instance, illegal trade refers to everything that is not considered a legal transfer.

²⁴ United Nations, 'Report of the Secretary-General to the Security Council on the protection of civilians in armed conflict', op. cit.

²⁵ International Action Network on Small Arms, 'The Tools for Arms Project in Mozambique', *IANSA Newsletter*, May 2000, vol. 4 [www.iansa.org].

²⁶ United Nations Development Programme, 'Light Weapons and the Proliferation of Armed Conflicts', UNDP, April 1999.

²⁷ International Action Network on Small Arms, 'Weapons Reduction in Cambodia', *IANSA Newsletter*, May 2000, vol. 4.

²⁸ Chachiua, Martinho, 'Operation Rachel 1996-1999', Institute for Security Studies, Pretoria, Monograph 38, June 1999.

²⁹ United Nations, Security Council President's Statement on the role of the Security Council in prevention of armed conflicts, S/PRST/2000/25, United Nations, New York, 20 July 2000.

– United Nations, Security Council President's Statement on the maintenance of peace and security and post-conflict peace-building, S/PRST/2000/10, United Nations, New York, 23 March 2000.

– United Nations, 'Report of the Secretary-General on the role of United

Nations peacekeeping in disarmament, demobilization and reintegration', S/2000/101, United Nations, New York, 11 February 2000.

– United Nations, Security Council President's Statement on the role of the Security Council in the prevention of armed conflicts, S/PRST/1999/34, United Nations, New York, 30 November 1999.

– United Nations, Security Council President's Statement on small arms, S/PRST/1999/28, United Nations, New York, 24 September 1999.

– United Nations, Security Council President's Statement on maintenance of peace and security and post-conflict peace-building, S/PRST/1999/21, United Nations, New York, 8 July 1999.

– United Nations, Security Council President's Statement on the protection of civilians in armed conflict, S/PRST/1999/6, United Nations, New York, 12 February 1999.

[30] Association of Southeast Asian Nations, Jakarta Regional Seminar on Illicit Trafficking in Small Arms and Light Weapons, Jakarta, Indonesia, 3-4 May 2000 [www.aseansec.org].

[31] See the IANSA website [www.iansa.org].

Chapter 11: Protecting children from sanctions

[1] 'Iraqi youth pay price for UN sanctions', *Toronto Star*, 25 June 2000.

[2] Garfield, Richard, 'The Impact of Economic Sanctions on Health and Well-being', Paper no. 31, *Relief and Rehabilitation Network Paper*, November 1999.

[3] United Nations, 'Supplement to an Agenda for Peace: Position paper of the Secretary-General on the occasion of the fiftieth anniversary of the United Nations', A/50/60-S/1995/1, United Nations, 3 January 1995.

[4] United Nations, Security Council Resolution S/RES/1265 (1999), adopted by the Security Council at its 4046th meeting on 17 September 1999.

[5] 'When Sanctions Don't Work', *The Economist*, 8-14 April 2000.

[6] Center for Economic and Social Rights, *Unsanctioned Suffering: A Human Rights Assessment of United Nations Sanctions on Iraq*, New York, May 1996, p. 1.

[7] Ministry of Health (Government of Iraq) and UNICEF/Iraq, 'Child and Maternal Mortality Survey 1999, Preliminary Report', Iraq, July 1999.

[8] Office of the High Commissioner for Human Rights, 'The Human Rights Impact of Economic Sanctions on Iraq', background paper prepared for the meeting of the Executive Committee on Humanitarian Affairs, 5 September 2000, p. 4.

[9] United Nations, Security Council Resolution S/RES/706 (1991), adopted by the Security Council at its 3004th meeting on 15 August 1991; United Nations, Security Council Resolution S/RES/712 (1991), adopted by the Security Council at its 3008th meeting on 19 September 1991.

[10] United Nations, Security Council Resolution S/RES/1284 (1999), adopted by the Security Council at its 4084th meeting on 17 December 1999.

[11] United Nations Foundation, *UN Wire*, 20 March 2000, quoting letter to the editor of *The New York Times* by Denis Halliday, former UN Coordinator of Humanitarian Affairs in Iraq, 15 March 2000.

[12] Food and Agriculture Organization of the United Nations (FAO), 'Technical

Report prepared for the Government of Iraq by the Food and Agriculture Organization of the United Nations', ES:TCP/IRQ/8924, Rome,13 September 2000, p. 17.

[13] United Nations Foundation, 'Iraq: Blasts United States on Sanctions Policy', *UN Wire*, 27 August 1999, quoting Edith Lederer, Associated Press, 26 August 1999.

[14] Minear, L., et al., *Toward more Humane and Effective Sanctions Management: Enhancing the Capacity of the United Nations System*, Occasional Paper No. 31, Thomas J. Watson Jr. Institute for International Studies, 1998.

[15] Center for Economic and Social Rights, *Unsanctioned Suffering*, op. cit., p. 6.

[16] 'When Sanctions Don't Work', *The Economist*, op. cit.

[17] United Nations Foundation, 'Iraq: Blasts United States on Sanctions Policy', op. cit. See also Minear et al., op. cit.

[18] United Nations, Office of the Iraq Programme, Oil-for-Food Basic Figures [www.un.org/depts/oip/latest/basicfigures.html].

[19] United Nations, 'Report of the Secretary-General to the Security Council on the Protection of Civilians in Armed Conflict', S/1999/957, United Nations, 8 September 1999.

[20] United Nations, Security Council Resolution S/RES/1173 (1998), adopted by the Security Council at its 3891st meeting on 12 June 1998; United Nations, Security Council Resolution S/RES/1306 (2000), adopted by the Security Council at its 4168th meeting on 5 July 2000.

[21] United Nations, Security Council Resolution S/RES/1306 (2000), adopted by the Security Council at its 4168th meeting on 5 July 2000.

[22] United Nations, Press Release SC/6825, 'Chairman of Security Council's Angola Sanctions Committee briefs Council on Expert Panel Report investigating sanctions violations', 15 March 2000.

[23] United Nations, Security Council Resolution S/RES/1295 (2000), adopted by the Security Council at its 4129th meeting on 18 April 2000.

[24] 19 July 2000: International Diamond Manufacturers' Association (IDMA) and World Federation of Diamond Bourses (WFDB), meeting in Antwerp, adopt resolution cutting off trade from Angola, the Democratic Republic of the Congo and Sierra Leone. Measures include:

– Importers of rough diamonds to legislate for sealing and registering exported stones by accredited export authorities.

– Legislation to be passed in all States involved in the diamond trade to make involvement in dealing illegal rough diamonds a criminal offence.

– Systematic monitoring and accounting of import/export data by a new International Diamond Council.

[25] United Nations, 'Statement dated 29 December 1997 by the Inter-Agency Standing Committee to the Security Council on the humanitarian impact of sanctions', S/1998/147.

[26] United Nations, Strategic Planning Unit, Executive Office of the Secretary-General, 'UN Sanctions: How Effective? How Necessary?', United Nations, New York, March 1999.

[27] Minear et al., op. cit.

[28] Hufbauer, Gary Clyde, Jeffrey J. Schott and Kimberly Ann Elliott, *Economic Sanctions Reconsidered: History and Current Policy*, Institute for International

Economics, Washington, DC, 1990 (2nd ed.).

²⁹ Koppel, Naomi, 'UN Report: Sanctions Ineffective', Associated Press, Geneva, 15 August 2000; Reuters, 'US hits at UN expert calling Iraq sanctions illegal', Geneva, 17 August 2000. The background paper 'The Human Rights Impact of Economic Sanctions on Iraq', prepared by the Office of the High Commissioner for Human Rights, op. cit., found that economic sanctions almost always have a dramatic impact on the rights recognised in the International Covenant on Economic, Social and Cultural Rights.

Chapter 12: Raising standards for child protection

¹ Save the Children, 'Eye to Eye: Photostories' [www.savethechildren.org.uk/eyetoeye/photo/play.html].

² United Nations Office for the Coordination of Humanitarian Affairs (OCHA), 'An Easy Reference to International Humanitarian Law and Human Rights Law', second edition, OCHA, New York, 1999.

³ United Nations, Secretary-General's Statement to the Security Council at its 4046th meeting, S/PV.4046, United Nations, New York, 16 September 1999.

⁴ Médecins Sans Frontières (MSF), *Alert*, MSF, New York, vol. 5, no. 2, Summer 2000.

⁵ United Nations Children's Fund (UNICEF) Staff Working Papers, 'The International Criminal Court', Evaluation, Policy and Planning Series EPP-00-007, UNICEF, New York, 2000.

⁶ United Nations Foundation, 'Cambodia: Top Khmer Rouge leader's health failing', *UN Wire*, 15 September 2000; United Nations Foundation, 'Cambodia: Commitment to try Khmer Rouge leaders questioned', *UN Wire*, 7 September 2000.

⁷ The Security Council asked the Secretary-General to negotiate an agreement with the Government of Sierra Leone to create an independent special court, consistent with Security Council Resolution 1315, S/RES/1315 (2000), adopted by the Security Council at its 4186th meeting on 14 August 2000. By the terms of Resolution 1315 (2000), the Council recommended that the subject matter jurisdiction of the special court should include crimes against humanity, war crimes and other serious violations of international humanitarian law. That jurisdiction should also include crimes committed in Sierra Leone under that country's national law. The Council further recommended that the special court should have personal jurisdiction over persons who bore the greatest responsibility for the commission of crimes referred to in the resolution. That would include those leaders who, in committing such crimes, had threatened the establishment and the implementation of the peace process in Sierra Leone.

⁸ See ICRC website [www.icrc.org].

⁹ United Nations, 'Report of the Secretary-General to the Security Council on the protection of civilians in armed conflict', S/1999/957, United Nations, New York, 8 September 1999.

¹⁰ United Nations, Report of the Secretary-General to the General Assembly, 'Renewing the United Nations: A programme for reform', A/51/950, United Nations, New York, 14 July 1997.

[11] Ibid.

[12] United Nations, 'Report of the Panel on United Nations Peacekeeping Operations', A/55/305-S/2000/809, United Nations, New York, 21 August 2000.

Chapter 13: Women and the peace process

[1] Heyzer, Noeleen, Executive Director, United Nations Development Fund for Women (UNIFEM), Statement to the International Conference on War-affected Children, Winnipeg, Canada, 17 September 2000.

[2] United Nations, Security Council Press Release, SC/6816, 8 March 2000.

[3] United Nations, Security Council Resolution, adopted at its 4213th meeting, S/RES/1325 (2000), United Nations, New York, 31 October 2000.

[4] United Nations Development Fund for Women's gender budget analysis of the 2001 United Nations Consolidated Appeals Process (CAP); information supplied by UNIFEM, May 2001.

[5] Gurirab, Dr. Theo-Ben, Message of the President of the United Nations General Assembly, United Nations Press Release, GA/SM/157 OBV/133 WOM/1191, 7 March 2000.

[6] Byanyima, Winnie, Member of Parliament (Uganda), Speech addressing the Burundi peace talks, 26 July 2000.

[7] Ibid.

[8] United Nations Development Fund for Women, 'Against all odds: The lives of women and girls in south Sudan', UNIFEM, New York, 2000.

[9] Brownell, Mary, Statement at UNIFEM panel, 'Women at the peace table', Commission on the Status of Women, New York, 1 March 2000.

[10] Anderlini, Sanam Naraghi, *Women at the peace table: Making a difference*, UNIFEM, New York, 2000.

[11] International Alert, 'The role of women in achieving peace and maintaining international security', NGO Statement to meeting of the United Nations Security Council on the Arria Formula, 23 October 2000 [www.international-alert.org].

[12] Anderlini, op. cit., p. 10.

[13] United Nations International Research and Training Institute for the Advancement of Women (INSTRAW), *Engendering the Political Agenda: The Role of the State, Women's Organizations and the International Community*, INSTRAW, Santo Domingo, Dominican Republic, 2000, chapter 3.

[14] Heyzer, Noeleen, Executive Director, United Nations Development Fund for Women, Statement to the United Nations Security Council, United Nations, New York, 24 October 2000.

[15] Ending impunity for gender-based war crimes was discussed in more detail in chapter 5, 'Ending sexual violence and exploitation'.

[16] Electoral Institute of Southern Africa (EISA), information obtained from website [www.eisa.org.za].

[17] Mahoney, Kathleen E., 'Gender and the Judiciary: Confronting gender bias', in Adams, Kirstine and Andrew Byrnes, eds., *Gender Equality and the Judiciary: Using international human rights standards to promote the human rights of women and the girl-*

child at the national level (papers and statements from the Caribbean Regional Judicial Colloquium, Georgetown, Guyana, 14-17 April 1997), London, Commonwealth Secretariat, 1999.

[18] United Nations, Security Council Resolution, adopted at its 4213th meeting, S/RES/1325 (2000), United Nations, New York, 31 October 2000.

[19] United Nations, Windhoek Declaration and Namibia Plan of Action on Mainstreaming a Gender Perspective in Multidimensional Peace Support Operations, United Nations, Windhoek, Namibia, 31 May 2000.

[20] United Nations, 'UN Site for Special and Personal Representatives and Envoys of the Secretary-General' [www.un.org/News/ossg/srsg.htm], website update of 15 March 2001.

Chapter 14: Media and communications

[1] Human Rights Watch (HRW), *Easy Prey*, HRW, New York, 1994, p. 46.

[2] United Nations, Security Council Resolution adopted by Security Council at its 4130th meeting, S/RES/1296, United Nations, New York, 19 April 2000.

[3] International Federation of Journalists, *Children's Rights and Media: Guidelines and Principles for Reporting on Issues Involving Children*, Recife, Brazil, May 1998.

[4] Committee to Protect Journalists (CPJ), *Attacks on the Press in 2000: A Worldwide Survey*, CPJ, New York, 2000 [www.cpj.org].

[5] Hay, Robin (Global Affairs Research Partners), 'The Media and Peacebuilding: A discussion paper (and draft operational framework)', Institute for Media, Policy and Civil Society, Vancouver, Canada, 8 July 1999.

[6] The Communication Initiative, 'Radio Kwizera, 1995, Tanzania: Basic Facts' [www.comminit.com/11-342-case_studies/sld-636.html].

[7] United Nations Children's Fund (UNICEF) discussion website, *Voices of Youth* [www.unicef.org/voy/chat/].

[8] The Communication Initiative, 'Media and Children in Need of Special Protection: Guidance notes for UNICEF staff', slide 2 of 21, The Communication Initiative [www.comminit.com/other_presentations/guidance_07-07-99/].

[9] Associated Press, 'International Coalition Says Palestinian Youth Not Recruited to Fight', 8 April 2001.

[10] International Telecommunication Union [www.itu.int/ti/industryoverview/at_a_glance/basic98.pdf].

[11] United Nations Secretary-General Boutros Boutros-Ghali, quoted in: Minear, Larry, Colin Scott and Thomas G. Weiss, *The News Media, Civil War and Humanitarian Action*, Lynne Reiner, Boulder, Colorado, 1996.

Chapter 15: A children's agenda for peace and security

[1] Save the Children (UK), 'Back to reality in Kosovo: Case stories', *What we do, Feature stories*, February 2000 [http://193.129.255.93/functions/wedo/features/koso-

vo2.html].

[2] Arria Formula briefing with Graça Machel, November 1996.

[3] United Nations, Security Council Resolution 1314 (2000), adopted by the Security Council at its 4185th meeting, on 11 August 2000; United Nations, Security Council Resolution 1261 (1999), adopted by the Security Council at its 4037th meeting, on 25 August 1999.

[4] United Nations, Security Council Resolution 1314 (2000), adopted by the Security Council at its 4185th meeting, on 11 August 2000; United Nations, Security Council Resolution 1296 (2000), adopted by the Security Council at its 4130th meeting, on 19 April 2000; United Nations, Security Council Resolution 1308 (2000), adopted by the Security Council at its 4172nd meeting, on 17 July 2000; United Nations, Security Council Resolution 1261 (1999), adopted by the Security Council at its 4037th meeting, on 25 August 1999; and others.

[5] United Nations, Report of the Secretary-General, 'Children and armed conflict', A/55/163-S/2000/712, United Nations, 19 July 2000, box 7.

[6] Mydans, Seth, 'Emerging From its Crisis, East Timor Rebuilds', *The New York Times*, 18 October 2000.

[7] United Nations Children's Fund (UNICEF), *The State of the World's Children 2000*, UNICEF, New York, 1999, p. 42.

[8] Ibid., p. 43.

[9] Carnegie Commission on Preventing Deadly Conflict, *Toward a Culture of Prevention, Statements by the Secretary-General of the United Nations*, Carnegie Corporation of New York, New York, December 1999, p. 7.

[10] United Nations Children's Fund, *The State of the World's Children 2000*, op. cit., p. 44.

[11] Oxfam, 'An end to forgotten emergencies?', briefing, May 2000, p. 2.

[12] Net ODA for 1990, available in current US dollars from the Organisation for Economic Co-operation and Development/Development Assistance Committee (OECD/DAC), was converted to 1999 dollars using the US GDP deflator from the International Monetary Fund's *International Finance Statistics Yearbook 2000*. No adjustments for exchange rates were made.

[13] Oxfam, 'Make debt relief work: Proposals for the G7', Oxfam Policy Papers, Oxfam International Policy Paper, July 2000.

[14] United Nations Children's Fund, *The State of the World's Children 2000*, op. cit., p. 13.

[15] United Nations, Report of the Secretary-General, 'We the Children: End-Decade Review of Follow-up to the World Summit for Children', advance unedited copy, United Nations, 16 May 2001, pp. 49 and 52.

[16] United Nations, 'Report of the Secretary-General to the Security Council on the Protection of Civilians in Armed Conflict', S/1999/957, United Nations, 8 September 1999.

[17] Organization of African Unity (OAU), Report of the International Panel of Eminent Personalities to Investigate the 1994 Genocide in Rwanda and the Surrounding Events, OAU, 7 July 2000, Executive Summary, E.S.44 [www.oau-oua.org/Document/ipep/ipep.htm].

[18] Carnegie Commission on Preventing Deadly Conflict, *Preventing Deadly Conflict*, Carnegie Corporation of New York, December 1997, p. xvii.

[19] Stockholm International Peace Research Institute (SIPRI), *SIPRI Yearbook 2000: Armaments, Disarmament and International Security*, Oxford University Press, Oxford, 2000 [http://editors.sipri.se/pubs/yb00/ch5.html]; Lynch, Colum, 'Rising US Debt to UN Spurs Fight Over Funds', *Washington Post*, 9 August 2000.

[20] United Nations, Secretary-General's report, 'Renewing the United Nations: A Programme for Reform', A/51/950, United Nations, 15 July 1997, para. 199 [www.un.org/reform/track2/focus.htm].

[21] Forum on Early Warning and Early Response (FEWER), website [www.fewer.org].

[22] Stockholm International Peace Research Institute, *SIPRI Yearbook 2000*, op. cit.

[23] United Nations Development Programme (UNDP), *Human Development Report 2000*, Oxford University Press, New York, 2000, table 16, p. 217.

[24] United Nations, 'The causes of conflict and the promotion of durable peace and sustainable development in Africa', A/52/871-S/1998/318, United Nations, New York, 13 April 1998, para. 27.

Afterword

[1] United Nations Children's Fund (UNICEF), *The State of the World's Children 2000*, UNICEF, New York, 1999, p. 43.

Abbreviations

AIDS	acquired immune deficiency syndrome
ASEAN	Association of Southeast Asian Nations
CAP	Consolidated Appeals Process (United Nations)
CCO	Committee of Co-sponsoring Organisations (UNAIDS)
CEDAW	Convention on the Elimination of All Forms of Discrimination against Women
CRC	Convention on the Rights of the Child
DAC	Development Assistance Committee (OECD)
DD&R	disarmament, demobilisation and reintegration (programmes)
DDA	Department for Disarmament Affairs (United Nations)
ECHO	European Community Humanitarian Office
ECOWAS	Economic Community of West African States
EU	European Union
FAO	Food and Agriculture Organization of the United Nations
FAWE	Forum for African Women Educationalists
GDP	gross domestic product
GNP	gross national product
G7	Group of Seven donor countries
HIPC	heavily indebted poor countries
HIV	human immunodeficiency virus
HRW	Human Rights Watch
IANSA	International Action Network on Small Arms

IASC	Inter-Agency Standing Committee (United Nations)
ICBL	International Campaign to Ban Landmines
ICC	International Criminal Court
ICRC	International Committee of the Red Cross
ICTY	International Criminal Tribunal for the former Yugoslavia
IDP	internally displaced person
IFRC	International Federation of Red Cross and Red Crescent Societies
ILO	International Labour Organization
INSTRAW	International Research and Training Institute for the Advancement of Women (United Nations)
IPAA	International Partnership Against AIDS in Africa
IRC	International Rescue Committee
ISCA	International Save the Children Alliance
MINUGUA	United Nations Verification Mission in Guatemala
MSF	Médecins Sans Frontières
NATO	North Atlantic Treaty Organization
NGO	non-governmental organisation
NID	National Immunisation Day
NRC	Norwegian Refugee Council
OAS	Organization of American States
OAU	Organization of African Unity
OCHA	Office for the Coordination of Humanitarian Affairs (United Nations)
ODA	official development assistance
OECD	Organisation for Economic Co-operation and Development

OHCHR	Office of the High Commissioner for Human Rights
OSCE	Organization for Security and Cooperation in Europe
SADC	Southern African Development Community
SIPRI	Stockholm International Peace Research Institute
STI	sexually transmitted infection
UNAIDS	Joint United Nations Programme on HIV/AIDS
UNDP	United Nations Development Programme
UNESCO	United Nations Educational, Scientific and Cultural Organization
UNFPA	United Nations Population Fund
UNHCR	Office of the United Nations High Commissioner for Refugees
UNICEF	United Nations Children's Fund
UNIFEM	United Nations Development Fund for Women
UNMAS	United Nations Mine Action Service
UNRWA	United Nations Relief and Works Agency for Palestine Refugees in the Near East
UNSECOORD	United Nations Security Coordinator
UNTAC	United Nations Transitional Authority in Cambodia
UNTAG	United Nations Transition Assistance Group in Namibia
USAID	United States Agency for International Development
UXO	unexploded ordnance
WFP	World Food Programme
WHO	World Health Organization

In 1994, the United Nations Secretary-General appointed **Mrs. Graça Machel** as an independent expert to carry out an assessment of the impact of armed conflict on children. Her groundbreaking report was presented to the United Nations in 1996 and set out a comprehensive agenda for the protection of children in armed conflict. Mrs. Machel, the former Minister of Education in Mozambique, is a well-known international advocate for children. She is the founder and president of Fundacao para o Desenvolvimento da Comunidade, a community foundation in Mozambique. She is a member of numerous international boards, including the United Nations Foundation, the International Crisis Group, ACCORD, the South Centre and the Forum for African Women Educationalists. She is currently the Chancellor of both the University of Cape Town and the United Nations University for Peace.

Sebastião Salgado has dedicated his nearly 30 years as a photographer to chronicling the lives of the world's dispossessed. The Brazilian photographer has won numerous awards for his imagery. Among his published works are *Other Americas*, about the peasant communities in Latin America; *Workers: An Archeology of the Industrial Age*, on manual labour around the world; and *Migrations* and *The Children*, on the global phenomenon of mass displacement of people. A UNICEF Special Representative, Mr. Salgado has collaborated with a number of international humanitarian organisations throughout his career. He is presently documenting the global campaign to eradicate polio.